THE EVERYTHING
Wicca & Witchcraft
Book

Dear Reader,
What comes to mind when you hear the word witch? A cackling old hag with a long nose, warts, and a pointy black hat? An evil sorceress stirring a strange brew in a cauldron? Those negative stereotypes are rapidly being replaced with more accurate images as Wicca and witchcraft "come out of the broom closet." Today's witches are doctors, computer programmers, teachers, landscapers, and flight attendants. The person who cuts your hair or repairs your car might be a witch. Wicca, in fact, is one of the fastest-growing religions in the Western world.

That's all fine and well, but what can Wicca and witchcraft do for you? First, let's consider what it won't do. It won't solve all your problems overnight; it won't give you perfect hair; it won't do your housework. But it will provide a framework for living the life you really want and the tools to achieve your fondest dreams. It will open new horizons for you, bring you myriad opportunities, and change your life in incredible ways. It will show you how to control your own destiny.

Maybe you'd like to learn to do magick spells. Maybe you're seeking a community of people who share your reverence for the earth and all life. Maybe you want to connect with a deeper part of yourself and with the divine forces in the universe. If so, Wicca and witchcraft can guide you to become what you already are in your heart and soul—a powerful, magickal, spiritual person. This book can lead you as you take the first steps. Blessed be.

Skye Alexander

Welcome to the EVERYTHING® Series!

These handy, accessible books give you all you need to tackle a difficult project, gain a new hobby, comprehend a fascinating topic, prepare for an exam, or even brush up on something you learned back in school but have since forgotten.

You can choose to read an *Everything*® book from cover to cover or just pick out the information you want from our four useful boxes: e-questions, e-facts, e-alerts, e-ssentials. We give you everything you need to know on the subject, but throw in a lot of fun stuff along the way, too.

We now have more than 400 *Everything*® books in print, spanning such wide-ranging categories as weddings, pregnancy, cooking, music instruction, foreign language, crafts, pets, New Age, and so much more. When you're done reading them all, you can finally say you know *Everything*®!

QUOTE

Words of wisdom
from experts
in the field

FACTS

Important snippets
of information

ALERTS!

Urgent
warnings

ESSENTIALS

Quick
handy tips

DIRECTOR OF INNOVATION Paula Munier

MANAGING EDITOR, EVERYTHING SERIES Lisa Laing

COPY CHIEF Casey Ebert

ACQUISITIONS EDITOR Lisa Laing

DEVELOPMENT EDITOR Brett Palana-Shanahan

THE
EVERYTHING®
WICCA & WITCHCRAFT BOOK

2ND EDITION

Rituals, spells, and sacred objects
for everyday magick

Skye Alexander

Avon, Massachusetts

Dedication
To the Kerrville Cowgirls

An Everything® Series Book.
Everything® and everything.com® are registered trademarks of F+W Media, Inc.

Published by Adams Media, a division of F+W Media, Inc.
57 Littlefield Street, Avon, MA 02322 U.S.A.
www.adamsmedia.com

ISBN 10: 1-59869-404-9
ISBN 13: 978-1-59869-404-8

Printed in the United States of America.

10 9 8 7 6 5 4 3 2

Library of Congress Cataloging-in-Publication Data
is available from the publisher.

This publication is designed to provide accurate and authoritative information with regard to the subject matter covered. It is sold with the understanding that the publisher is not engaged in rendering legal, accounting, or other professional advice. If legal advice or other expert assistance is required, the services of a competent professional person should be sought.

—From a Declaration of Principles jointly adopted by a Committee of the American Bar Association and a Committee of Publishers and Associations

Many of the designations used by manufacturers and sellers to distinguish their products are claimed as trademarks. Where those designations appear in this book and Adams Media was aware of a trademark claim, the designations have been printed with initial capital letters.

This book is available at quantity discounts for bulk purchases.
For information, please call 1-800-289-0963.

Contents

Acknowledgments

I'd like to thank Paula Munier, Lisa Laing, Brett Palana-Shanahan, and Casey Ebert at Adams Media.

The Top Ten Ways Wicca and Witchcraft Can Help You

1. They give you the tools to create your own reality.

2. They allow you to take greater control over your life.

3. They provide a framework for living in harmony with nature and the cosmos.

4. They strengthen your mental skills.

5. They can enhance your relationships with other people.

6. They broaden your perspective of the universe.

7. They put you in touch with the nonphysical realms of existence.

8. They heighten your intuition.

9. They can improve your health.

10. They connect you with a network of like-minded people worldwide.

Introduction

▶ LATELY, YOU MIGHT have noticed that the words *Witch*, *Witchcraft*, and *Wicca* pop up everywhere—on television and radio programs, in movies, at bookstores, in magazines, on the Internet, and even in casual conversations. These terms are not new, but they have finally lost their negative connotations. TV witches are no longer portrayed as ugly, evil crones—no more warts, wrinkles, and pointy black hats. Instead, the characters and people presented could live next door—and some probably do!

Surprised? Don't be. Wicca is among the fastest-growing religious systems in the United States; it is even recognized by the U.S. military. Similarly, witchcraft is a rapidly growing practice/methodology in which magick (manipulating energies) plays a key role.

Notice the important difference between Wicca and witchcraft: although the two are related, and share similar practices, the beliefs behind them are often different. To keep it simple, remember that Wicca is a religion, like Christianity, while witchcraft is a methodology. Wiccans generally practice witchcraft, but witches may not necessarily share Wiccan beliefs and therefore would not consider themselves Wiccan.

Confused? That's okay; sometimes even those who have been practicing magick for decades still have to pause and consider how to define themselves in easily understood terms. *The Everything® Wicca & Witchcraft Book* is one such pause for explanation and definition.

This book's goal is to provide you with a plethora of useful information. It is, in fact, a guide that will cover everything you need to know in order to better understand both Wicca and witchcraft, and even learn some magick to practice yourself. Here you'll discover where these two systems fit into the broad-based Neo-Pagan community, and you'll get an overview of their origins. You'll also find out how each system is practiced and who, exactly, is shaping this swelling spiritual wave.

Are you curious about elemental and planetary correspondences for plants and animals, or how to effectively construct a ritual in a truly magickal way? Would you like to know whether witches are psychic, what kinds of ethics Wiccans hold dear, what divinatory tools magickal folk prefer (and why), or if any of the superstitions about witches are true? The answers are all here!

In this book, as in most others on this topic, you will read about the many personalities (mentioned or quoted directly) who have contributed in one way or another to what Wicca and witchcraft are today. Who are these people, what walks of life do they come from, and why are they important to the Craft? To fully understand Wicca and witchcraft, you will need to get a good feel for the real people leading these movements.

As you read, keep in mind that Wicca and witchcraft are composed of many vision-based faiths and practices, shaped intimately by the individuals walking their chosen paths. This means that no book can be the "final authority" on Wicca and witchcraft. The information provided here is generalized—a picture painted with a broad brush, if you will, of what's common and popular in Wicca and witchcraft. It's quite possible that you could meet a witch or Wiccan who does things differently than what's portrayed in these pages. There's a lot of room for improvising, borrowing from other cultures and paths, and personalizing these practices. In fact, the ability to transform and adapt with the earth, society, and each person's individuality is among the cornerstones of eclectic witchery and Wicca, as well as of many Neo-Pagan traditions.

Having the option of adapting custom and heritage does not mean traditional concepts and practices should be tossed out with the proverbial bath water. Some witches and Wiccans only follow older or familial systems with specific rules and rites. They honor tradition, believing that it draws its power from use and refinement over generations. But nevertheless, even the most stringent of magickal traditions has room for spontaneity and ingenuity at suitable moments.

Finally, I should point out that both my perception of and my communication about Wicca and witchcraft are certainly influenced by my own experiences. I consider myself a witch and a magician. Magick is an intimate part of my everyday life, and I am very pleased and excited to be sharing its wonders and blessings with you.

CHAPTER 1

And Harm None: Philosophy and Ideology

As is true of followers of all religions and cosmologies, witches and Wiccans share some beliefs and disagree on others. Their ideas may be influenced by their cultural traditions and backgrounds, personal life experiences, or individual temperaments. In general, most seek to improve themselves and humankind as a whole, and to live in harmony with the universe. This means working for the greater good—often through the use of magick—and harming none.

Which Is the Witch?

Despite the ugly face that other religions have tried to put on witches, historically most have been concerned with helping individuals and communities. Of course, there are some "wicked witches" just as there are greedy evangelists and pedophile priests. It's important to remember that fear and misunderstanding underlie the misconceptions many people hold about witches. Once you get to know them, witches and Wiccans are pretty much like everyone else; they just see the world a little differently.

FACT

The words *Wicca* and *witch* come from the Anglo-Saxon term *wicce* meaning "to bend or shape." The term was used to refer to a female witch. *Wicca* referred to a male witch; the plural is *wiccan*. The Old English word *wiccacraeft* meant "witchcraft."

In the past, many witches learned their art as part of a family tradition in which they were carefully trained. (For more about the history of witchcraft, see Chapter 2.) Villages and cities alike had their honored cunning folk to whom people would turn for all kinds of help, from encouraging crops to grow to fixing a broken heart. Healing made up a large part of the witch's work, and many witches were knowledgeable herbalists and midwives. In exchange for such services, the witch might receive a chicken, a measure of grain, or other necessities. (The barter system is still alive and well in witchcraft.)

Witches learned their skills as a craft, just as someone might learn carpentry or masonry. Religious constructs weren't linked with the practice of witchcraft itself, though individual witches may have followed the beliefs of their families or culture. Witches do not need to believe in divine beings in order to use magick. They do not necessarily have a dogma to which they adhere in order to perform their work, just as computer programmers and auto mechanics don't have to be members of a particular faith to do their jobs.

Witches are not necessarily Wiccan. Witchcraft implies a methodology (for example, the use of magick), whereas the word *Wiccan* refers to a person who has adopted a specific spiritual philosophy. Witches can follow any religion, or none. Wiccans practice specific rituals and moral codes just as people of other world faiths do.

However, the lack of an ethical or religious construct does not mean witches are without ethics or religion. The use of magick is simply a means to an end and is, in itself, morally neutral. Ethics get involved only in how magick is wielded. (More about this later.)

For the most part, both witches and Wiccans believe in religious tolerance and respect every path as having potential for human enlightenment. Most Wiccans have come from other religious backgrounds and believe that people must choose their own paths. You're not likely to find a Wiccan standing on a street corner trying to convert passersby to her faith.

Who's Who?

By the way, it's good to remember that a male witch or Wiccan is not called a warlock. He is a witch or Wiccan, too. *Warlock* derived from an Old English word for *oath breaker*; later, during the mid-1400s, the word came to mean *liar* (whether the person was male or female). So to call a male witch a warlock is a nasty insult. For the purposes of simplicity, this book will use the word *witch* for both male and female witches or Wiccans.

The words *wizard* and *sorcerer* can be used for a man or a woman. *Wizard* derives from a term meaning "wise," and *sorcerer* means "witch" or "diviner." Writers Gerald Gardner and Sir James Frazier are commonly given credit for coining the term Wiccan and kick-starting the modern movement in the 1950s. The word *magician* is also appropriate for both sexes and for both witches and Wiccans.

Zoroaster, in ancient Persia, taught priests called magi who relied heavily on astrology as an art. The "wise men" mentioned in the Christmas story are sometimes referred to as magi—they gained knowledge of Jesus's birth by watching the stars. Depending on the cultural setting, *magician* came to mean people adept in astrology, sorcery, or other magickal arts. Note that the word *magick* in Wicca and witchcraft is spelled with a *k*, to differentiate it from stage magic (or sleight of hand).

FACT

Wicca and witchcraft share some core concepts, and practitioners use some of the same tools. However, witches come from a wide array of schools, belief systems, and traditions of magick that are distinctive and unique.

Gods and Goddesses

Another difference between witches and Wiccans is that many Wiccans recognize a specific god or goddess, or honor several deities. Which beings or personages someone follows may be chosen by the individual, or dictated by a group, magickal tradition, or cultural standard. Wiccans look to "the Divine" as the source of life energy, a guide in the spiritual quest, and a helpmate in the use of magick.

Several divine figures show up as popular favorites in the Wiccan community. Among them are:

- Apollo (Greece and Rome)
- Bast (Egypt)
- Brigid (Celtic Europe)
- Ceres (Rome)
- Ceridwen (Celtic Europe)
- Dagda (Ireland)
- Diana (Rome)
- Hecate (Greece)
- Ishtar (Middle East)
- Isis (Egypt)
- Kuan Yin (Asia)
- Pan (Greece)
- Ra (Egypt)
- Tara (India and Tibet)

Wiccans tend to see a particular divine energy expressed in many faces; for example, the Eleusian mother goddess Demeter was called Ceres by the Romans. The Triple (or Tripart) Goddess is depicted as the three phases of womanhood: maiden, mother, and crone.

Karmic Law

A third distinction is that witches may or may not concern themselves with the potential results of a spell or ritual. Wiccans are bound by what's known as the threefold law. Thus, Wiccans and witches may view the cause and effect of their magick differently. This doesn't mean that witches don't respect magickal power, however, nor does it suggest that they are unethical.

The threefold law has similar overtones to the concept of karma. The law basically states that whatever you do, whatever energies you "put out," return to you threefold (three times over) in this lifetime or the next.

The threefold law translates as *What goes around comes around, not just once but three times*. This seems to be a very good reason to make sure your motives are positive. Although karma is an Eastern term, you can see versions of karmic law expressed in the Christian concept that what you sow so shall you reap. Essentially, it's the idea that for every action there's a reaction, and that your individual actions will redound to you, if not in this incarnation then sometime in the future.

Wiccans believe you create your own destiny with your thoughts, words, and deeds. Because they subscribe to this idea, Wiccans tend to be more conscious and conscientious in their behavior and thinking than many other individuals are. Although the idea of reincarnation cannot be validated, many Wiccans and witches seriously consider the karmic implications of their actions or inactions.

Different Strokes for Different Folks

Witches and Wiccans approach magick in very personal ways—ways that can be incredibly complex or very simple. Kitchen and hedge witches, for example, generally practice pragmatic, uncomplicated magick, much of which originates in folklore. Hedge witches traditionally do not belong to a coven. Solitary practitioners, they depend on self-study, insight, creativity, and intuition for their guideposts. Hedge witches may be self-dedicated, but they are rarely publicly initiated. Similar to village shamans and cunning folk, they often provide spells and potions for daily needs. Their practice usually includes plant and herbal magick, often for the purpose of healing.

Others practice magick with more ritualistic overtones, drawing inspiration from various mystical and spiritual movements, such as the Kabbalah (Jewish mysticism and magick). Ritualistic witches look at every aspect of a spell or a working as being part of a huge picture. Each piece must be in the right place for everything to work as it should. For example, the astrological phase of the moon during which the spell is performed should be suited to the task. Every part of the working should be carefully contrived to build energy toward a desired goal.

Shapes, numbers, colors, movements, objects, and sounds can all play parts in the construction of a spell or ritual. Each action or ingredient is considered to represent or embody a specific energy. The magician carefully chooses these for their symbolic value and how they relate to her intention.

A large majority of such workings have been used for a long time and are honored as part of the tradition the witch follows. This is not to say that a ritualistic school has no room for variety or improvisation. It's just that the improvisation usually happens within a set framework.

Good Witch, Bad Witch

Are there "bad" witches who use their knowledge and power for personal gain and ill will? Yes, of course, just as there are "bad" Christians, "bad" Muslims, and so on. People are people. If you shake any figurative tree hard enough, a couple of rotten apples are liable to fall off. That's just human nature. The good news is that these rotten apples are the exception, not the rule.

Just like everyone else, witches confront issues that require them to make ethical choices. For instance, should magick be used as a weapon, even if it's only to fight back?

ALERT!

Some witches believe that you cannot effectively bless if you do not know how to curse. The reasoning behind this belief is quite simple: If you don't recognize the cause of a hex and fully comprehend the magickal processes used to enact it, how can you possibly hope to disarm it?

Wiccans and witches alike see magick as ethically neutral, even as electricity is neutral. Both magick and electricity can be used to help or to harm. Magick is simply the intentional use of energy. The witch directs energy by willpower toward a goal. How a person uses magick—the witch's intention—is what colors it white, black, or gray. To complicate matters, people's perceptions of what constitutes white, black, and gray aren't the same. Followers of any religion or belief system face a similar conundrum. Defining anything in concrete terms is nearly impossible.

Black, White, and Gray Magick

Your motive for doing a spell determines whether it's "white" or "black" magick, or somewhere in between. Magick spells can be grouped into three basic categories:

- Any spell done to harm someone else is **black magick**.
- Spells and rituals performed for the purpose of connecting with the Divine or to obtain higher knowledge are considered **white magick**.
- Everything else falls into the **gray** area.

As you might imagine, most magick that witches perform fits in the gray category. This doesn't mean it's wrong to do gray magick. Tapping your magickal skills to get a better job or improve your love life is like using any other talent to enhance your situation. As long as you don't harm someone else in the process, you're operating in safe territory.

FACT

Some people call themselves "white witches," meaning they abide by a simple code that instructs them to work for the good of all. White witches believe it's highly unethical to attempt to manipulate another person or to use magick to interfere with his free will. This kind of manipulation occurs most commonly in love magick, when one person tries to force another's attentions.

Many witches end a spell or ritual with the words, "This is done for the greatest good and may it harm none." Because it's sometimes hard to determine whether what you're doing is for the good of all concerned, this phrase invites the universe to step in and guide energy to keep it from being misdirected.

Magicians recognize that they may not be able to foresee all possible outcomes of their magick. Human beings are not omniscient, and sometimes good intentions lead to terrible results. By requesting that higher (and wiser) powers direct their magick toward the best possible outcome, witches remove any selfish attachments and desires from their spellworking. The phrase "harm none" also pertains to the person doing the spell and protects the magician from any unwanted ramifications of a spell.

This brief overview is a broad generalization at best. Each witch relies on her inner voice (or conscience, if you will) in determining how she wields magick. There is no cut-and-dried answer to whether anyone is a good or a bad witch. Most witches hope and try to be the best witches—and the best people—they can be.

The Wiccan Rede

"The Wiccan Rede" is a guide for practitioners of Wicca. This short rhyme sums up the basic code of ethics Wiccans try to follow, in their magickal work and in their everyday lives.

The Wiccan Rede

Bide the Wiccan law ye must
In perfect love, in perfect trust,
Eight words the Wiccan Rede fulfill:
An' ye harm none, do what ye will.
What ye send forth comes back to thee,
So ever mind the Rule of Three.
Follow this with mind and heart,
And merry ye meet, and merry ye part.

Immanence, Interconnectedness, and Community

Starhawk, one of the foremost figures in the modern revival of witchcraft, lists immanence, interconnectedness, and community as the three core principles or values of Goddess-based religion. Immanence means that all life on earth is an embodiment of the Divine and therefore sacred. You and everyone else are manifestations of the God and Goddess.

Interconnectedness means that all things in heaven and earth are linked and interrelated, energetically. "What affects one of us affects all," writes Starhawk in her landmark book *The Spiral Dance*. Harming or healing any life form, anywhere on the planet, has an impact on all other life forms, at the level of spirit even if physically the impact is not noticeable.

As community-oriented faiths, Wicca and Goddess-based spiritual traditions see the growth, safety, and well-being of all beings as a goal. Instead of being concerned only with individual happiness and success, followers of these belief systems see themselves as members of a global community and seek to live in harmony with all people, animals, plants, and other life forms.

Heaven and Earth

Christianity has its heaven. Buddhism has nirvana. Where do witches go when they die? Many of them believe that their souls go to Summerland, a resting place before reincarnation into new bodies, in an ongoing cycle of birth, life, death, and rebirth.

Generally speaking, witches and Wiccans accept the idea of reincarnation, a belief that has also existed in numerous cultures and faiths for a very long time. Some African tribes claim the soul goes into the belly of the earth to await rebirth. In China, the spirits of the dead are said to wait in the underworld (which is not hell, but simply a place for spirits). Hindus believe that the spirit, freed from the physical body, waits to be reborn from the stars.

If your soul previously inhabited other bodies, why can't you remember your previous lives? It seems that between death and rebirth memories of past lives are veiled, perhaps to prevent confusion or to enable you to enter into a new lifetime with a fresh perspective. Many people say their memories of previous existences have reawakened in dreams, during meditation, through hypnosis or regression therapy, or as a result of some type of traumatic experience.

Perhaps you've had a *déjà vu* experience or encountered someone you felt you'd known forever, even though you'd just met. These common occurrences are often explained as evidence of reincarnation. Indeed, a great deal of research has been conducted over the years that supports the idea. Regardless of whether you recall your past lives, the events of previous incarnations shape your present existence.

Memories of previous incarnations may be awakened by someone or something that ties into the past life experience. The information that comes through from that past life is usually pertinent to what is happening in the here-and-now.

And what about animals? Do they come back? Can humans be reborn as animals? No one knows for certain. If you ask some pet owners, they'll tell you animals display uncanny psychic abilities and seem to have a soul or spirit. Witches often have exceptionally strong ties with animal companions whom they call "familiars." Although Hindus believe humans can reincarnate as other species, witches generally accept that human souls come back to earth in human bodies.

Earth as a Classroom

The witch's body houses his soul. Witches who believe in reincarnation—and most do—regard earth as a place of learning. Their time on this planet is spent gaining and applying knowledge in ways that can only be accomplished on the physical plane. The eventual goal, however, is to stop the cycle of reincarnation so the soul can return to the Source. The earth, its creatures—everything in this world—are seen as teachers, and all experiences are considered opportunities for growth.

How long a soul waits between incarnations is uncertain. Several years, or perhaps decades or centuries, may pass between sojourns in this world. Many people believe you choose the time, place, and conditions into which you are born, or that you decide in concert with a divine plan that extends throughout the universe.

Gnostics, Hindus, Buddhists, Kabbalists, and Druids alike subscribe to the idea that human beings are not merely mortal shells. After the body dies, the indestructible soul is released into another dimension, where it waits to be reborn on earth and begin the process of learning again.

You may have a specific "task" or "reason" for assuming a particular lifetime. Karmic issues incurred during previous existences influence your present and future lifetimes. Consequently, your soul might have to wait until conditions on earth are optimal for you to undergo the spiritual growth you seek before you can re-enter a physical form.

Reverence for Nature

The worldview of most witches bears a similarity to that of the shaman. Like shamans, witches see the earth as a living, breathing entity to be honored and protected, not a place to conquer and control. Every living thing in this world—and the planet itself—possesses a spirit, a unique energy pattern or resonance. As a result, witches tend to think globally, and attempt to live in harmony with nature and the universe.

FACT

The word *shaman* is thought to derive from either of two sources. In Tunquso-Manchurian, the word *saman* means "one who knows." In Sanskrit, the term *sranaba* was used to describe an ascetic who depended on spirits to provide information, insight, and guidance.

With this in mind, most witches strive to weave their magick in accordance with natural laws, working in partnership with the planet instead of fighting it. Many witches are strong proponents of protecting the land and wildlife, feeling that the destruction of either is a crime against Gaia (or Gaea), one name for the earth's spirit; in Greek mythology, the goddess of the earth.

Stewardship of this planet doesn't end with donations to environmental causes or recycling efforts. It also involves magickal practices. Witches often send out positive energy through spells and rituals to help heal the planet and its inhabitants. The energy may be aimed at protecting a particular place or species or the whole world. Perhaps that sounds rather grand, but magick is only limited by the practitioner's perception of what it can and cannot do. If, as the Buddha said, "With our thoughts we create the world," there is no reason magickal energy cannot encompass the whole globe, like a giant hug.

"It's sacred ground we walk upon with every step we take," many witches sing. The idea is that you need to move gently, to respect all life, and to honor the sacredness in all things and in each other, in both your magickal and mundane life.

The Next Generation

"Teach your children in the way they should go," instructs a biblical writer. Does this idea apply to followers of Wicca and witchcraft, too? What are the karmic implications of "teaching" a child magickal methods and ideology? The magickal community continues to struggle with these types of questions. In part, a Neo-Pagan parent doesn't want to close the world of magick to his or her child. Young children, because they have wonderful imaginations and lack skepticism, can achieve amazing results from their magick. On the other hand, does teaching children magick interfere with their free will to choose their own paths?

One school of thought maintains that many witches were brought up in the Judeo-Christian tradition and now walk a different path; likewise, their children can change direction and choose their own faith as they mature. Magick was historically a family trained craft, so learning from a parent or grandparent is part of the witch's legacy.

A second school of thought says that children should find their own way, and parents should not influence their search for a personal path. Many witches have difficulty comprehending this approach because a parent teaches by example. How can a child *not* be influenced by a Wiccan parent who is truly walking the walk?

The answer for most parents lies somewhere between the two extremes. The primary consideration seems to be teaching children tolerance, respect for all life, earth-awareness, compassion, and self-confidence—in effect, teaching them to be good human beings. These basic values can be found in virtually every faith and worldview. Spirituality need not be colored by specific religious beliefs, dogma, and practices.

Many Wiccan and Neo-Pagan circles welcome children into magickal celebrations. Bardic circles invite children to sing or tell stories. In some rituals, each child present stands hand in hand between two adults, as an important part of the whole. Usually children enjoy participating in magick rituals when they are given the opportunity.

Another reason to teach children a magickal path is that they take to it quite naturally. There is passion in Wicca and witchcraft, a zest for life, and an appreciation for living that's refreshing. Children's joy and innocence can also teach adults much about magick and happiness.

Folklore and Superstitions

As you have seen, the roots of witchcraft and Wicca reach back to the origins of humanity. The magickal heritage carefully preserved by witches throughout the ages includes a rich body of folklore as well as tales of divine and legendary figures. Ancient rituals and practices, along with many, sometimes odd, superstitions, have also been handed down through generations.

Witchy Lore and Superstition

Fantastical tales and superstitions about witches and magick derive from various sources. Some beliefs developed from simple misunderstandings. For example, a witch might use a broom to vigorously sweep a space, in order to clear away any unwanted or disruptive energies. Observers of such a magickal rite, not realizing what they were seeing, misunderstood the witch's intent and may have thought she was trying rise off the ground. Thus, the idea that witches fly on their broomsticks was born.

Mainstream religions that intentionally wished to demonize the "Old Religion" also put forth erroneous concepts about witches. Still other ideas grew directly out of ancient magickal customs, country sayings, and primitive conventions.

FACT

Some modern witches make light of the nonsensical images most people hold. For example, as you drive to work one day, you might see a witch's car bearing a tongue-in-cheek bumper sticker that reads "Real witches don't melt in the rain" or "My other car is a broom."

Although some superstitions are rooted in truth, many are simply mis-representations of witches and what they do. Halloween is a good example. Pointy hats, costumes, and black cats—the symbols of this holiday—are misinterpreted by holiday revelers. Pointed hats, for instance, actually represent a cone of power and wisdom flowing from a higher source into the mind of the witch or wizard. Black cats aren't harbingers of bad luck; they have long been the faithful companions and familiars of witches. Donning a costume on Halloween (or Samhain, in witch-speak) serves as a visual affirmation to show what you hope to become in the next year—sort of a New Year's resolution, for Halloween is the witch's New Year's Eve.

Common Misconceptions

Witches do not eat babies, and they're not Satanists. They're more likely to wear a business suit than a pointy black hat. Most drive cars rather than ride broomsticks and prefer pizza to eye of newt any day.

Here are some common stereotypes:

- *Witches sell their souls to the devil in return for special powers.* This folkloric image is erroneous and has been fostered by mainstream religions.
- *Witches are humans who have psychic abilities.* This assumption may or may not be true. Some psychics may be witches; some but not all witches are psychic.
- *Witches are sorcerers.* This term is accurate from an anthropological point of view.
- *Witches are modern worshipers of ancient gods and goddesses.* This description is fairly accurate for Wiccans but not always for witches.
- *Witches cast evil spells on people, either for fun or revenge, such as turning men into toads.* Although witches do cast spells for people (with their permission), these spells are done to help others, not to harm them. And if they could, most witches would rather turn frogs into princes!
- *Witches are old, ugly hags.* Witches come in all shapes, sizes, and ages—many are quite beautiful, and young women are eagerly

joining the ranks of Wicca. This stereotype is inspired by the crone, a woman whose child-rearing responsibilities are behind her and who can now devote herself to her Craft.

Only education and understanding can uproot misconceptions and prejudices about witches. Many universities now offer classes in the history and practice of magick and witchcraft. Wicca is the fastest-growing religion in America—even the U.S. Armed Forces now officially recognizes Wicca, according to a National Public Radio program. It's time to start thinking of witches and Wiccans in a whole new sense—as people who are simply living their lives in a uniquely magickal way.

CHAPTER 2

A Brief History of Magick and Witchcraft

Witches have a rich cultural heritage that they continue celebrating today. Witchcraft's origins are hidden in antiquity—most likely, people around the world have practiced magick and witchcraft in some form since the beginning of time. Anthropologists speculate that Stonehenge may have been a sacred site where magickal rituals were performed, and the cave paintings in southern France might have been expressions of sympathetic magick. Today interest in the Craft is reawakening as contemporary witches put a modern spin on an ancient worldview.

The Old Religion

It's impossible to separate magick and witchcraft. Although not all magick falls under the broad title of witchcraft, all witches practice magick in one form or another. At the dawn of the human race, when people first came to understand cause and effect, they began trying to explain the mysteries of earth and the heavens. If a wind blew down a tree and hurt someone, the wind might be characterized as "angry" or considered to be a spirit worthy of appeasement. In this manner, aspects of nature were anthropomorphized and the first vestiges of magickal thinking were born.

As civilizations developed, each brought a new flavor and tone to magickal ideas. One of these ideas was that the universe is a web composed of all kinds of invisible interlocking strands or connections. If humans could learn to influence one of these connections, they could affect the whole web.

At first, these attempts to influence the world were very simple: one action to produce one result. The action usually corresponded symbolically to the desired result. For example, to bind an angry spirit, a person might tie a knot in a piece of rope. If the action worked, or seemed to work, it was used again. Eventually a tradition developed.

ALERT!

Modern Wicca and witchcraft have departed from the custom of handing over magickal authority to a select few. Today, everyone is welcome to explore these paths and processes, not just an elite group. In fact, utilizing one's personal power is encouraged—through individual exploration, the field of magick has evolved and expanded greatly.

Our ancestors delegated the tasks of influencing the universe to a few wise individuals, who were elevated to positions of authority in their community. These people existed in diverse cultures and under various names—shaman, priest, magus, or witch. They all performed the same basic functions, though their specific actions and observances generally depended on their particular culture and era. Here are some titles of magickal practitioners from around the world:

- A ba'alath ob: mistress of talismans (Hebrew)
- Cyrabderis: witchdoctor (Mexican Spanish)
- Kashaph: magus and sorcerer (Hebrew)
- Magos: wise person (Greek)
- Maleficus: diabolical witch (Latin)
- Strega: witch (Italian).
- Volvas: sorceress (Norse)

Over time, attempts at influencing fate became more elaborate and included ritualistic attempts to coerce the ancestors, powerful spirits, or gods into action. The community placed a few venerated people in charge of such sacred duties. In early Celtic communities, for example, the Druids who served as seers, healers, advisors, and spiritual leaders were second in power only to the clan's chieftain.

Witchcraft in Europe

It's been said that history is written by the victors. History is imperfect and is often clouded by societal, personal, or political agendas; therefore, the study of magickal history is no easy task. To trace the course of events to modern Wicca and witchcraft, one can begin by examining the early manifestations of witchcraft in Europe.

"History is the witness that testifies to the passing of time; it illumines reality, vitalizes memory, provides guidance in daily life and brings us tidings of antiquity."

—Marcus Tullius Cicero (106–43 B.C.E.),
Roman orator, statesman, and philosopher

There are at least four competing interpretations of how witchcraft took root in Europe. The first view, which most in the magickal community have rejected, is that witches never really existed. According to this opinion, witchcraft was simply an invention of the Church authorities, used specifically to gain power and wealth.

The second view suggests that witchcraft developed out of European fertility cults that emphasized a goddess as a central deity. Although this concept has some merit, historians have yet to substantiate it with written chronicles.

The third view says that the idea of witchcraft was a social convention and superstition. When people could not explain an unpleasant event, they blamed someone whom they labeled a witch. This perspective traditionally does not allow for the existence of real witches, but instead considers them to be merely superstition.

The last theory describes how witchcraft evolved gradually from a wide variety of practices and customs. Many of these customs are rooted in paganism, Hebrew mysticism, Celtic tradition, and Greek folklore surrounding sorcery. Many of these customs carried through to Christianity—vestiges of magickal and pagan practices were prevalent in the early Church, and some remain to this day.

Saint Brigid was a Celtic goddess so beloved by the common people that the Church adapted her story and canonized her. This is an excellent example of pagan beliefs and symbolism that the early Church "borrowed" and incorporated into its own traditions.

Despite the Church's obvious connection to paganism, early Christians did everything in their power to discourage the old ways. Books of penance from the Middle Ages frequently speak of punishments for people caught practicing magick. For example, a mother caught putting her daughter on the roof to cure sickness was commanded to do penance for seven years (penance generally consisted of some type of fasting or other restriction).

Witchcraft was also influenced by the myths that traveled from one culture to the next. As the Vikings and the Romans invaded the British Isles, their legends, gods, and goddesses mixed with the beliefs of the indigenous people. Traders and travelers, too, brought stories and ideas to the lands they visited, so that cross-pollination occurred.

Additionally, because most people in earlier centuries were illiterate, magickal traditions were handed down through generations by oral teaching. The few individuals who did possess the ability to read and write probably recorded information according to their own views. Therefore, it's difficult to ascertain what's true and what's fantasy regarding long-ago magickal practices.

FACT

St. Patrick is lauded in Catholicism for having driven the snakes out of Ireland. Snakes are symbols of occult wisdom, kundalini energy, sexuality, and the Old Religion that existed for thousands of years in Ireland, Britain, and Europe before the ascent of Christianity; therefore, St. Patrick is actually revered for driving out the spiritual beliefs that predated Christianity.

Witchcraft Outlawed

During the eighth and ninth centuries, laws regulating witchcraft became much more prevalent. Some of these laws made sense and seem reasonable by today's standards. For example, Charlemagne made human sacrifice a crime punishable by death.

Other laws, however, began to undermine the customs and traditions of the common people. For example, in 743, the Synod of Rome declared it a crime to leave offerings to spirits. In 829, the Synod of Paris passed a decree proclaiming that the Church no longer tolerated incantations and idolatry. By 900, Christian scholars were devoting much time and effort to writing about how women were supposedly being led astray by the devil. These events helped prepare the scene for the fury of the Inquisition.

The Inquisition

Between the 1100s and 1300s, the Church continued to discredit witches. Christian zealots presented a picture of witches as evil creatures who cavorted with the devil, despised all things sacred, ate children, and held wild orgies to seduce innocents. Stories of sorcerers who required that supplicants renounce the Church or Christ as payment for their services ran rampant.

The tales and heinous charges ascribed to medieval witches were nothing new. Similar accusations happened when the Romans and the Christians first clashed, and when the Syrians fought against the Jews. Even today, religious extremists hurl malicious charges at one another. Every group, it seems, wants its beliefs to be upheld as the one "true" religion.

Members of the European learned community railed against the evils of witchcraft in flowery language, and preachers disseminated these ideas among the common folk. In effect, the Church labeled everything magickal as heresy. Witchcraft became a crime against God and the Church. From the twelfth century onward, both clerical and civil law grew harsher toward witchery. Between 1317 and 1319, Pope John XXII authorized a religious court, known as the Inquisition, to proceed against sorcerers and all persons who were believed to have made a pact with the devil.

Thousands of trials proceeded. Punishments included burning and excommunication, as well as hanging. The interrogation process involved torturing people to get them to confess the "truth"—that is, to force them to admit to whatever the inquisitor wished—and to name other witches.

"In 1484, the Papal Bull of Innocent VIII unleashed the power of the Inquisition against the Old Religion. With the publication of the *Malleus Maleficarum*, 'The Hammer of the Witches,' by Dominicans Kramer and Sprenger in 1486, the groundwork was laid for a reign of terror that was to hold all of Europe in its grip until well into the seventeenth century."
—Starhawk, *The Spiral Dance*

In the process, accusing someone of witchcraft became a bureaucratic convenience. Not only those who actually practiced the Craft were tortured, imprisoned, and killed—anyone whom the authorities disliked or feared might be accused of being a witch. Conviction rates soared as many "undesirables" fell prey to the Inquisitors.

The atmosphere in England was less radical than on the continent. Because Henry VIII had separated from the Catholic Church, practicing witchcraft was regarded as a civil violation, and fewer instances of death sentences were handed out. In part, this may have been due to the influence of John Dee, a wizard of some renown, who served as an advisor to Queen Elizabeth I.

The Burning Times

The witch-hunt craze picked up speed during the Reformation period. The intellectual leaders of this religious movement, which sought to reform the Christian practices of Europe and reject the Catholic Church as the only true Christianity, offered no protection to those accused of witchcraft. The public, confused and struggling with the new religious ideas being put forth, was only too willing to blame anyone whose opinions and traditions differed. Anybody with a grudge against a neighbor might denounce her as a witch. It was the perfect environment for mass persecution. The legal sanctions against witchery became even harsher than before, and the lengths to which authorities would go to secure a confession grew even more malevolent.

The infamous *Malleus Maleficarum*, a guidebook for Inquisitors, added fuel to the fires of Christian righteousness. The torturers believed that if an accused person was not guilty, God would certainly intervene. When divine intervention didn't happen, the subsequent confessions and deaths increased the Inquisitors' fervor and power.

FACT

As occurs in all tragedies, some individuals profited from the witch hunts. Payments were given to informants and witch hunters who produced victims. In some instances, male doctors benefited financially when their competitors—female midwives and herbalists—were condemned as witches.

During the so-called Burning Times in Europe, which lasted from the fourteenth until the eighteenth centuries, at least tens of thousands and possibly millions of people were executed as witches, depending on which source you choose to accept. The majority of these were women and girls. So thorough were the exterminations that after Germany's witch trials of 1585 two villages in the Bishopric of Trier were left with only one woman surviving in each.

During the Burning Times, cats were feared as witches' familiars and destroyed by the thousands. It's been theorized that the Black Plague, which devastated Europe's human population, resulted in part because the rat population increased and spread disease when their natural predators were eliminated.

It's hard to know for certain why the witch hysteria finally subsided. Part of it may have been that people grew weary of the violence. In England, the hunts declined after the early 1700s, when the witch statute was finally repealed. The last execution on record occurred in Germany in 1775.

Witchcraft in the New World

In the New World, witchcraft evolved as a patchwork quilt of beliefs and practices. Many different concepts, cultures, and customs existed side by side, sometimes overlapping and influencing one another. Each new group of immigrants brought with them their individual views and traditions. Over time, they produced a rich tapestry of magickal thought.

Medicine men and women of the native tribes in North, Central, and South America had engaged in various forms of magick for centuries. They tapped the plant kingdom for healing purposes and divined the future. They communed with spirits, ancestors, and other nonphysical beings, seeking divine aid with crops and the hunt. Like pagans of other lands, these indigenous people honored Mother Earth and all her creatures. And, like magicians everywhere, they manipulated the forces of nature to produce results.

When white settlers migrated to the New World, they infused their concepts and customs into the territory. Not all of the early European immigrants were Christians. Some followed the Old Religion and sought freedom to practice their beliefs in a new land. Old World pagans continued with their magickal workings as they had in their native countries. Evidence suggests that some of these people joined Indian tribes whose ideas were compatible with their own.

The African slave trade brought the traditions of African witches to the Americas. Followers of voudoun, Santeria, macumba, and other faiths carried their beliefs and rituals with them to the Caribbean and the southern states of the United States, where they continue to flourish today.

The Salem Witch Trials

When William Griggs, the village doctor in colonial Salem Village (now Salem), Massachusetts, couldn't heal the ailing daughter and niece of Reverend Samuel Parris, he claimed the girls had been bewitched. Thus began the infamous Salem witch hunt that remains one of America's great tragedies. Soon girls in Salem and surrounding communities were "crying out" the names of "witches" who had supposedly caused their illnesses.

Between June and October of 1692, nineteen men and women were hung and another man was crushed to death for the crime of witchcraft. More than 150 other victims were thrown into prison, where several died, on charges of being in league with the devil.

FACT

Today, the victims of the Salem Witch Trials are commemorated by engraved stones nestled in a small, tree-shaded park off Derby Street, near the city's waterfront and tourist district. Visitors are invited to walk through the memorial and remember Salem's darkest hour.

Religious and political factors combined to create the witch craze in Salem. A recent smallpox epidemic and attacks by nearby Indian tribes had left the community deeply fearful. Competition between rivals Rev. James Bayley of neighboring Salem Town (now Danvers) and Rev. Parris exacerbated the tension as both ministers capitalized on their Puritan parishioners' fear of Satan to boost their own power.

The hysteria also enabled local authorities to rid the community of undesirables and dissidents. Economic interests, too, played a role in the condemnation of Salem's "witches"—those convicted had their assets confiscated and their property was added to the town's coffers. A number of the executed and accused women owned property and were not governed by either husbands or male relatives.

Witchcraft's Rebirth

Despite centuries of persecution, witchcraft never died. It just went underground. Witches continued to hand down teachings, concepts, and practices from mother to daughter, father to son, in secret. Through oral tradition, rituals, codes, and symbols, magickal information passed from generation to generation, at every level of society.

Some parts of the world, of course, never experienced the witch hysteria that infested Europe and Salem, Massachusetts. But even in those places where persecution once raged, witchcraft and magick reawakened during the nineteenth and twentieth centuries.

Magick in the Victorian Era

Interest in magick, mysticism, spiritualism, and the occult in general blossomed toward the end of the nineteenth century, perhaps as a reaction to the Age of Reason's emphasis on logic and empiricism. The magicians of this era had a strong impact on the evolution of contemporary witchcraft and magick.

One noted figure of the time was Charles Godfrey Leland, a Pennsylvania scholar and writer who traveled widely studying the folklore of numerous cultures. His most famous book, *Aradia*, or the *Gospel of the Witches* became an important text that influenced the development of Neo-Paganism and modern-day witchcraft. Another was Madame Helena Blavatsky, a Russian-born medium who moved to New York and founded the Theosophical Society with Henry Steel Olcott. Theosophy, which means "divine wisdom," combines ideas from the Greek mystery schools, the Essenes, Gnostics, Hindus, Buddhists, Christians, Neoplatonists, and others, as discussed in her best-known books *The Secret Doctrine* and *Isis Unveiled*.

The Hermetic Order of the Golden Dawn, begun by Englishmen William Wescott, S. L. MacGregor Mathers, and William Woodman, was the most important magickal order to arise in the West during the Victorian period. All three men were Freemasons and members of the Rosicrucian Society, which influenced their beliefs and practices. The order's complex teachings drew upon the ideas and traditions of numerous ancient cultures and melded them into an intricate system of ceremonial magick.

The most significant symbol in the Golden Dawn's magickal repertoire was the Tree of Life from the Hebrew kabbalah. This geometric figure depicts the stages of personal transformation that a magician must go through to achieve illumination. The order also incorporated elements from Hindu mythology, yoga, astrology, alchemy, the tarot, ancient languages, and many other subjects into its ideology and rituals.

The Golden Dawn's magick rituals were written by the noted British poet and mystic, William Butler Yeats, who was one of the order's most prominent members, in collaboration with founding father S. L. MacGregor Mathers.

The most notorious member of the Golden Dawn was Aleister Crowley, a controversial and charismatic figure who many say was the greatest magician of the twentieth century. After breaking with the Golden Dawn, he formed his own secret society, called Argenteum Astrum, or Silver Star, and later became the head of the Ordo Templi Orientis (Order of the Templars of the Orient or OTO). Much of his magick centered upon the use of sexual energy. The author of numerous books on magick and the occult, Crowley also created one of the most popular tarot decks with Lady Frieda Harris, known as the Thoth Deck.

Neo-Paganism

Pagan was originally a derogatory term used by the Church to refer to people, often rural folk, who had not converted to Christianity. Generally speaking, today's Neo-Pagans can be described as individuals who uphold an earth-honoring philosophy and attempt to live in harmony with all life on the planet as well as with the cosmos. Pagans tend to be polytheistic rather than worshiping only a single god or goddess, although some pagans may not revere any particular deity. Like Wiccans, they celebrate nature's cycles and the eight holidays discussed in Chapter 4.

The pagan and Wiccan communities overlap a great deal and share many beliefs, interests, and practices. Not all pagans are witches or Wiccans, although Wiccans and witches are pagans. Because of the similarities between them, pagans and Wiccans often combine their resources for political, humanitarian, environmental, and educational objectives.

Wicca and Feminism

It's no surprise that Wicca gained popularity during the 1960s and '70s as feminism emerged. For women who were raised in patriarchal religions, Wicca offers balance and equality. It is one of the few faiths that honors a feminine deity. In fact, many women probably became interested in Wicca during those decades because of its feminist appeal rather than its spiritual tenets.

"In Wicca, the Goddess is seen as the creator of all that is," explains Debbie Michaud in *The Healing Traditions & Spiritual Practices of Wicca*. "She represents the power of the feminine, and a way to connect to all life on this planet."

Hungarian hereditary witch Zsuzsanna Budapest was one of the early influences in feminism's link with Wicca. Other pioneers, including California writer Starhawk, author of the bestseller *The Spiral Dance*, and Margot Adler, journalist for National Public Radio and author of several books including *Drawing Down the Moon*, also guided Wicca's growth through the

'70s and '80s. In the early days of the women's movement, some witches found it difficult to separate the political from the spiritual nature of Wicca. Over time, however, many of Wicca's followers—and many feminists—have broadened and deepened their understanding of women's power as well as their relationship with the Goddess.

Dianic covens, named for the independent Roman goddess Diana, are feminist in orientation and place more importance on the female principle than the male. If you consider feminism beyond its limited, political sense, however, and see it as a worldview that equally values both women and men, feminine and masculine energies, then Wicca is inherently a feminist religion.

ALERT!

It's important to note, as Starhawk points out in *The Spiral Dance*, that Wiccans don't see the Goddess as ruler of the world—she is the world. She is the divine energy and power manifest in all things and in each of us.

In Wiccan terms, the Goddess is often depicted in three aspects—maiden, mother, and crone—that signify the three phases of womanhood. Wiccans also see Mother Earth as a manifestation of the Goddess. God, the masculine principle, is considered to be the Goddess's equal and is often viewed as her consort. The Goddess is linked with the moon, the God with the sun. Many Wiccan rituals and sabbats are based on the changing relationships between the earth, the sun, and other heavenly bodies.

Wicca and Witchcraft Today

In the last few decades, the ranks of Wicca and witchcraft have swelled rapidly. Although it's impossible to accurately determine how many people practice witchcraft, a study done in 2001 by City University of New York found 134,000 self-described Wiccans in the U.S.

The American Academy of Religions now includes panels on Wicca and witchcraft. The Defense Department recognizes Wicca as an official religion and allows Wiccan soldiers to state their belief on their dog tags. As of 2006, an estimated 1,800 Wiccans were serving in the U.S. military.

Undoubtedly, the Internet has been instrumental in bringing the pagan and Wiccan communities together, and in spreading information about the Craft. By enabling witches around the world to connect with one another in a safe and anonymous manner, the Internet has helped extend witchcraft's influence to all corners of the globe. Today you'll find thousands of Web sites and blog sites devoted to the subjects of Neo-Paganism, Wicca, witchcraft, and magick, along with lots of intelligent, thought-provoking ideas and scholarship. Witchcraft isn't a static belief system or rigid body of rules and rituals; it's a living entity that's continually evolving and expanding. As education dissolves fear and misconceptions, magickal thinking and practices will gain greater acceptance among the general populace and influence the spiritual growth of all people, regardless of their specific faiths.

CHAPTER 3

The Divine Realm

Throughout history, virtually every culture has entertained visions of a divine realm populated by one or more beings with supernatural powers. Depicted in these divine beings are archetypes that transcend the boundaries of time and location. The great Mother Goddess, for example, appears as Mary, Demeter, Ceres, Isis, and many other female creator figures. Wiccans honor both a God and a Goddess; Neo-Pagans often recognize a number of deities. Some witches follow a specific faith and worship one or more gods or goddesses; some aren't religious at all.

One Deity or Many?

Early people connected spirits with the wind, nature, the stars, and the forces behind seemingly inexplicable phenomena. These divine beings were said to watch over creation and guide human destiny. As the earth's population grew and cultures interacted with one another—though war, trade, and migration—humankind's conceptions of the heavenly realm evolved.

Some spirits fell out of favor as our ancestors learned more about the actual workings of the physical world and the universe. In some instances, small tribal gods and goddesses merged with or gave way to deities with more extensive powers. Some deities went by different names and faces in different countries—Venus in Rome, Aphrodite in Greece, Amaterasu in Japan—although their attributes were essentially the same.

Whether you choose to honor a single god or goddess or many different deities is purely a personal choice. Witches, Wiccans, and Neo-Pagans—just like followers of other faiths—often disagree about the nature of the Divine. Many people believe that all spiritual paths are equally valid and all lead to the same place.

The ascendance of Judaism and Christianity, which extolled a single God, pushed out polytheistic religious beliefs in most of the Western world. The growth of Neo-Pagan, Wiccan, and Goddess-based spirituality, however, has reawakened an interest in polytheism and led many people to consider multiple aspects of the Divine.

How do you envision the Divine? How do you integrate sacred energy into your own life? Do you believe in many gods and goddesses, one deity with many faces, or a single Supreme Being?

Divine Trinities

Even religions that uphold a belief in one Supreme Being distinguish different facets of that entity. Often the Divine is viewed as a holy trinity. Christianity, for instance, envisions God as having three distinct aspects: Father, Son, and Holy Spirit. Wiccans portray the Goddess as Maiden, Mother, and

Crone. Islam talks of the three daughters of Allah, the eldest of whom presides over fate.

The early Greeks built three separate temples to Hera: one for the child, one for the wife, and one for the widow. Isis, Osiris, and Horus composed the ancient Egyptians' divine trio. The Zoryas (Slavonic warrior goddesses) represented dawn, dark, and midnight in one power. Carmenta (the Roman goddess of childbirth) had two sisters with whom she worked constantly: Antevorta (looking forward) and Postorta (looking back).

Choosing Gods and Goddesses

It is natural for humans to want to make gods and goddesses in their image, which is why there are literally thousands of names for the divine beings honored around the world. As you explore the myths and traditions of various cultures, you may feel an affinity with certain deities whose attributes correspond to your own spiritual vision. Some witches naturally relate to the gods and goddesses that are part of their personal heritage. Italians might gravitate to Strega, Scandinavians to Freya, Greeks to Sophia, Irish to Brigid.

A specific god or goddess might appear to a witch in a dream, meditation, or vision. Countless people throughout history have experienced visitations from divine beings. Myths and legends from many cultures speak of gods and goddesses interacting with humans. Such appearances aren't just a thing of the past—they can happen to anyone, anytime.

ALERT!

Some gods and goddesses may be "right" for you at one period in your life, while others seem appropriate to your path at other stages of your development. Young women, for instance, might admire Diana's vitality and independence; older women can relate to the wisdom of Hecate.

Once you've familiarized yourself with a number of gods and goddesses, you may opt to petition one or more for help with a specific task. If you are facing a formidable challenge or obstacle, you could call on the Hindu god Ganesh to assist you. Perhaps you wish to incorporate a certain deity's attributes into your own character. If you want to develop qualities of compassion you might align yourself with the Kuan Yin, the Asian goddess of mercy.

How Do Gods and Goddesses Reveal Themselves?

The answer depends on the person asking the question. If you tend to be a visual person, you might see a vision that you associate with a particular god or goddess. Isis, for instance, might send an image of winged arms or appear as a great bird. If your auditory sense is strong, you may hear a deity speak to you. Brigid might invite you to stir her cauldron or Yemaya's song might penetrate your dreams. Apollo may make his presence known via the scent of bay leaf, one of his sacred plants. Suffice it to say that the Divine knows how to connect with each person through a medium that he or she will understand.

Frequently, deities communicate with humans through dreams. While sleeping, you're more receptive to symbols and signs than you are in your ordinary waking state. Gods and goddesses may slip you messages while you're meditating, too. Perhaps you may receive insights while you're engaged in mundane tasks, such as putting on makeup or washing dishes—when your mind is only partly focused on the familiar activity, allowing room for spiritual discourse to take place.

Many people believe that higher powers are always trying to communicate with us and are eager to assist us in our spiritual development. As Carol K. Anthony says in her book *A Guide to the I Ching*, "the light is always there, but we must be open to see it."

Pay attention to signs. To American Indians, the appearance of an animal or bird may be a signal from a divine being who has assumed the creature's form in order to convey information. Listen to your intuition, too—hunches can be messages from a higher source.

The Divine Feminine

Perhaps the most profound and omnipresent symbol of the Divine Feminine is Mother Earth herself. Concern for the environment and "green" practices demonstrate respect for the Goddess, who is manifest in all of nature. It's no accident that movements honoring the earth and the Goddess evolved simultaneously. Indeed, many witches believe that unless Goddess energy reawakens within each of us and in the world as a whole, the planet may be destroyed.

Witches often depict the Goddess in three stages that represent the three phases of a woman's life: maiden, mother, and crone. Celtic art illustrates this tripart nature as three interlocking pointed loops called *vesica piscis*, which symbolize the opening to the womb. Others show the feminine trinity as three phases of the moon: waxing, waning, and full.

The Maiden

The Maiden Goddess signifies youth. In this aspect, she symbolizes innocence, hope, joy, curiosity, flexibility, courage, and enthusiasm. Greco-Roman mythology expressed this phase of the Goddess as Luna, the chaste moon goddess. Diana, Artemis, Eos, Renpet, Bast, and Persephone also characterize the maiden aspect of the Divine Feminine.

In magickal work, the following can serve as symbolic associations for the Maiden:

- Baby animals (before puberty)
- The colors silver, white, and light blue
- Lightweight clothing and delicate fabrics such as gauze, lace, thin cotton, and silk
- Clear quartz, pearl, diamond, aquamarine
- The chaste tree, meadowsweet, lemongrass, white rose, hyacinth, narcissus, crocus, apple blossoms, peach blossoms, lilac, gardenia
- The morning hours of the day, from dawn until noon
- The spring months
- The waxing moon

The Mother

The Mother Goddess signifies maturity. Her attributes include fertility, creativity, nurturing, comfort, abundance, strength, sensuality, confidence, and power. Pele, Gaia, Freya, Isis, Ceres, Demeter, Brigid, Oshun, Yemaja, Aphrodite, Venus, Tara, and Mary are among the goddesses who personify the mother phase of the Divine Feminine.

In magickal work, the following can serve as symbolic associations for the Mother:

- Pregnant or nursing animals
- Rich colors: ruby red, forest green, royal blue, and amber
- Luxurious clothing and fabrics including velvet, damask, cashmere, silk, and mohair
- Geode, emerald, turquoise, opal, coral, rose quartz, amber
- Apple, pomegranate, peach, raspberry, strawberry, red clover, red rose, mint, iris, jasmine, cinnamon, parsley, daisy, myrtle, orchid, saffron
- The afternoon hours, from noon to sunset
- Summer through the harvest season
- The full moon

The Crone

The Crone signifies the years after menopause. In some traditions, a woman is considered a Crone after she has experienced her second Saturn Return (usually at about age fifty-eight). The attributes inherent in this aspect of the Divine Feminine include wisdom, intuition, prophecy, stability, pragmatism, patience, detachment, and fortitude.

The last phase of womanhood, the crone period, is the one usually associated with witches. The traditional images of the ancient crone or hag aren't attractive, but that reaction is not surprising. Humans are afraid of mortality and the Crone reminds one of old age and death.

Sophia, Hecate, Ceridwen, White Buffalo Woman, Butterfly Woman, Kali, Lilith, Baba Yaga, and Kuan Yin are among the goddesses who personify the crone phase of the Divine Feminine. In magickal work, the following can serve as symbolic associations for the Crone:

- Old animals
- Dark colors: brown, black, midnight blue, purple
- Heavy clothing (often robes) and fabrics including wool, linen, and velvet
- Smoky quartz, jet, onyx, amethyst, fossils
- Holly, mandrake, pine, juniper, mistletoe, nightshade, nuts, oak, moss, wintergreen, ginseng; also dried or withered plants
- The hours from sunset to dawn
- Late fall and winter
- The waning moon

Goddesses and Their Attributes

Cultures around the world have long viewed the Goddess in many forms, with many faces. Our ancestors divided the Divine Feminine into lots of different deities and assigned certain attributes, powers, and responsibilities to each. Thus, individual goddesses express the various aspects of the feminine archetype.

Some depictions of the Goddess embody characteristics that are unique to the national or religious traditions of the people who worshiped her. In most cases, however, goddess figures express similar qualities, regardless of the country or faith with which they are associated.

FACT

The Greek goddess Aphrodite and the Romans' Venus both represent love and beauty. Pele, the Hawaiian fire goddess, has much in common with Kali, the Indian goddess of destruction and rebirth. The Buddhist Kuan Yin and the Christian Mary both symbolize compassion.

Whatever she's called, however her story is told, the inherent features of the Divine Feminine—fertility, creativity, compassion, wisdom, beauty, love, healing—can be seen in the deities of all cultures. Here are some of the world's many goddesses and the attributes usually associated with them.

GODDESSES OF THE WORLD		
Name	**Culture**	**Attributes**
Aino	Finnish	beauty
Amaterasu	Japanese	beauty, leadership, brightness
Aphrodite	Greek	love, beauty, sensuality
Artemis	Greek	courage, independence, protection
Axo Mama	Peruvian	fertility
Bast	Egyptian	playfulness, joy
Brigid	Celtic	creativity, smithcraft, inspiration, healing
Calypso	Greek	music
Ceres	Roman	nourishment, health
Ceridwin	Celtic	inspiration, wisdom
Concordia	Roman	peace
Cybele	Asia Minor	fertility
Diana	Roman	hunting, purity, independence
Freya	Norse	love, healing, sensuality
Hathor	Egyptian	love
Hecate	Greek	magick, death, wisdom

Inanna	Sumerian	journeys, facing fears, courage, grief
Isis	Egyptian	art, nourishment, wholeness, awakening
Kali	Indian	transformation, destruction, change
Kuan Yin	Chinese	compassion, humanitarianism, mercy
Lakshmi	Indian	wealth, abundance
Medea	Greek	magick
Pele	Hawaiian	fiery spirit, destruction and rebirth, vitality
Sekmet	Egyptian	grace, dignity, strength
Siva	Slavic	fertility
Sophia	Greek	wisdom, primal power
Uttu	Sumerian	creativity
Tara	Indian	nourishment, protection, compassion
Tiamet	Babylonian	power, magick, protection
Wang-mu	Chinese	immortality
Yemaja	Nigerian	secrets, dreams, childbirth, purification

On days when a witch wishes to connect with certain qualities in herself or wants to strengthen abilities she feels are weak, she can ask for help from a goddess who embodies those beneficial qualities. Say you have an important business meeting coming up and you want to make a good impression. The Egyptian sun goddess Sekmet, depicted as a lioness, symbolizes the attributes you desire to accomplish your goals. Align yourself with her energy to accomplish your aims.

The Divine Masculine

The feminine is not complete without the male; together, these energetic polarities form a whole. Before the re-emergence of goddess-centered spirituality, only the male divinity's face was present in most parts of the world. Some Wiccans and witches concentrate on the Divine Feminine. Others, however, believe that the Divine expresses as both male and female.

Witches often depict the Divine Masculine as having three faces, which represent the stages of a man's life: youth, maturity, and old age. However, witches aren't the only ones who envision a tripart God. Christians honor the male trinity of Father, Son, and Holy Spirit. In the Hindu religion, Brahma represents the creative principle of God, Vishnu is considered the preserver, and Shiva is the destroyer. Although the cultural aspects of these deities may differ, they still recognize the tripart expression of the masculine force.

The Son

The youthful aspect of the God is depicted as the Son. He signifies naiveté, daring, a sense of adventure, vitality, action, exuberance, and freedom. The ancient Egyptians expressed this archetype as Horus, who flies through the sky freely, with the sun in one eye and the moon in the other.

In magickal mythology, the Oak King represents the waxing year. This rather cocky young male takes over from the elder aspect of the God at year's end by battling him for the crown. The tale of Sir Gawain and the Green Knight is an excellent illustration of this concept, the Green Knight being the elder god.

The Horned God that witches honor also symbolizes this facet of the Divine Masculine. His wildness, sensuality, and passion make him brashly attractive. This deity expresses the witch's connection to nature as well, and to all the primal magick therein. Cupid (the son of Venus) is another easily discernible example of the youthful virility associated with the Son.

The Father

In the Father, the mature face of God is emphasized. This aspect of the Divine Masculine represents strength, power, authority, leadership ability, protection, responsibility, and courage. He is viewed as the warrior king in some cultures, the wise ruler in others. In modern Western society, he could be seen as the capable corporate executive.

FACT

Mars, the god of war in Roman mythology, was a staunch protector of the land. He symbolizes the transition from the son aspect of the God to the father phase. Interestingly enough, another name for Mars was Marpiter (Father Mars), implying an older, more experienced deity.

Like the Goddess, the God possesses a creative aspect. Indeed, both forces are necessary for creation. The Father God in some early cultures oversaw the crafts, such as those of the smiths who were regarded as magick workers in their own right. Hephaestus, originally a fire god in Lycia and Asia Minor, eventually became the god of craftspeople in Greece. He earned this reputation by constructing palaces for the gods and fashioning Zeus's thunderbolts. This creative aspect of the Father can also be seen in the figure of Bahloo, the Australian aborigine All-Father, whose job was to create all animals and people with his consort.

The Grandfather

The elder aspect of the masculine deity, or Grandfather, is as wise and wily as his female consort. He oversees the underworld (the place where souls are said to go between lives), destiny, death, resurrection, and justice. Like the Crone's, his concerns extend beyond the physical world and involve the process of transformation, assimilation of knowledge, and movement between the various levels of existence.

In the tarot, the grandfather aspect of the God energy is illustrated as The Hermit. This card usually shows a bearded old man dressed in long robes, retreating into the darkness. However, he holds a lantern high, shining light to illuminate the way for those who wish to follow and learn what he knows.

The mythological elder god, known as the Holly King, who battles with the Oak King is one version of the grandfather archetype. Truthfully, the grandfather could win this battle with his wits if he so chooses. Nonetheless, he allows himself to lose so that the Wheel of Life will keep turning.

Gods and Their Attributes

Since the beginning of time, cultures around the world have honored a masculine force. The *yang* energy of the universe has been depicted in various guises and personalities, as individual deities with specific natures, powers, and responsibilities. The many faces of the God express qualities associated with the male archetype: strength, virility, daring, leadership skills, logic, protection, knowledge, and courage. Here are some of the god figures found in various cultures around the world and the attributes connected with them.

GODS OF THE WORLD		
Name	**Culture**	**Attributes**
Adibuddha	Indian	ultimate male essence
Aengus	Irish	youth, love
Agassou	Benin	protection, guidance
Ahura Mazda	Persian	knowledge

Aker	Egyptian	gatekeeper
Anu	Babylonian	fate
Apollo	Greek	beauty, poetry, music, healing
Bes	Egyptian	playfulness
Bunjil	Australian	vital breath
Byelbog	Slavonic	forest protector
Damballah	Haitian	wisdom, reassurance
Ea	Chaldean	magick, wisdom
Ganesa	Indian	strength, perseverance, overcoming obstacles
Green Man	Celtic	fertility, nature, abundance, sexuality
Hanuman	Indian	learning
Horus	Egyptian	knowledge, eternal life, protection
Itzamna	Mayan	written communication
Lugh	Celtic	craftsmanship, healing, magick
Mars	Roman	aggression, war, vitality, courage
Mercury	Roman	intelligence, communication, trade, travel
Mithras	Persian	strength, virility, courage, wisdom
Odin	Scandinavian	knowledge, poetry, prophesy
Osiris	Egyptian	vegetation, civilization, learning
Pan	Greek	woodlands, nature, fertility
Shiva	Indian	destruction, transformation

Sin	Chaldean	time, life cycles
Thoth	Egyptian	knowledge, science, the arts
Tyr	Teutonic	law, athletics
Vishnu	Indian	preservation, stability
Zeus	Greek	authority, justice, abundance, magnanimity

Archetypes transcend nationalities and religions, appearing in various yet similar forms in many different cultures. For example, the Greek god Zeus corresponds to the Roman god Jupiter. You can see overlaps between the Egyptian god Thoth and the Greeks' Hermes. Mars and Mithras, both gods of war, were worshiped by soldiers in Rome and Persia, respectively.

On days when a witch wishes to identify with certain god-like qualities, she can ask for help from a deity who embodies those attributes. If you want to ace an exam, you could call on Mercury, Thoth, or Hermes to assist you. If you hope to overcome a formidable challenge or adversary, Ganesh is the god with whom to ally yourself. Regardless of your goal or concern, you'll find a deity who can provide the help you need.

Honoring and Invoking Deities

How can you get a god or goddess on your side? Many witches believe that divine assistance is always available to you and that the deities gladly offer their guidance, help, and energy to humans to use for positive purposes. Some view divine beings as higher aspects of human consciousness, which can be accessed and activated through magickal means.

If you want to connect with a particular entity, first ask that god or goddess to listen to your request and come to your aid. One theory states that deities will not interfere with your own free will—you must ask them sincerely for help.

If you aren't used to considering a divine being as a partner in your spiritual and practical pursuits, you may wonder how to go about petitioning your favorite god or goddess for assistance. Here are a few suggestions:

- Make an offering of some sort to the deity. Burning incense is a popular offering, although you may wish to choose an offering that more specifically corresponds to the nature of the deity whose help you seek.
- Place a figurine of the chosen deity on your altar and focus your attention on it.
- Use an oracle, such as tarot cards or runes, to access Divine Wisdom and open your mind to messages from the deities.
- Pray.
- Meditate.
- Light a candle in honor of the deity you wish to petition.
- Design and perform a ritual to the deity.
- Write your request on a slip of paper, then burn it.
- Choose a crystal or gemstone that relates to the deity. Carry the stone in your pocket and touch it periodically.
- Plant herbs or flowers in honor of the god or goddess. Choose plants that correspond to the deity's nature and your intent, such as roses for love or mint for prosperity.

Other Spiritual Entities

Although ordinarily you can't see them, many beings share your world with you. Perhaps you're aware of spirits around you—you may see or hear them, or simply sense their presence. Some of the entities reside here in the physical realm, others exist in what is often thought of as heaven. These distinctions, however, are a bit misleading, as the various levels of existence aren't really separate—they interact with and permeate one another.

Folklore and fairy tales frequently refer to nonphysical entities. Seafaring legends, for instance, often mention mermaids. Leprechauns appear with regularity in Irish lore. Angels and spiritual guardians are discussed in the mythologies of most religions. So many people—not just witches—claim to have witnessed these beings that it's hard to dismiss them as pure fantasy.

Elementals

Elementals are so named because they represent the four elements: earth, air, fire, and water. Most of the time you can't see them, though occasionally they cross over into human beings' range of vision. If you befriend them, elementals can serve as devoted helpers who will eagerly assist you in performing magick spells.

Make sure to treat elementals with consideration and respect—if they don't like you, they might play tricks on you. Always remember to thank the elementals who assist you in your spell working, too, and perhaps offer them a small gift to show your appreciation.

Gnomes are earth spirits. Sometimes called trolls or leprechauns, these creatures can assist you with practical matters and prosperity magick. *Salamanders* are fire spirits. When you need inspiration, courage, or a boost of vitality, call upon these lively beings. *Sylphs* are air spirits; their specialty is communication. Seek their aid when you need help with negotiating contracts, legal issues, or other concerns that involve communication. *Ondines* are water spirits. They can help you with emotional matters, especially love spells.

Faeries

Most people think of faeries as tiny Tinkerbell-like creatures, but that's not an accurate perception—those delicate, winged beings are probably sylphs. Opinions vary regarding the true nature of faeries. By some accounts, faeries evolved from the Picts, the indigenous people who lived in Ireland and parts of Britain before the Saxons invaded the Isles. Morgan Le Fay, King Arthur's sister, may have been a *bean-sidhe* or faery woman.

Another theory suggests that faeries are the energetic prototypes from which humans developed. These beings look like beautiful people whose forms are virtually perfect. Faeries are said to live almost forever—in the faery world time as you know it has no meaning.

Regardless of which view you accept, you'll want to proceed cautiously if you decided to deal with faeries. Clever shapeshifters, these beings can be tricksters who might help or harm you, depending on how they feel about you. It's said that life with the faeries is so seductive you won't want—or be able—to return to an ordinary earthly existence once you enter their world. Legend warns that eating or drinking with them will trap you in the faery realm forever.

Ancestors

Native Americans and Asians, in particular, often call upon the ancestors for guidance and assistance. "Ancestors" may be actual, deceased relatives of the person who petitions them, or they can be spirits the person never knew on earth. These wise, compassionate entities serve as guardians and guides, offering healing, protection, and other benefits to human beings. The "Sage" referred to in the *I Ching* is a good example of an ancestor figure.

You could choose to meet with your ancestors by going on a shamanic journey, mentally traveling to the spirit world as you would physically travel on earth to visit friends or relatives. Unlike faeries and elementals, the ancestors don't play tricks on humans; they are concerned with the well-being and spiritual advancement of earth's creatures. In return for an ancestor's help, you may want to offer a gift to express your thanks. Native Americans frequently make offerings of tobacco in gratitude.

Angels

Virtually every faith speaks of angels in its legends, myths, and religious texts. According to most views, angels are considered to be cosmic messengers and spiritual guardians. They protect and guide human beings. They also serve as celestial helpers who carry requests between earth and the divine realm.

Pictures almost always depict angels with glowing haloes and beautiful feathered wings, and people usually describe them as having these features. However, this may be an illusion. Most likely, haloes and wings are vital energy fields or auras emanating from an angel's form.

Spiritual and magickal traditions present many different conceptions of angels. The most common image is the guardian angel. Many people believe that everyone has a personal angelic guide, a benevolent being who may or may not have been human at one time. Your angel hears your prayers, watches over you, and helps you handle the challenges in your life.

Another theory proposes the existence of an angelic hierarchy, composed of many types of angels with varying roles and powers. This hierarchy includes seven levels of angelic beings, the lowest level being personal guardian angels (which are just above humans). Archangels, including Michael, Gabriel, Raphael, and Uriel, occupy the second level. Above them come the Principalities, then the Powers, Virtues, Dominions, and Cherubim. The Seraphim reside on the topmost tier. These heavenly hosts combat evil forces and keep the universe functioning.

How you choose to view spirits is up to you. You may accept or reject the existence of any or all nonphysical entities. Most witches believe in at least some of these spirits, although their ideas often differ. If you are among the "believers," you might want to work with some of these spiritual beings. In the magickal view of the world, all entities—physical and nonphysical— are linked energetically. When you improve your relationships with angels, faeries, elementals, and others in the spirit realms, everything in the universe benefits.

CHAPTER 4

The Wheel of the Year

For centuries, earth-honoring cultures have followed the sun's apparent passage through the sky. Your ancestors divided the Wheel of the Year, as the sun's annual cycle is known, into eight periods of approximately six weeks each. Each "spoke" corresponds to a particular degree in the zodiac. Wiccans and other pagans call these eight holidays (or holy days) "sabbats." It's no coincidence that many modern-day holidays fall close to these ancient, solar dates. Each of these special days affords unique opportunities for performing magick spells and rituals.

Samhain

The most holy of the sabbats, Samhain (pronounced SOW-een) is usually observed on the night of October 31, when the sun is in the zodiac sign Scorpio. Better known as Halloween or All Hallow's Eve, this is the holiday people usually associate with witches and magick. Most of the ways the general public marks this sabbat, however, stem from misconceptions—it's a solemn and sacred day for witches, not a time for fear or humor. Some religious groups that don't understand its true meaning feel threatened or offended by Halloween and have even tried to ban it.

The Holiday's Significance

Considered to be the witches' New Year, Samhain begins the Wheel of the Year. Thus, it is a time of death and rebirth. In many parts of the Northern Hemisphere the land is barren, the last of the crops have been plowed under for compost, and the earth rests in preparation for spring. Witches often choose to shed old habits or attitudes at this time, replacing them with new ones in connection with the ongoing cycle of destruction and renewal. Samhain is also a good time to perform banishing spells.

Magicians believe the veil that separates the seen and unseen worlds is thinnest at Samhain. Consequently, many witches do divination during Samhain, because insights and information can flow more easily on this sabbat than at any other time of the year.

For witches, Samhain is a time to remember and honor loved ones who have passed over to the other side. That's why Halloween is associated with the dead. No, skeletons don't rise from graves, nor do ghosts haunt the living on Samhain, as movies and popular culture tend to portray it. Witches may attempt to contact spirits in other realms of existence, however, or request guidance from ancestors or guardians.

Ways to Celebrate

What would Halloween be without colorful costumes? This practice stems from the early custom of making wishes on Samhain, similar to making New Year's resolutions. Wearing a costume is a powerful magick spell, a visual affirmation of your intentions. No witch would portray herself as a hobo or ghost! Instead, try dressing up as the person you'd like to be in the coming year.

FACT

The Halloween customs of bobbing for apples and giving apples as treats have their roots in the Old Religion. According to mythology, the apple is one of the Goddess's favorite fruits. If you cut one in half, you'll see that the seeds form a pentagram inside.

Samhain is a good time to do a psychological housecleaning. On a slip of paper, write whatever you want to leave behind when the old year dies— fear, self-limiting attitudes, bad habits, and so on. Then burn the paper in a ritual fire.

Southwestern witches sometimes combine features from the Mexican Day of the Dead with Celtic pagan customs on Samhain. In central Texas, people decorate their altars to mark the sabbat, often displaying photos of deceased loved ones whom they wish to honor. During the week before Samhain, they go house to house, visiting the altars of friends and relatives, offering prayers and paying respects.

Winter Solstice or Yule

The Winter Solstice occurs when the sun reaches 0 degrees of the zodiac sign Capricorn, usually around December 21. This is the shortest day of the year in the Northern Hemisphere. Also known as Yule, the holiday marks the turning point in the sun's descent into darkness; from this point, the days grow steadily longer for a period of six months. Thus, witches celebrate this sabbat as a time of renewal and hope.

The Holiday's Significance

Pagan mythology describes the apparent passage of the sun through the heavens each year as the journey of the Sun King, who drives his bright chariot across the sky. In pre-Christian Europe and Britain, the Winter Solstice celebrated the Sun King's birth. This beloved deity brought light into the world during the darkest time of all.

It's easy to see parallels between the Old Religion's myth and the Christmas story. You can also see the light theme expressed in the custom of lighting candles during Hanukkah and Kwanzaa, both of which fall near the Winter Solstice. In all these religious practices, light symbolizes blessings, joy, and promise.

Ways to Celebrate

Before the Victorian era, Christians didn't decorate their homes at Christmas with ornamented pine trees and holiday greenery. That's a pagan custom. Because evergreen trees retain their needles even during the cold winter months, they symbolize the triumph of life over death. Holly was sacred to the Druids. According to Celtic mythology, holly bushes afforded shelter for the earth elementals during the wintertime. The Druids valued mistletoe as an herb of fertility and immortality. It has long been used in talismans as an aphrodisiac—perhaps that's the reason people kiss beneath it today.

In a magickal sense, pine is used for its cleansing properties. The crisp, clean scent of pine needles can help eliminate negative energies from your home. You don't have to wait for Yule to clear bad vibes from your home, however. Burning pine-scented incense or candles can do the trick, too.

Burning the Yule log is another ancient tradition with which pagans mark the Winter Solstice. On the eve of Yule, witches build a fire from the wood of the nine sacred trees. The central figure in the Yule fire is an oak log, for the oak tree represents strength and longevity. After the fire burns down, anyone who wishes may collect ashes and wrap them in a piece of cloth. If you place the package under your pillow, you'll receive dreams that provide guidance and advice for the coming year.

Imbolc, Brigid's Day, or Candlemas

This sabbat honors Brigid, the beloved Celtic goddess of healing, smithcraft, and poetry. A favorite of the Irish people, Brigid was adopted by the Church and canonized as Saint Brigid when Christianity moved into Ireland. Her holiday is celebrated either on February 1 or around February 5, when the sun reaches 15 degrees of Aquarius. In the Northern Hemisphere, daylight is increasing and the promise of spring is in the air. Therefore, Imbolc is celebrated as a time of hope and renewal.

The Holiday's Significance

Brigid is one of the fertility goddesses, and Imbolc means "in the belly." This holiday honors all forms of creativity, of the mind as well as the body. Illustrations of Brigid sometimes show her stirring a great cauldron, the witch's magick tool that symbolizes the womb and the receptive, fertile nature of the Divine Feminine. As goddess of inspiration, Brigid encourages everyone, regardless of gender, to stir the inner cauldron of creativity that exists within.

ALERT!

Brigid goes by many names, including Lady of the Flame, Goddess of the Hearth, and Bright One. Her feast day is sometimes called Candlemas due to her association with fire. In magickal thinking, the fire element is believed to fuel inspiration and creativity.

Although Brigid is an aspect of the Divine Feminine, her day falls under the zodiac sign Aquarius, a masculine air sign in astrology. Her blazing hearth is both the metalsmith's forge and the homemaker's cook fire. Thus, she represents mind and body, a blend of yin and yang energies, and the union of polarities that is necessary for creation.

Ways to Celebrate

On Imbolc, the Sun King's chariot ascends in the sky; the sun's rays grow stronger and days grow longer. Witches celebrate this spoke in the Wheel of the Year as a reaffirmation of life and a time to plant "seeds" for the future. You may wish to build a fire in a magick cauldron to honor Brigid. On a piece of paper, write wishes you want to materialize during the year, then drop the paper into the cauldron. As the paper burns, the smoke rises toward the heavens carrying your requests to Brigid.

In keeping with holiday's theme of fire, many people light candles to honor the Goddess. Candles are the most common tool in the witch's magickal tool box, used in all sorts of spells and rituals. Engrave words that represent your wishes—love, prosperity, health, etc.—into the candle's wax. Then light the candle and focus your attention on its flame, while you envision your wishes coming true.

Spring Equinox or Ostara

Pagans and witches celebrate Ostara (also known as Eostre) when the sun enters 0 degrees of Aries, around March 21. In the Northern Hemisphere, the Spring Equinox ushers in warmer weather, days that are longer than nights, and the advent of new life. Christianity adopted this joyful period of the year for the celebration of Easter (which usually falls near the Spring Equinox). Ostara gets its name from the German fertility goddess Ostare; the word *Easter* derives from the same root. Both holidays celebrate the triumph of life over death.

The Holiday's Significance

The Sun King's chariot continues climbing higher in the sky, reaching the point at which day and night are of equal length on Ostara. Therefore, this sabbat is associated with balance, equality, and harmony.

The Spring Equinox marks the first day of spring and the start of the busy planting season in agrarian cultures. Farmers till their fields and sow seeds. Trees begin to bud, spring flowers blossom, and baby animals are born. Ostara, therefore, is one of the fertility holidays and a time for planting seeds—literally or figuratively.

Ways to Celebrate

On Ostara, sow seeds that you want to bear fruit in the coming months. This is an ideal time to launch new career ventures, move to a new home, or begin a new relationship. If you're a gardener, you'll start preparing the soil and planting flowers, herbs, and/or vegetables now. Consider the magickal properties of botanicals and choose plants that represent your intentions. Even if you aren't a gardener, you could plant seeds in a flowerpot to symbolize wishes you hope will grow to fruition in the coming months.

Witches connect each plant—herb, flower, and tree—with specific magickal properties. Sage, for example, is used for purification rituals. Mint and parsley can be added to prosperity talismans to attract wealth. White snapdragons insure protection and roses play an important role in love magick.

FACT

In an old German story, a rabbit laid some sacred eggs and decorated them as a gift for the fertility goddess Ostara. Ostara liked the beautiful eggs so much that she asked the rabbit to share the eggs with everyone throughout the world.

Some popular Easter customs have their roots in Ostara's symbolism. Eggs represent the promise of new life, and painting them bright colors engages the creative aspect of the sabbat. You might enjoy decorating eggs with magickal symbols, such as pentagrams and spirals. And rabbits, of course, have long been linked with fertility.

Beltane

Witches usually celebrate Beltane on May 1, although some prefer to mark it around May 5, when the sun reaches 15 degrees of Taurus. The sabbat is named for the god Baal or Bel, sometimes called "the bright one." In Scottish Gaelic, the word *bealtainn* means "fires of Belos" and refers to the bonfires pagans light on this sabbat. The joyful festival celebrates the earth's fertility, when flowers bloom and plants begin sprouting in the fields. The Christian Church adopted this ancient holiday as May Day, and some of Beltane's old rituals (sans the overt sexuality) are still enacted today.

The Holiday's Significance

The second fertility holiday in the Wheel of the Year, Beltane coincides with a period of fruitfulness. To ancient and modern pagans alike, this holiday honors the earth and all of nature. In early agrarian cultures, farmers built fires on Beltane and led livestock between the flames to increase their fertility.

Sexuality is also celebrated on this sabbat—the Great Rite has traditionally been part of the holiday's festivities. In pre-Christian days, Beltane celebrants engaged in sexual intercourse in the fields as a form of symbolic magick to encourage fertility and a bountiful harvest. Children who were conceived at this time were said to belong to the Goddess.

Ways to Celebrate

It's best to celebrate Beltane outside in order to appreciate nature's fullness. Because Beltane is a fertility holiday, many of its rituals contain sexual symbolism. The Maypole, around which young females dance, is an obvious phallic symbol. Witches often decorate the Maypole with flowers in recognition of the earth's beauty and fruitfulness. Sometimes a woman who seeks a partner will toss a circular garland over the top of the pole, signifying the sex act, as a way of asking the Goddess to send her a lover.

Beltane's connection with the earth and fullness makes this sabbat an ideal time to perform prosperity magick. Incorporate peppermint, parsley, lavender, alfalfa, cedar, or money plant into your spells. This is also a good time to make offerings to Mother Earth and the nature spirits.

Another fertility ritual utilizes the cauldron, symbol of the womb. Women who wish to become pregnant build a small fire in the cauldron, then jump over it. If you prefer, you can leap over the cauldron to spark creativity in the mind instead of the body.

Summer Solstice or Midsummer

In the Northern Hemisphere, the Summer Solstice is the longest day of the year. The Sun King has now reached the highest point in his journey through the heavens. Witches generally celebrate Midsummer around June 21, when the sun enters 0 degrees of the zodiac sign Cancer. This is a time of abundance, when the earth puts forth her bounty.

The Holiday's Significance

In early agrarian cultures, Midsummer marked a period of plenty when food was abundant and life was easy. Our ancestors celebrated this joyful holiday with feasting and revelry. At this point, however, the sun has reached its pinnacle and begins its descent once again. Celtic pagan mythology depicts this as the end of the Oak King's reign as he is overthrown by the Holly King, who presides over the waning part of the year.

Folklore says that at Midsummer earth spirits abound—Shakespeare's delightful play *A Midsummer Night's Dream* was inspired by this belief. Apparently, life on every level rejoices in the fullness of the season. If you wish, you can commune with the elementals and faeries at this time.

Ways to Celebrate

Just as they've done for centuries, witches today celebrate the Summer Solstice with feasting, music, dancing, and thanksgiving. Remember to share your bounty with the animals and birds, too, and to return something to Mother Earth as a sign of gratitude.

Midsummer is also a good time to collect herbs, flowers, and other plants to use in magick spells. Some say that if you wish to become invisible, you must wear an amulet that includes seeds from forest ferns gathered on Midsummer's eve. Spells for success and abundance are best done on the Summer Solstice.

Lughnassadh or Lammas

Named for the Irish Celtic god Lugh (Lew in Wales), this holiday is celebrated either on August 1 or around August 5, when the sun reaches 15 degrees of Leo. According to Celtic mythology, Lugh is an older and wiser personification of the god Baal or Bel (for whom Beltane is named). Lughnassadh (pronounced LOO-na-saad) is the first of the harvest festivals. The early Christians dubbed the holiday *Lammas*, meaning "loaf-mass," because the grain was cut at this time of the year and made into bread.

The Holiday's Significance

Corn, wheat, and other grains are typically harvested around Lughnassadh. In agrarian cultures, this was the time to begin preparing for the barren winter months that lay ahead. Our ancestors cut, ground, and stored grain, canned fruit and vegetables, and brewed wine and beer in late summer. The old English song "John Barleycorn Must Die" describes the seasonal ritual of rendering grain into ale.

> "Threshing of the harvest was considered a sacred act and the threshing barn a sacred place. An old fertility custom is still practiced when a new bride is carried over the threshold."
> —Debbie Michaud, *The Healing Traditions & Spiritual Practices of Wicca*

Early pagans sold their wares at harvest fairs and held athletic competitions at this time of the year. You can see this age-old tradition carried on today at country fairs throughout rural parts of the United States.

Ways to Celebrate

Today, witches enjoy sharing bread and beer with friends on Lughnassadh, just as they've done for millennia. You might like to bake fresh bread from scratch or even brew your own beer as part of the celebration. While you're kneading the bread, add a dried bean to the dough. When you serve the bread, whoever gets the bean in his piece will be granted a wish.

If you like, you can fashion a doll from corn, wheat, or straw to represent the Sun King. To symbolize the time of year when his powers are waning, burn the effigy in a ritual fire as an offering to Mother Earth. The custom of decorating your home with dried corncobs, gourds, nuts, and other fruits of the harvest is also connected to Lughnassadh.

Autumn Equinox or Mabon

The Autumn Equinox usually occurs on or about September 22, when the sun reaches 0 degrees of Libra. Once again, day and night are of equal length, signifying a time of balance, equality, and harmony. Mabon is also the second harvest festival, and witches consider it a time for giving thanks for the abundance Mother Earth has provided.

The Holiday's Significance

This sabbat marks the last spoke in the Wheel of the Year. From this day until the Winter Solstice, the Sun King's path arcs downward toward earth. As the days grow shorter and the cold, barren winter approaches, witches reflect on the joys and sorrows, successes and failures of the year that is nearing its conclusion.

Mabon is a good time to do magick spells that involve decrease or endings. Do you want to let go of self-destructive beliefs? Lose weight? End an unfulfilling relationship? Now is the time to break old habits and patterns that have been limiting you.

Anything you wish to eliminate from your life can now be released safely, before the New Year begins with Samhain. In keeping with the theme of balance, witches also attempt to align themselves with the forces of nature on Mabon and to unite the disparate parts of themselves in order to achieve peace and harmony within.

Ways to Celebrate

Because the Equinox is a time of balance, try to balance yin and yang, active and passive on this day. Seek rest and activity, solitude and socializing in equal portions. Engaging in creative endeavors of all kinds is also a good way to mark the sabbat.

CHAPTER 5

Meditation and Visualization

Many witches consider meditation and visualization essential to the practice of magick. In order to perform spells, you must shift your ordinary, everyday consciousness and thinking to another level. One of the easiest and safest ways to enter this elevated state of awareness is through meditation. Meditation also enables you to clear your mind and calm your body. In this relaxed, centered condition, you can receive information and insights from the divine realm.

What Is Meditation?

For many people, the word meditation conjures up images of Buddhist monks sitting cross-legged, intoning "ooooommmm." However, meditation in one form or another has been a part of every major religion throughout the world. In the past few decades, conventional Western medicine, professional sports, correctional facilities, and the business world have also discovered the benefits of meditation. Meditation is sometimes described as listening to God, whereas prayer is talking to the Divine.

According to Dr. Martin Hart, President of the American Society of Alternative Therapists, meditation "provides a direct access route into the unconscious, without using artificial means." Because the unconscious stores everything we've ever experienced, Hart says in meditation "a greater level of information is available to us and this allows us to make better choices in the conscious state."

When you meditate, you empty your mind of all thoughts and become receptive, allowing impressions and inspiration—from your subconscious or from a higher source—to flow into your awareness. The body's processes slow down. You feel calm, relaxed, and centered.

According to Jeremy Taylor, a seventeenth-century English prelate and author, "Meditation is the tongue of the soul and the language of our spirit." Perhaps that sounds somewhat lofty, but meditation isn't a high-and-mighty process, and you don't need to be a monk to do it. In time, with a little practice, virtually anyone who wants to can learn to meditate.

Why Do People Meditate?

People who practice transcendental meditation (or TM), the most widespread type of meditation in the United States, say their goal is to achieve inner connection and focus. Taoists and Buddhists meditate to reach a place of total stillness within. Others seek to clarify their vision of the universe and Spirit. How a person approaches meditation depends on her cultural, religious, spiritual, or philosophical perspective.

Meditation enables you to contemplate ideas at a deeper level and better comprehend them. In meditation, you can explore the great mysteries that have engaged human hearts and minds for eons. Some people choose to ponder a single concept, word, or image, such as the Zen saying "one hand clapping," during meditation. This technique strengthens your mental muscles and expands your perception.

According to Eddie and Debbie Shapiro, authors of *The Meditation Book*, "Meditation is not a goal in itself." Rather, meditation's purpose is "to bring about the transformation of our perception of ourselves and our world—from that of skepticism and doubt to acceptance and kindness."

Witches find meditation useful because it helps them gain mental and emotional clarity. Daily meditation clears the clutter from your mind, balances the relationship between the inner and outer worlds, disperses tension, centers the spirit, and creates a positive atmosphere for working magick. From this hushed state of the body and soul, you can channel energy more easily. Stress and anxiety dam up the flow of creative energy. As magicians know, a clear, still, focused mind and a quiet heart are necessary to perform effective spells.

Historical Background

The roots of meditation are impossible to trace. The first time a human being gazed thoughtfully into the night sky or paused to reflect upon the beauty of a flower, he was meditating. The dancer twirling near a tribal fire who suddenly felt outside herself, the bard who gave himself over fully to his song and the muse—these people and others like them moved into a meditative state without trying.

The first written texts that link meditation (as an altered state of consciousness) to various therapeutic benefits appeared around three thousand years ago among Indian yogis. Early Christian mystics also practiced meditation, in connection with prayer, contemplation, and fasting, as a way to achieve a direct experience of God. The Bible contains numerous references to states of awareness that sound very much like those achieved through meditation.

In 1959, Maharishi Mahesh Yogi introduced TM into the United States. During the 1960s and '70s, as the New Age movement grew and Westerners sought natural ways to achieve greater peace and well-being, meditation's popularity expanded rapidly.

A few decades ago, medical institutions began examining meditation more seriously. Studies clearly showed the physical benefits of meditation. Today, many hospitals and medical facilities offer instruction in meditation, and many doctors recommend it to their patients.

Health Benefits of Meditation

The benefits of meditation aren't merely subjective; they can be measured physically. During meditation, you move from your ordinary beta state of awareness to alpha. Brainwave frequencies shift from the usual 13 to 30 cycles per second to 8 to 13 cycles per second. Heart rate and respiration slow. The brain also steps up production of endorphins, the proteins that enhance positive feelings.

FACT

The American Heart Association reports that daily meditation can reduce the risk of heart attack and stroke. Health insurance statistics show that people who meditate regularly are less prone to illness—87 percent fewer are hospitalized for coronary disease and 55 percent fewer for cancer.

Clinical studies at Charles Drew University of Medicine and Science in Los Angeles and the University of California, Los Angeles have demonstrated that regular meditation can lower high blood pressure and help alleviate many other stress-oriented problems. People who suffer from chronic pain have discovered that meditation can reduce their discomfort. Every day you are bombarded with sights, sounds, and hundreds of pieces of information that keep your mind buzzing at warp speed. When you meditate, all that busyness slows down; you stop worrying about work, money, relationships, and daily responsibilities, and allow yourself to exist only in the moment. It's like going on a short retreat without ever leaving home.

Regular meditation also aids:

- Mental clarity
- Emotional detachment and objectivity
- Awareness of the body-mind-spirit connection
- Inner peace and harmony
- Creativity and imagination
- Intuition
- Instincts (and control over those instincts)
- Sports performance
- Balance between heart and mind
- Sense of purpose
- Anger management
- Work proficiency
- Feelings of well-being and self-esteem
- Relationships with others, the environment, and the world

You don't need to subscribe to a particular religious or philosophical belief system to benefit from meditation. Whether you're seeking spiritual, mental, emotional, or physical benefits, meditation can be the "soul food" you need to live a healthier, happier life.

How to Meditate

So exactly where should you begin? Do you have to sit in a lotus position, like a human pretzel? Should you press your thumbs and index fingers together and chant *OM*? Well, first of all, just relax. If you can do that much, you're well on your way. The following directions offer suggestions and guidelines to help you get the most out of meditation. You don't have to follow them exactly. Trust your instincts; if something feels awkward, don't do it. And remember, give yourself a chance—meditation isn't something you'll master overnight.

Your mind is accustomed to thinking of dozens of things at once; now you're asking it to stop multitasking and hone in on one particular idea or goal. That's why the Buddha recommended three things for successful meditation (or any spiritual pursuit): Practice, practice, practice!

Let go of any preconceptions about how fast you should be "getting it," or what kind of magickal experiences might result. If you set a lot of expectations for yourself, you're likely to be disappointed and make learning more difficult. Meditation isn't something you strive or push yourself to excel at. You ease into it.

Find a convenient place and a comfortable position that you can sit in for a while. The more comfortable your body is, the easier it becomes for your mind to direct its attention toward the purpose you've intended. At first, your mind is going to jump about from thought to thought, like a butterfly flitting from flower to flower. Everything from a little twitch in your leg to a dog barking down the road can potentially break your concentration. That's why meditation is considered a discipline.

Close your eyes and give yourself permission to put the world around you "on hold" for a bit. Breathe slowly and deeply; pay attention to your breath. It may help to shake out your arms and legs or stretch a bit before you sit down to meditate. Some people like to do some light exercise, such as yoga or walking, to release tension prior to meditation.

Begin by committing yourself to just five minutes of meditation a day, then increase the amount of time over a period of weeks. Just sit quietly, with your eyes closed. At first five minutes may seem like an eternity, but soon you'll stop glancing at your watch and simply enjoy taking a brief time out to relax.

What to Expect

Each person's experience of meditation is unique, depending on personality, concentration level, and the goal of the meditation. Furthermore, your own experiences may not always be the same. Most meditators say they feel a sense of calm and inner peace. Some individuals report body sensations, such as warmth, a slight tingling in the extremities, or light-headedness.

FACT

Experts on meditation recommend meditating either first thing in the morning when you're fresh or right before your main meal of the day. Some people like to meditate twice a day, in the morning and in the evening before going to bed. Experiment and see what works best for you.

At deeper levels, you may experience a connection with Spirit (however you interpret that connection). You might also witness dreamlike visions or creative insights. Perhaps you'll achieve a sense of purpose or receive clarity that helps you resolve problems. This kind of inner knowing can't easily be described in words—but you'll know it when you feel it. Over time, meditation can help you resolve issues or change patterns in your life.

Aids to Meditation

Metered breathing is the most universally suggested meditation aid. Here's how it goes. Take three cleansing breaths in through your nose and out through your mouth. Continue to breathe slowly. Let one breath naturally lead to the next, so there's no break in the rhythm. Focus your attention on your breathing.

Now, just for the fun of it, breathe a little more quickly than normal for about ten seconds and see if your senses heighten or diminish. Inhale, hold that breath for a beat or two, then exhale normally. Repeat this for about five minutes and note the results. Now mix and match the breathing: inhale slowly, exhale quickly; exhale slowly, inhale quickly. Finally, try the slow, regular breathing again and notice how you feel. There's no right way—use whichever breathing pattern works best for you.

ALERT!

Aromatherapy can help calm and center you. Buddhists often burn incense in conjunction with meditation. If you prefer, you can place a few drops of essential oil on your pulse points. Lavender, sandalwood, clary sage, frankincense, vanilla, and pine are good choices. Only pure essential oils produce beneficial aromatherapy effects—synthetic scents won't work.

Some people find it useful to gently press the tips of the thumbs and forefingers together while meditating. Activating the acupressure points in the fingertips can encourage mental relaxation and insights. Others like to ring a bell prior to meditation as a cue or prompt.

Practice Makes Perfect

The more you exercise any skill, the better you'll get at it. The same is true of meditation. Here are some additional tips to improve the results you get from meditation.

- Meditate at the same time every day. Establishing a routine trains the mind to anticipate relaxation at a certain time.
- Eliminate all distractions (phone, TV, etc.).
- Create a sacred space for your daily meditations.
- Listen to soothing music without a melody, lyrics, or rhythmic beat.
- Gaze at a candle flame—the flickering produces a hypnotic effect.
- Design a ritual around your meditation.
- If you wish, smudge the area or cast a circle around the place where you meditate.
- Record your experiences and insights in a journal.

Be patient with yourself and keep practicing. It's not unusual to fall asleep during meditation (in fact, meditation is frequently prescribed for people with sleep disorders). You wouldn't expect to run a marathon without training, and you shouldn't expect to reach intense altered states of consciousness the first time you meditate, either.

End your meditation gently. Slowly bring your awareness back to normal. Open your eyes a little at a time. Wiggle your body a bit. Stay seated quietly for a few moments to give yourself a chance to adjust and return to everyday reality—don't get up too quickly, or you may become dizzy.

Different Types of Meditation

The best-known form of meditation is TM. This technique involves the repetition of a *mantra*—a meaningful word, sound, or phrase. A mantra gives your mind something to focus on while you're meditating. If you choose to repeat a phrase, make sure it's a short, positive statement such as an affirmation. (You'll learn more about affirmations and mantras in the next chapter.)

Buddhists often chant as part of their meditation practice. When you chant, you repeat a word, phrase, blessing, or prayer in a rhythmic, singsong manner. The repetitive nature of a chant, as well as the actual words that compose it, act on your subconscious to generate the desired result.

Harmonious sounds can help disperse blocked energy and promote the flow of beneficial *ch'i*, the vitalizing force that the Chinese believe animates all life. Playing or uttering pleasant sounds not only improves meditation, it's good *feng shui* and can enhance your whole environment.

Contemplation involves focusing on a particular object, idea, or image in order to gain greater insight into it. Zen *koans* (riddles) are sometimes used as topics for contemplation. Choose a thought or subject you wish to understand more deeply, such as love, peace, acceptance, or forgiveness, then focus your attention on it while meditating. Keep your mind open to receive insights.

In creative visualization, you form a mental picture that conveys relaxation, such as waves breaking gently on the sand. Hold the image in your mind in order to improve your focus. Creative visualization is an important part of working magick, as you'll learn shortly.

Active meditation sounds like an oxymoron, but that's exactly what you're doing when you rake a Zen garden, walk a labyrinth, or stroll peacefully through the woods. The key is to move slowly, mindfully, remaining attentive to your motions.

Drumming can also stimulate deep meditative states and even astral travel. The vibrations and resonance of drumsong mirror those of your own heart. Start out with slow, regular beats. Then let the sensations and your intuition guide you.

The Importance of Meditation in Magick

It's been said that magick is all in your mind—and it's true. Your mind is the most important ingredient in working magick. If you're distracted or your mind keeps jumping about from thought to thought, your spells won't be very effective. Mental clarity and concentration are essential to performing safe, powerful magick. That's why witches and other magicians often practice meditation—it trains and disciplines your mind.

Meditation also strengthens the link between you and the Divine. When your mind is calm and receptive, you can get messages from your angels, guides, or whatever higher power you recognize. Meditation expands your capacity for communication with unseen forces by shifting your brainwave activity into alpha rather than the usual beta. When all the daily chatter is silenced, you can hear "the still small voice within."

Meditation enhances your personal power, too, by connecting you with the higher forces. You feel more self-confident. Little things don't bother you so much. You sense that a divine energy is working through you and that you are part of a greater whole. You can let go and stop trying to control things and/or people. You become more accepting and can forgive others, thereby dissolving one of the obstacles to successful magick.

Creative Visualization

Before a house can be built or a dress can be fabricated, someone had to imagine it. The architect or the fashion designer first created a mental image of the finished product. That's what creative visualization means. The same is true in magick: visualization precedes manifestation.

Whether you realize it or not, you're constantly visualizing. When you read the word "apple" you instantly form an image in your mind. When you converse with someone, you mentally witness the scenarios being described.

Creative visualization isn't merely running pictures randomly across the landscape of your mind, however. The images you create have specific purposes. Some years ago, researchers discovered that cancer patients could improve their health by visualizing Pac-Man-type creatures gobbling up cancer cells. You can use visualization to facilitate relaxation, as mentioned earlier, to get a better job, to protect yourself and your loved ones—just about anything you desire.

The Power of Imagination

As a child, you probably played make-believe and imagined all sorts of fanciful situations. Perhaps you still spin out vivid daydreams or indulge "what if" scenarios in great detail. Conjuring up images at will and directing them toward carefully chosen objectives is the essence of creative visualization.

Most people underestimate the power of thought and the ability to change reality by changing your mind. But when you get right down to it, most of the decisions you make—especially the life-altering ones—are shaped in your mind long before you take any action. You might imagine a number of possibilities in detail before finally selecting one route to follow.

Sometimes the things you fear most come to pass, because you keep worrying about them and investing them with emotional energy. This is an example of the power of imagination at work, in a negative way. A witch never puts her mind on something she doesn't want to happen.

Your thoughts and visualizations guide energy in a particular direction. The Buddha said, "We are what we think. All that we are arises with our thoughts. With our thoughts, we make the world." Metaphysicians believe all thoughts resonate in the cosmic web that links human beings with everything else in the universe. When you form an image in your mind, you plant a seed in the web's energy matrix. The more you nourish that seed, focusing on the idea with deep feeling, the more likely it is to grow into something tangible.

Visualization in Magick

Visualization is a key component in magickal work. You must be able to form a picture in your mind of the result you intend to manifest. Clear, simple, vivid images generate faster and more satisfactory results than indistinct or confused concepts. First envision what you desire, then fuel the vision with your willpower to cause your intention to materialize. Your will animates the image and moves it from the realm of spirit to the physical realm.

FACT

Author Shakti Gawain brought the concept of creative visualization into widespread public awareness. Her bestselling book *Creative Visualization* contained ideas that witches have long utilized, and presented them in a way that virtually anyone could easily understand and apply in their daily lives.

Of course, there are right ways and wrong ways to use visualization in magick. The most important rule is to envision the outcome you desire. Don't focus on the problem or condition you wish to change. For instance, if your goal is to heal a broken leg, don't think about the injury—envision the leg strong and healthy. Don't concern yourself with the steps that lead to your destination, either. Just concentrate on the end result and the rest will fall into place.

Make sure to include yourself in your visualization. See yourself rolling in a pile of hundred-dollar bills or happily performing the job you desire.

Imbue your visualizations with as much sensation as possible. Instead of only seeing something occurring, allow yourself to hear, taste, smell, and touch as well.

Don't keep changing your mind or the images you've created. It's okay to refine and enrich them, but if you keep putting out new and different visions you'll confuse the matter.

Be patient. Some intentions take a while to manifest, especially complex goals or ones that involve other people.

You can create visualizations for yourself or for others, but if someone else is involved you should get permission first. Otherwise, you may be interfering with that person's free will or manipulating her. Visualizations for the good of all, such as envisioning world peace, are generally okay.

If you have trouble visualizing, here are a few tips that may help you improve your imaging skills:

- Think about your intention as you fall asleep and bring it into your consciousness as soon as you wake up in the morning.
- Use photos or pictures cut from magazines to strengthen your visualization process.
- Display images in a place where you'll see them often throughout the day, to continually remind you of your objective.
- Connect physical objects symbolically to your mental images. For instance, in a love spell two candles could symbolize you and your beloved.

Above all, believe that your visualization will bear fruit. As motivational speaker Denis Waitley puts it, "If you believe you can, you probably can. If you believe you won't, you most assuredly won't. Belief is the ignition switch that gets you off the launching pad."

Journeying to Other Worlds

As you become more adept at meditation and visualization, you may decide to take a journey in imagination. This type of journeying allows you to access other levels of awareness and interact with spirit beings who reside in these different worlds.

From the shamanic perspective, the universe is like a great castle with millions of rooms. When a human being assumes a physical body on earth, he enters one of those rooms. Most people never realize that countless other rooms exist. By shifting your perspective, you can journey to those rooms and discover what lies within.

A journey can be a guided meditation, led by a priest, priestess, shaman, or other facilitator. The person leading the journey may drum or play music to direct others in a type of astral travel. Sometimes the leader describes vivid imagery, which the travelers envision to help them move through various states of being.

Meet Your Spirit Guides

Frequently, witches journey to meet entities in the spirit world who can offer advice and guidance. When you journey, you may ask a guide or ancestor with whom you have already established rapport to accompany you. Or you might begin the journey with a purpose in mind and invite any spirit who wishes to help to come to you.

It's considered good manners to offer a gift of thanks to a spirit guide or animal you meet during a journey. Some Native Americans carry tobacco with them when they journey to give to their ancestors. After the journey, you can present an offering by leaving food outside for the "four-legged" and "winged" beings to carry to the spirits.

It's not uncommon to meet animals, birds, or other creatures during a journey. These spirit or totem animals usually appear in order to convey information that corresponds to their innate characteristics. For example, an elephant might inspire strength, a snail might suggest that you slow down. If you encounter an animal while journeying, ask it what message it brings—the insights you receive will be quite revelatory. Remember to thank the animal for its assistance.

CHAPTER 6

Sacred Sounds: Prayers, Affirmations, and Incantations

The universe constantly pulses with energy—everything is linked via an elegant network of vibrations. The so-called "music of the spheres" may be the resonances produced by the planets' energetic vibrations. Throughout history, human beings have used music, prayers, and chants as a way of communicating with the Divine. Sacred sounds, as witches know, ripple through the cosmic web to produce magickal results. Indeed, sound could be the catalyst that sparks creation and brings about harmony and healing on many levels.

Prayer

The religious community has never doubted the power of prayer to heal body, mind, and spirit. For thousands of years, in cultures around the world, the faithful have sought divine intervention to relieve suffering and attract blessings. Witches view prayer as a means of communicating with the Divine. That communication may take the form of a request, gratitude, worship, or simply opening up to Spirit.

John Bunyan, a seventeenth-century English preacher and writer, said that prayer is "sincere, sensible, affectionate pouring out of the soul to God." American poet Ralph Waldo Emerson described prayer as "a study of truth." The Unity Church calls prayer an "inward, silent knowing of the soul . . . of the presence of God."

Like meditation, praying calms the mind and body, placing you in a gently altered state of consciousness where you can receive insights and guidance. On the physical level, blood pressure drops, heartbeat slows, breathing rate is lowered, and the adrenal glands secrete fewer of the stress-response hormones.

The Components of Prayer

Many prayer groups believe forgiveness is also an important ingredient in prayer. According to C. Norman Shealy, M.D., Ph.D., founder of the American Holistic Medical Association, "Forgiveness produces miracles; lack of forgiveness inhibits miracles." Others suggest that prayer is a demonstration of hope. As magicians know, hopefulness and a positive attitude have the power to manifest beneficial results.

Surrender is another important component of prayer. In her bestselling book *A Return to Love*, Marianne Williamson writes, "Through openness and receptivity on the part of human consciousness, spirit is allowed to infuse our lives, to give them meaning and direction."

Prayer, of course, is more than mere words. It is part of a complete, unified attitude that brings body, mind, emotions, and spirit together. Prayer fosters a state of receptivity, awareness, trust, forgiveness, and gratitude, from which all things are possible.

How to Pray

Prayer can take many forms, from the formal repetition in a church or temple of memorized verses taken from a religious text to feeling grateful for a beautiful sunny day. You can pray silently or aloud, alone or with others, for yourself or someone else. You can pray to God, the Goddess, a Divine Spirit, the All-knowing Power of the Universe, your guardian angels, the ancestors—whatever presence you feel guides your life. You can pray first thing in the morning, before meals, at bedtime—or when you're stuck in traffic, in the shower, at your computer, or taking a walk in the park.

You can even join an online prayer group. The Internet offers hundreds of sites where you can post a prayer request, respond to others who currently need help, or read the personal testimonies of people who believe they've been helped by prayers. Some prayer groups "meet" in online chat rooms, blog sites, and specialized prayer subgroups for women, children, etc.

The Power of Prayer

Whether you pray for yourself or someone else, your words have amazing power. According to Larry Dossey, M.D., in cases of intercessory prayer (praying for someone else at a distance) the consciousness of whoever is doing the praying actually influences the body of the person who is being prayed for. Though this may sound strange to some people, shamans and witches have utilized this phenomenon for centuries to aid the healing process.

One highly visible case is that of former New York Jets football player Dennis Byrd, who broke his neck in a game and was paralyzed. Byrd's doctors thought he'd never walk again, but he does and he credits prayer with being a factor in his remarkable recovery.

FACT

Effective Prayer

Prayer is a highly personal matter and you can pray in myriad ways. However, certain practices and attitudes are more likely to produce beneficial results than others. Prayer isn't begging or pleading with the God or Goddess to give you what you want—it's humbly aligning your personal will with Divine Will. When you pray, you commit yourself to co-creating the best possible outcome, in conjunction with and under the guidance of a higher power.

Here are some guidelines that can help you pray effectively.

- Relax and "let go" (through breathing, meditation, yoga, music, etc.), so that you can still the mind and shift your awareness from the mundane world to the world of Spirit.
- Forgive yourself and others.
- Release fears and doubts.
- Give thanks for the blessings in your life and for Divine Intervention in previous situations.
- Be clear about what you want and hold this image in your mind's eye as intensely as possible.
- State your request aloud or silently, but try not to be so specific that you don't allow room for God to work "in mysterious ways."
- Turn over your request to a higher power, trusting that it will be taken care of in accordance with Divine Will.
- Be willing to do your part to bring about what you've asked for. If you have no power to influence what happens, release it and be willing to accept whatever Divine Will decides.

- Listen for a response or guidance in some form—an impression, insight, vision, awareness, physical sensation, even actual words.
- When your prayer is answered, express your gratitude. Rejoice and be thankful.

Perhaps the most important part of effective prayer—and the most difficult part—is faith. You may have heard the biblical saying that if you have faith the size of a mustard seed you can move mountains. If you don't truly believe your prayers will be answered—even if the outcome isn't quite what you envision—your skepticism will interfere with the prayer's success.

Prayers and Magick

Although some witches may resist the idea of prayer, associating it with organized religion, many are reclaiming prayer as a key ingredient in working magick. Prayers are a kind of respectful, deity-directed spell. When you pray for something, you indicate your desire for something to manifest. That's what you do when you utter a spell, too. Although not all witches believe in a higher power, if a magician honors Spirit in any form, prayer certainly has a place in her magick.

Witches often use ritual to put themselves in the right frame of mind to work magick, incorporating prayers into the ritual. Some people light candles, chant, play music, dance, drum, or move in special ways. Some invite various gods and goddesses to participate in the ritual. A Wiccan might call the quarters to bless and guide the ritual, an invocation that qualifies as prayer.

Some witches direct prayers to a particular deity whose attributes are in harmony with the request. For instance, you might petition Aphrodite for help in matters of the heart. Other witches pray in a more general manner, such as asking for world peace, trusting a higher power to intervene in whatever way is appropriate.

Because it's impossible for humans to realize all the facets of a situation, witches often end their prayers (and spells) with the phrase "for the good of all, and may it harm none." This phrase releases the prayer's energy to the Divine, so it can be guided toward the best possible outcome, even if the result isn't exactly what is expected.

Chanting

Each human being is born with a wonderful instrument that can be used for healing, transformation, and magick: the voice. Since the dawn of time, people have employed this oldest and most accessible of musical instruments to praise deities, interact with each other, and celebrate the cycles of life. Recently, Western healers have rediscovered what witches and shamans have understood for millennia. By harnessing the power inherent in the human voice, you can balance body, mind, and spirit.

Chants are typically words or syllables repeated aloud for a particular purpose. Saying a rosary is a form of chanting. Witches sometimes chant rhymes in their rituals. The repetitive nature of a chant, as well as the actual words that compose it, act on your subconscious to generate the desired result.

Chanting may be accompanied by drumming, clapping, rattles, dancing, or playing musical instruments, specifically for the purpose of increasing psychic energy. At its height, chanting can stimulate altered states of awareness, including ecstatic trances.

FACT

Some chants have a religious focus. *Om mani padme hum* is a Sanskrit chant Buddhists sometimes utter in meditation. Another chant that is believed to align the body's energy centers involves repeating the Hebrew names for God: *Yod Hey Shin Vahv Hey.*

Gregorian chants seem to be particularly effective at charging the mind and body, probably because they include a nearly complete spectrum of vocal frequencies. Dr. Alfred Tomatis, a French eye, ear, and nose specialist affectionately known as "Dr. Mozart," noticed that the ear was the first sense organ to develop. According to Tomatis, frequencies in the range of 2,000 to 4,000 cycles per second—those found in the upper range of the human speaking voice—are the most beneficial. These resonances stimulate vibrations in the cranial bones and the ear muscles, which then revitalize or "charge" the brain.

Mantras

Some people prefer to intone a word from a language other than their native tongue, perhaps one with a religious connotation. A mantra is a group of sacred sounds repeated for spiritual purposes. The word *mantra* comes from Sanskrit and translates as "delivering the mind." Among Hindus, it means "the learning." Lama Govinda, a Tibetan Buddhist, taught that mantras are a tool for thinking, but thinking in a distinctively different way in which truth supersedes prejudice, preconditioning, and personal agendas.

The mantra is a mechanism through which you begin to see the spirit housed within your body. This spirit is also consciousness, and the essence that makes each person unique. By recognizing this spirit and returning to connectedness with it, you move from the material world into the magickal realm.

In the Upanishads, *Om* is thought to be the basis of all sacred sounds. This word contains the alpha and omega of energy—transformation and enlightenment. In the popular chant *Om mani padme hum*, *Om* represents the perfected mind, body, and speech that Buddha advocated. *Mani* signifies compassion; *padme* represents knowledge; and *hum* is the infinity within the finite.

Yogis use mantras in performing many amazing physical feats. Western witches intone mantralike words or songs to raise power and focus the mind. Speaking a mantra delivers the mind from mundane pursuits and enables you to reach a heightened state of awareness more easily. It also cleanses sacred space and fills it with supportive energy.

Benefits of Chanting

To understand the implications of sacred sounds a little better, consider the sounds that assail you every day. How does sound affect you? A honking horn will make you jump, for example, while the sounds of tinkling bells may inspire a smile. Through the use of sacred sounds, you massage your spirit with joyful noises that are uplifting and positive.

Dr. Alfred Tomatis developed a form of therapy that has been used in the United States and Europe to treat physical and psychological problems ranging from depression to autism. His techniques help patients improve their listening abilities and recapture the restful, sonic environment of the womb.

Chanting shifts consciousness because the vibration of sound has a measurable effect on the nervous system. Sound healers, including Colorado's Jonathan Goldman, use sound to activate and balance the body's energy centers, known as the *chakras*. Each chakra resonates with its own unique tone. Goldman says that the vowel sounds can be used as mantras to open up and "tune" the chakras, thereby enabling them to transmit harmonious, healing energy to the body.

"We can change our vibrational rate through our own self-generating sounds," sound healer Jonathan Goldman believes. As individuals, we can use our voices to affect our own frequencies and energy levels. As a group, we can "adjust the planet to a new level of consciousness."

Goldman recommends starting with the deepest "UH" sound you can make while focusing your attention on the root chakra, the energy center at the base of the spine. Then, at a slightly higher pitch, vocalize "OOO" and feel it vibrating in the sacral chakra. Next, direct the sound "OH" to the solar plexus. Continue moving up the body and the register, uttering "AH" in connection with the heart chakra. Let "EYE" resonate in the throat chakra, then "AYE" at the brow chakra or third eye, and finally "EEE" at the crown chakra.

The concept isn't so strange, really. You've probably had the experience of feeling joyful, invigorated, and rejuvenated when singing your favorite music. Sound waves can be focused to produce a range of remarkable effects, from a singer shattering glass with a clear, high note to a doctor using ultrasound to break up kidney stones.

Even the universe sings. Many people describe having heard the voice of the earth as a low, resonating hum. According to the ancient Greek philosopher Pythagoras, the planets revolving in their orbits around the sun produce sounds that he called "the music of the spheres." Perhaps by attuning themselves to these universal vibrations, human beings can create harmony on this planet.

Chanting and Magick

"In the beginning was the Word," the Bible says. According to Christian tradition, the voice of God is the instrument of creation, the source of all that exists on earth and in the cosmos. The Hopi believe the universe was created by Spider Woman, who sang the sun, moon, earth, and stars into being, then animated earth's creatures with her voice. According to Sufi mythology, God fashioned the first human from clay, then asked the angels to sing the person's soul into a state of ecstasy so that it would enter and enliven the clay.

These creation stories express the power of the voice and the magick inherent in sound. Witches and other magicians often chant, sing, and intone special words or phrases to create the circumstances they desire. Most spells and rituals involve affirmations, incantations, prayers, or invoking spiritual beings for assistance. Chanting can also dispel unwanted energies and break down obstacles that might otherwise impede a spell's success.

Some shamans even use chanting and singing to reconnect the soul with the physical body after a trauma has caused a separation. Singing to the missing parts of the soul/self is believed to create a pathway or bridge so the wandering parts can find their way back home.

As musician Steven Halpern puts it, sound is the "carrier wave of consciousness," capable of transmitting information from one life form to another. Sound can even carry intentions between the visible and nonvisible realms.

In a magickal setting, chanting can be done solo or in a group. In a group setting, chanting provides the additional benefit of uniting the people in attendance and charging their emotions at a concurrent rate. This process generates what's known as a cone of power, an energy field that the attendees will send out toward their goal.

Words of Power

Spiritual and occult literature abounds with references to the power of the human voice. For millennia people have been reciting magickal words as a way of invoking supernatural forces and petitioning them for assistance. This is usually done by calling out the deities' names. Speaking someone's name is said to be an act of power, giving the namer influence over the named (which is why in some belief systems, individuals have "public" names and "private" names that are kept secret). In the Genesis story, Adam was allowed to name the animals on earth and thus was given dominion over them.

Witches and magicians recognize the power inherent in some words, incorporating them into spells and rituals. Abracadabra, for instance, is universally associated with magick, by the public as well as occult practitioners. But the word isn't just part of the stage illusionist's repertoire. Derived from the Aramaic *Avarah K'Davarah*, which translates "I will create as I speak," it expresses a magician's intention to manifest a result. As long ago as the second century the word was written as an inverted pyramid and used in amulets to protect the wearer from illness.

One of the most powerful and sacred statements is also one of the shortest: I am. This magickal combination connects you with your divine essence for creative purposes. You can intone the words to balance your vital energy, center yourself, and generate power, much as you might chant the word Om. Or you can consciously choose to form a magickal sentence that begins with "I am" in order to manifest a desired condition.

ALERT!

Be very careful how you use the phrase "I am." Whatever follows these words will be charged with magickal energy and intention. *Never* say hurtful or derogatory things such as "I am stupid" or "I am ugly"—these statements can materialize as unpleasant conditions.

Many witches end spells with the words "So mote it be." This phrase (like "so be it") seals a spell and instructs the universe to carry out the witch's will. If a witch wants to banish an entity or energy, he might order it to leave by saying, "Be gone." The expression "Blessed Be" is a favorite greeting among witches and a magickal exchange of positive energy.

Resonance and Vibration

Because the universe—and everything in it—is composed of vibrations, all sounds produce effects. Sound healers have demonstrated that the body's chakras can be balanced by playing certain notes on the musical scale. Don Campbell, musician and author of *The Mozart Effect*, believes he healed himself of degenerative bone disease by "making thunder"— singing, dancing, and vocalizing a loud, long, extended tone that expressed his deepest fears, tension, and joy.

FACT

On his CD *Holy Harmony*, sound healer Jonathan Goldman presents a compilation of nine powerful frequencies that are believed to be "related to the Creator's ancient musical scale used in creation, destruction, and miraculous manifestations . . . ." Goldman had special tuning forks cut to produce these frequencies, which align and heal the body's energy centers and transform consciousness.

Witches tap the power of resonance to raise energy, cleanse sacred space, focus the mind, and empower spells. Whether you use your own voice or a drum, gong, bell, tingsha, singing bowl, or other instrument, sound can increase the effectiveness of your magick and add beauty to your rituals.

Affirmations

Affirmations are a modern interpretation of chanting, prayers, and mantras. As the word implies, an affirmation is a short statement designed to support and affirm the individual and her intentions. In recent years, affirmations have been widely used to break the chain of negative thinking and replace it with empowering concepts.

Motivational speakers encourage the use of affirmations to change thinking and behavior. In her bestselling book, *You Can Heal Your Life*, Louise Hay writes extensively about the power of affirmations to heal psychological and physical ills. Witches use affirmations to manifest outcomes of all sorts, from attracting prosperity to promoting peace.

The Power of Positive Thinking

Henry Ford said, "Whether you think you can or think you can't—you are right." Most people's negative conceptions of themselves are rooted in the opinions of other people, usually authority figures such as parents and teachers. Overcoming those old attitudes and beliefs is essential to both healthy self-esteem and effective magick. Because your thoughts are the most important part of any magick spell, it stands to reason that positive thinking will generate positive results and negative thinking will produce negative results. Consequently, you will never see an affirmation that includes negative words.

ALERT!

Affirmations aren't a quick fix. The longer you've held on to a self-limiting idea or problem, the longer it's likely to take the affirmation process to replace it with something beneficial. Be realistic and persistent—otherwise you'll undermine what you had hoped to achieve.

Affirmations don't leave any room for doubt, fear, or ambiguity. Their purpose is to clearly and optimistically express whatever condition you desire to bring about. Whether you write your affirmations or say them aloud, putting your intentions into words helps focus your mind and empower your spells.

The Right Way to Design Affirmations

Whether you're using affirmations to change an attitude or as part of a magick spell, there's a right way and a wrong way to do it. As you already know, an affirmation contains only positive words and images. Here's an example:

Right: I am completely healthy in body, mind, and spirit.
Wrong: I don't have any illnesses or injuries.

See the difference? The first sentence affirms what you seek: health. The second focuses on conditions you don't want: illnesses and injuries. Additionally, an affirmation must be stated confidently and in the present tense, as if the outcome you desire already exists. For example:

Right: I now have a job that's perfect for me.
Wrong: I will get a job that's perfect for me.

Being specific is usually a good thing when creating affirmations. If your goal is to lose twenty-five pounds or you've got your heart set on acquiring a 1965 red Mustang convertible with black leather seats, for instance, list the pertinent details in your affirmation. But sometimes you don't know all the ins and outs of a situation, or you don't want to limit your options. Sometimes it's best to let a higher and wiser power work out the fine points. The earlier example "I now have a job that's perfect for me" covers the bases without being specific.

It's easy to formulate successful affirmations; just follow these points:

- Keep it short.
- Be clear and precise.
- Only include images and conditions that you desire.
- Express your desires with positive words.
- Always use the present tense.

After you've created your affirmation, write it down and post it where you will often see it, to remind yourself of your objective. Repeat your affirmation frequently throughout the day, especially first thing in the morning and last thing at night. Contemplate your affirmation while meditating. Associate an image or visualization with your affirmation; for instance, see yourself performing the job you desire or donning a new outfit that's the size you wish to wear.

Affirmations in Magick

In witchcraft, affirmations are frequently combined with spells and rituals. When you're casting a spell, you might opt to say your affirmation aloud, clearly stating what it is you intend to accomplish. You could even design a series of several affirmations that reinforce the active parts of your spellworking.

Written affirmations can also be an effective part of a magick spell. You can write an affirmation on a piece of paper and slip it into an amulet or talisman. Many witches like to write words that describe their intentions on candles, or you could incorporate affirmations into paintings and collages.

Combine verbal and written affirmations if you like. For instance, if you are performing a love spell, you could carve the word "love" on two candles. As you light the candles, say aloud "As these candles burn, love grows between my partner and me." Once you understand the basics of creating affirmations, you may find original ways to use them in your spells and rituals. Be creative.

Incantations

An incantation is a special type of affirmation. What's unique about incantations is that they are usually written as rhymes. The catchy phrasing and rhythm make it easy to remember an incantation. Don't worry about the literary quality of your incantations; just follow the same guidelines for creating affirmations, then make your statements rhyme.

Incantations can be as short as two lines or as long as your imagination and intention dictate. You can use an incantation in the same way you'd use any other affirmation. Although it's perfectly okay to merely write an incantation, more often they are spoken aloud. Because incantations feature both rhyme and meter, you may enjoy putting them to music and singing them.

Incantations in Magick

Like affirmations, incantations are often employed in magickal work. Some of the songs Wiccans and witches sing at celebrations are incantations. Chanting a love incantation while dancing around a Maypole on Beltane is a joyful and powerful form of magick. Here's an example of an incantation to attract love, from the book *Nice Spells/Naughty Spells*:

As the day fades into night
I draw a love that's good and right.
As the night turns into day
We are blessed in every way.

You may choose to speak an incantation as part of a ritual or to activate a spell. Incantations can also be recited at mealtime or before going to sleep, like prayers or blessings. In fact, many prayers are incantations. If you prefer, write your incantation and display it in a spot where you'll see it often. You might enjoy adorning your words with colorful pictures and framing your artwork. Creating incantations is fun—use your imagination. The more energy you infuse into your creation, the more effective it will be.

CHAPTER 7

Sacred Space

Anyone who has been in a church, temple, mosque, or shrine understands the meaning of sacred space. When you enter sacred space, you leave behind your everyday thoughts and concerns, immersing yourself in a place where Spirit abides. Sacredness, though, is more a matter of attitude and behavior than trappings. No structure, furnishings, or props are required. A grove of trees, a waterfall, or a spot in your own backyard can be a sacred space. The Buddha said, "Wherever you live is your temple if you treat it like one."

Establishing Sacred Space

The distinction between ordinary space and sacred space is an important one when it comes to magickal workings. Just as Christians go to a church to commune with God, Wiccans and witches practice magick in special areas designated for that purpose. The hallowed space may be a natural place, such as the oak groves where the early Druids performed rituals. Or it can be a structure built by human hands. Witches often erect altars in their homes; the place where the altar stands is considered sacred.

Many ancient ceremonial sites, such as Stonehenge, embody sacred space. Often Europe's cathedrals were constructed at places the early pagans considered sacred. In part, this was done to ease the transition as Christianity supplanted the Old Religion. But sacred sites, as anyone who's been to the Chalice Well in Glastonbury or Machu Piccu can attest, resonate with extraordinary energies that inspire reverence.

"Sacred space is a place where we honor the divine . . . . The purpose of sacred space is to awaken an awareness of our intimate connection to the spiritual world and to the universe as a whole."
—Carolyn E. Cobelo, *The Power of Sacred Space*

Within a sacred space, it's easy to sense the presence of a higher power and to connect with it. You step outside your ordinary world and move into a realm where wondrous possibilities exist. Many people experience physical and psychological changes, such as those that occur during meditation. At some sacred sites, such as Lourdes, miraculous healings are believed to occur.

Some sacred places are permanent—indeed, many have existed for millennia. Others are designed to be temporary, perhaps lasting only for the duration of a ritual or spell.

A Place for Magick

You'll probably want to designate a special place for working magick. Depending on your locale and personal preference, you can choose a spot outdoors or indoors—or both. It may be a private spot for your use only, or a public area that you feel drawn to.

Perhaps you've already chosen a place. If not, you might decide to dowse certain prospective sites to determine which is best for your purposes. You can dowse with special rods or with a pendulum. Many sensitive individuals simply tune in to the energies of places, without using a dowsing device. If a place feels right to you and the input you receive from your own guides, deities, or angels supports your choice, you can proceed to sanctify it for magick rituals.

FACT

Labyrinth-wright Marty Cain always dowses an area to locate the best spot for a labyrinth. She also asks for divine guidance and requests permission from the earth and earth spirits before she builds a labyrinth in a site she has chosen for this sacred circle.

Feng shui, the ancient Chinese art of placement, can also help you find the ideal place. Although there are many different schools of feng shui, each with somewhat different principles and perspectives, the most popular version in the United States utilizes a tool called a *bagua*. This simple device allows you to assess your home, a single room, your yard, or any other space. The bagua contains nine sectors that correspond to the various parts of your life. One sector relates to wisdom and spirituality. Aligning a bagua to your home or yard lets you instantly see which portion will best support your spiritual and magickal pursuits.

Some people like to site their sacred spaces along compass lines. This helps to ground you and align your own energies with those of the earth. It also makes it easy to call the four directions, which is part of many rituals (see "Calling the Four Quarters/Directions" later in this chapter).

Clearing Unwanted Vibrations

Whether you choose to establish a sacred space inside or out, you'll want to clear it of unwanted energies before you begin doing magick there. According to feng shui, all objects contain energy and affect the overall environment. If possible, remove items—furniture, artwork, equipment, etc.—that you find distracting or that aren't harmonious with your intentions. Everything that remains in your sacred space should pertain to your spiritual and magickal path.

ALERT!

Don't use chemical insecticides or other poisons in your sacred space. Whatever you put into sacred space—physical, emotional, and mental— is amplified. Outside, use natural insect repellants, and salt or mulch to inhibit weed growth. Inside, use only "green" cleaning materials.

Perform a cleansing ritual to get rid of ambient vibrations. The most popular way to do this is called "smudging." Light some dried sage and allow the aromatic smoke to waft through the area, purifying it. (You can purchase sage wands for this purpose at stores that sell New Age or Native American products.) Burning incense will work, too.

If you prefer, you can play a bell, gong, or drum to break up old energy patterns and chase away unwanted influences. Some people sprinkle salt in the corners of a room or mist the area with saltwater. Witches often use brooms to sweep sacred space clean. In conjunction with any of these clearing rituals, consider chanting an affirmation such as "This space is now cleansed of all harmful, disruptive, and unbalanced energies."

It's a good idea to clear your sacred space regularly, especially after other people have entered it.

The Circle

Traditionally, many rituals and spells are performed in a circle. In a group setting, participants stand or sit in a circle that allows each member to see and interact with everyone else. The circle shows that each person present is important to the success of the overall working.

A physical circle may be constructed for the purpose of working magick. Stones, plants, lights, fencing, or other structures might form the circle's perimeter, providing a clear boundary between mundane and sacred space. Great stone circles, such as those found at Stonehenge and nearby Avebury, offered sanctuary for the enactment of ancient rites and rituals.

Many circles, however, aren't physical—they exist as energy patterns created by the magician's imagination. A witch simply envisions a circle surrounding a designated area, usually for a brief period of time, and shifts the vibrations inside the circle for a specific purpose. Within the area defined as sacred by the circle, witches and Wiccans perform their rituals and spells.

The Circle's Symbolism

The circle represents unity, completion, continuity, and wholeness. To witches, the circle also corresponds to the annual cycle known as the Wheel of the Year (discussed in Chapter 4). In magickal work, a circle signifies protection.

When doing magick, witches frequently cast circles around themselves and the space where a ritual or spell will be performed. This practice serves two purposes: to keep out unwanted influences and to contain magickal energy until it's time to release it into the universe.

Ritual Circles

Before enacting a ritual, witches usually create a circle to provide a safe haven. The circle may or may not be visible. Sometimes a circle is cast with words, gestures, and visualizations. Participants know the boundary is there—they might even see a faint glow or sense different vibrations inside and outside the circle.

FACT

Some magicians actually draw a circle along with magickal symbols on the floor or ground before enacting a ritual. Others light candles or place symbolic objects to designate the sacred space within which a ritual will take place.

Whether you create a temporary or permanent circle is totally up to you. What's important is how you think, feel, and behave with regard to the sacred space you've established. Your circle is both a sanctuary and a place of power. Everything that transpires within it links you with the earth as well as with the worlds above, below, and within you.

Protocol and Practices

Sacred space is more than a physical place; it is also defined by the actions you engage in there and your state of mind. When the faithful enter a church, temple, or mosque, they often perform a ritual—removing their shoes, crossing themselves, kneeling, dabbing holy water on their foreheads, etc.—to signify a change in attitude and focus. The ritual act itself helps shift consciousness from that dominated by ego to that guided by Spirit.

ESSENTIAL

When Wiccans or witches come together to perform a ritual, they often enter the sacred space in single file, moving in a clockwise direction to form the circle. When the ritual is over, they close the circle and file out in a counterclockwise direction.

Some people like to take a purifying bath before performing a ritual or rite. Some change into special ritual clothing or don magickal jewelry. You might choose to take off your shoes so you feel more connected to the earth. The point is to do something to clearly demarcate—mentally as well as physically—sacred space.

Within the circle, participants observe certain practices and behavior conducive to the occasion. You want to keep the energy within the circle high: positive, harmonious, respectful, and joyful. Leave everyday worries, fears, anger, and negativity outside. Don't discuss mundane matters or engage in idle chit-chat. Remember, you are honoring the deities, your own magickal power, and the other members of the circle.

Casting a Circle

Even if you create a permanent physical circle within which to perform magick, you may still wish to cast a psychic circle around your sacred space prior to a ritual or spell. First, clear any unwanted energies from the space, using one of the techniques described earlier or one of your own design. Then invite everyone who will take part in the ritual or spell to enter the designated area.

To cast a circle, begin at the easternmost point of the space where you will be working. Move in a clockwise direction until you complete a circuit of the area and come back to the east, where you started. Make sure the circle is large enough to encompass everyone who will participate and everything that will be used in the spell or ritual.

Bring any magick tools or objects into the sacred space before you actually cast the circle. Bless and purify (by washing or smudging) items that will be used during the ritual. If you'll consume food or beverages inside the circle, bless them in advance.

An easy way to do this is to hold a wand or athame (ritual dagger) in your outstretched hand and walk slowly around the circle's circumference, while you envision drawing a wall of pure white light with the magick tool. (If you don't have a wand or athame, you can simply use your hand.) You should be *inside* the circle, with your tool or hand pointing outward. Another popular technique uses the four elements—earth, air, fire, and water—to cast the circle. Light a stick of incense (which represents air and fire) and walk around the circle, trailing fragrant smoke behind you. Next, sprinkle saltwater (signifying earth and water) around the perimeter.

You might like to cast a circle using materials that correspond to the season or your intention. For example, you could sprinkle cornmeal on the ground to draw a circle for a Lughnassad festival. At Yule, circle the sacred area with candles. If you are working a love spell, make your circle of rose petals.

Once a circle has been cast, no one should leave it. The circle brings the group's energy and magickal intention together, aligning them with higher powers. If a member leaves, it disrupts the dynamic that's been established. Occasionally, however, it happens that someone needs to go out of the circle. Instead of merely walking through the vibrational perimeter that's been created, thereby "breaking" the circle, use your hand or athame to "cut" a doorway in the circle. Pass through, then reseal the door by tracing the opening in reverse with your hand or athame.

Squaring the Circle

To honor the four elements and the four corners of creation, some witches erect four small altars within the circle. One altar is positioned at each of the four main compass points of the working space, known as the quarters. Wiccans frequently place items that represent the element of each quarter at the corresponding point of the sacred space. This honors the energies of that quarter.

"Squaring the circle" refers to the human body as the place where heaven and earth are united. The circle symbolizes heaven, the square represents earth. Leonardo da Vinci's famous drawing depicts a man with arms and legs outstretched, standing within a square and a circle. This shows that the circumference of the circle is the same as the square's perimeter.

Each altar may hold any number of objects, which represent the element of that direction. Here are some suggestions:

Direction	Element	Suggested Objects
East	Air	yellow candle, feathers, incense, wind chimes
South	Fire	red candle, marigolds, clear crystals, amber incense
West	Water	blue candle, shells, coral, bowl of water, fountain
North	Earth	green candle, stones, potted plants, marble or ceramic statue

You'll find more information about elemental correspondences in the next chapter. Once you become familiar with the elements, you can position symbolic items that hold meaning for you to mark the four corners of your own sacred space.

Calling the Four Quarters/Directions

Many magickal traditions "call the quarters" as part of casting a circle. Not everyone uses the same words or gestures, however. Wiccans probably won't perform this practice in exactly the same way as ritual or ceremonial magicians. Calling the quarters creates an invisible line of energy that marks the space between two worlds: the mundane and the spiritual, the temporal and the magickal.

Some people invoke angels when calling the quarters. Usually Raphael is associated with the east, Michael with the south, Gabriel with the west, and Uriel with the north. The deities are invoked in this order and released in the opposite order.

The following description is eclectic and generic, but nonetheless quite functional. As you call out to the four directions, visualize lines of pure white light connecting you to the powers of the universe. In time, you may wish to customize the ritual, adapting it to the season or intention, or even to design your own entirely.

Begin at the east (where the sun rises). Light a yellow candle here and face outward, with your back to the center of the circle. Call out to the forces of the east, saying: "Beings of Air, Guardians of the East, Breath of Transformation—Come! Be welcome in this sacred space. I/we ask that you stand firm to guard and protect, refresh and motivate. Support the magick created here by conveying my/our wishes on every wind as it reaches across the earth."

Move clockwise to the south and light a red candle. Invoke the deities of the south by saying: "Beings of Fire, Guardians of the South, Spark of Creation that banishes the darkness—Come! Be welcome in this sacred space. I/we ask that you stand firm to guard and protect, activate and fulfill. Support the magick created here by conveying my/our wishes to the sun, the stars, and every beam of light as it embraces the earth."

Continue to the west, light a blue candle, and call out: "Beings of Water, Guardians of the West, Rain of Inspiration—Come! Be welcome in this sacred space. I/we ask that you stand firm to guard and protect, heal and nurture. Support the magick created here by conveying my/our wishes to dewdrops, rain, and waves as they wash across the world."

Walk to the north, light a green candle, and say: "Beings of Earth, Guardians of the North, Soils of Foundation—Come! Be welcome in this sacred space. I/we ask that you stand firm to guard and protect, mature and provide. Support the magick created here by conveying my/our wishes to every grain of sand, every bit of loam that is our world."

Move into the center of the circle and intone: "Ancient One . . . the power that binds all the elements into oneness and source of my/our magick—Come! Be welcome in this sacred space. I/we ask that you stand firm to guard and protect, guide and fill all the energy created here. May it be for the good of all. So mote it be."

Closing the Circle and Releasing Magickal Energies

Releasing the sacred space is as important as erecting it. At the end of your workings, release the sphere you've created, thank the powers who've assisted you, ask them to keep guiding the energy you've raised, and bid them farewell until the next time.

Begin in the north quarter and move counterclockwise (as if you're unwinding something). Instead of envisioning the lines of energy forming, see them slowly evaporating back into the Void. Just because they leave your sacred space doesn't mean they're gone (energy can't be destroyed—it only changes form). They simply return to their source at the four corners of creation and attend to their tasks.

At the north point, say: "Guardians, Guides, and Ancestors of the North and Earth, I/we thank you for your presence and protection. Keep me/us rooted in your rich soil so my spirit/our spirits grow steadily until I/we return to your protection again. Hail and farewell!" Then extinguish the candle.

Move to the west and say: "Guardians, Guides, and Ancestors of the West and Water, I/we thank you for your presence and protection. Keep me/us flowing ever toward wholeness in body, mind, and spirit until I/we return to your protection again. Hail and farewell!"

Continue on to the south and say: "Guardians, Guides, and Ancestors of the South and Fire, I/we thank you for your presence and protection. Keep your fires ever burning within my/our soul to light any darkness and drive it away until I/we return to your protection again. Hail and farewell!"

Go to the east and say: "Guardians, Guides, and Ancestors of the East and Air. I/we thank you for your presence and protection. Keep your winds blowing fresh with ideas and hopefulness until I/we return to your protection again. Hail and farewell!"

In the circle's center say: "Great Spirit, thank you for blessing this space. I/we know that a part of you is always with us, as a still small voice that guides and nurtures. Help me/us to listen to that voice, to trust it, and trust in my/our magick."

Before leaving the circle, witches often join hands and chant: "Merry meet, merry part, and merry meet again."

Working with the quarters and the spirits is a lot like being in an evolving relationship with someone you respect and admire. If you treat these entities accordingly, you will rarely be disappointed.

Creating a Permanent Circle

If you have room, you might enjoy creating a permanent circle, either inside your home or outdoors. You could incorporate a circle into a garden, perhaps designing a grassy area surrounded by shrubs or flowers. Consider marking the four directions with appropriate symbols and objects, as described earlier. Large standing stones erected at each of the four main compass points—maybe even a complete ring of stones—would nicely define your circle. Depending on the site, you might wish to place an altar in the center of your circle and perhaps include a spot to light ritual fires. To emphasize the elements, you could position a fire pit (or barbecue grill) in the south, a fountain or pond in the west, a large shrub or tree in the north, and a windmill or whirligig in the east.

If a permanent circle isn't an option, consider cutting a circle from a large sheet of paper or fabric; you can store it in a closet when not in use. Decorate this portable circle with symbols and imagery to represent the four directions, along with other adornments that appeal to your aesthetic sensibility.

Inside your home, you may be able to turn an ordinary round rug into a magick circle. Place candleholders and flowers at each of the four directions. If you like, add other objects, artwork, or colors to symbolize the four elements. Use a cabinet, chest of drawers, table, or large trunk as an altar. The possibilities are limited only by your imagination.

Altars

Most witches include at least one central altar in a sacred space. Some witches believe it's important to place their altars in the east, where the sun rises. For practical purposes, placing the altar in the middle of your circle makes more sense, especially if a number of people will participate in rituals in your circle.

The altar provides a central focal point during spells and rituals. You can also display and store your magick tools here. You might consider decorating your altar with candles in attractive candleholders, flowers, statues of deities you feel close to, and crystals. Some witches like to leave their magick tools out on their altars at all times; others prefer to stash them away when not in use.

If you choose to leave your ritual tools out on your altar, be sure to display all four principal items—athame, pentagram, chalice, and wand—together to establish balance. These four implements represent the four elements: air, earth, water, and fire respectively.

In addition to the four primary tools, you'll probably want to keep a variety of other magick items and ingredients on hand for your workings. Most witches store a supply of candles in different colors, along with incense, essential oils, herbs, crystals, and gemstones. In time, you might also consider adding ribbons, parchment, mojo bags, a crystal ball, bells, a cauldron, tarot cards, runes, pendulum, ritual clothing and jewelry, and a grimoire for recording your spells.

Some witches change the decorations on their altars to coincide with the seasons and sabbats. This practice keeps your altar looking fresh and attractive, while also linking you with the Wheel of the Year and the cycles of life.

Your Personal Sanctuary: Auras and Sacred Psychic Space

Maintaining and respecting your own personal sacred space—and that of others—is essential to your emotional, psychic, and physical well-being. Many spiritual philosophies uphold the idea of the body as a temple. But your personal sanctuary extends beyond the limitations of the physical body.

You've probably heard of an aura, a subtle energy body that surrounds your physical form. This subtle energy field envelops you like a cocoon of light, radiating out from your physical body at least several inches to more than a foot in all directions. Sensitive individuals can actually see auras as shifting orbs of color and light. The haloes depicted in religious artwork around the heads of saints and spiritual beings are auras. Vibrational healers believe that imbalances in the aura eventually materialize as disease in the physical body. Meditation, chanting, music, prayer, and visualization can help balance and cleanse your aura.

At times, you may feel a need to enhance your personal sanctuary, either to establish inner peace or to protect yourself. The easiest way to do this is to envision yourself enclosed in a ball of pure white light, while you repeat the following affirmation: "I am surrounded by divine white light. I am safe and sound at all times and in all situations, now and always."

Some witches like to wear magickal jewelry or talismans to strengthen and safeguard their personal energy fields. Quartz crystals are often used for this purpose. You could fashion a harmonizing talisman and include items that correspond to the four elements. The following chapters will talk more about elemental connections and how to use gems, minerals, and plants for healing, protection, and other purposes.

CHAPTER 8

The Four Elements

When witches refer to the "elements," they don't mean the periodic table you learned about in science class. They're talking about the four cornerstones of creation—earth, air, fire, and water—the fundamental energies that exist in everything on earth. Magicians understand these energies and manipulate them to manifest the results they desire. In the previous chapter, you learned about the connection between the elements and the four directions, but there's more to it, as you'll soon discover.

The Cornerstones of Creation

It's easy to see the four elements as they physically exist on the planet. Witches, however, also concern themselves with the nonphysical aspect of the elements. Magicians consider the elements to be archetypal modes of expression and the foundation of occult science. Metaphysically, the elements correspond to astrological signs, lunar cycles, the seasons, the four directions, spiritual beings, human personalities, colors, shapes, the suits of the tarot, and a great deal more.

In his book *Astrology, Psychology, and the Four Elements,* Stephen Arroyo writes, "The four elements are not merely 'symbols' or abstract concepts, but rather they refer to the vital forces that make up the entire creation that can be perceived by the physical senses."

Knowledge of these elements has influenced many branches of philosophy and religion as well as magick. They also played an important role in alchemy. Although Aristotle is often credited with forming the concepts commonly accepted today in Western magick, references to the elements can be found in various ancient cultures and schools of thought.

Witches and other occultists recognize a fifth element, too: spirit. The five points of the pentagram symbolically depict all five elements. Spirit might be described as the essence underlying something; as Bill Whitcomb puts it in his book *The Magician's Companion,* spirit is "the seed (quintessence) necessary for the manifestation of the elements."

When you're doing magick, it helps to have a comprehensive understanding of the elements and how they operate in plants, minerals, animals, and other substances you may be using in a spell. Combining elemental energies correctly will enhance your workings and contribute to successful results.

Earth

You can easily understand the basic qualities of the earth element by looking at the ground beneath your feet. Earth's energy is stable, solid, practical, fertile, enduring, patient, and secure, depicted best by Mother Earth herself. You imply these characteristics when you describe someone as being "down to earth" or "earthy." Earth provides the substance that gives form to your intentions. It is linked with the physical body and the five senses.

Myths from ancient Sumer and Guatemala describe humankind as being shaped from soil. According to the ancient Greeks, the heavens were born into existence from the womb of Gaia, the mother who oversees all the earth's abundance. Some Native American stories speak about the soul waiting for rebirth in the earth's womb (under the soil). In Slavic tradition the soil was so sacred that a person placed one hand on the ground when making a promise.

The pentagram represents the earth element. In the tarot, the suit of pentacles relates to the element of earth. The cards in this suit describe material, physical, and financial conditions. In astrology, Taurus, Virgo, and Capricorn make up the earth signs. People born under these signs are usually practical, dependable, steady, persevering, sensual, and interested in financial and/or material matters.

Elemental Correspondences

As you become more familiar with the earth element and develop a deep, intuitive knowledge of the energy associated with it, you'll just naturally sense which things resonate with its vibration. Following are some things that witches associate with the element of earth:

- North
- Green
- The numbers four and eight
- Onyx, jet, turquoise, malachite, aventurine, jade
- Mint, sage, thyme, fennel, lavender, valerian, carnation, holly, oak, pine
- Cotton, hemp, leather
- Pewter, lead

Earth Magick

Usually earth magick is done to encourage abundance, financial or physical security, fertility, health, or protection. Hanging a pentagram on your front door to protect your home is a simple, yet effective, earth spell. Earth magick tends to operate at a slower rate than fire or air magick, but its results are likely to endure. Include items from the preceding list when working earth magick.

FACT

In early agrarian cultures, farmers gave offerings of bread or mead to the soil to ensure a good crop. People buried symbolic items in the ground to banish something or to encourage growth. A woman who wished to keep her lover from straying would gather a little soil from his shoe and place it in a white cloth bag.

Earth spells often draw upon the fertility of Mother Earth. Some prosperity spells, for instance, recommend planting seeds to represent your wishes. As you care for the seeds, you symbolically nurture your intentions. As the plant grows and flourishes, your intentions will bear fruit.

Air

Observe the wind and you will understand the basic qualities of the air element. It's linked with the mind and communication. Air's energy is changeable, light, flexible, ethereal, insubstantial, and cerebral. You imply these characteristics when you describe someone as being "flighty" or "an airhead."

Air is the most elusive of the elements because it is invisible, intangible, and inconsistent: like the wind, it can be gentle or fierce, damp or dry. Never still, it can quickly change from a balmy breeze to a gusty gale. The wind also carries pollen to fertilize flowers and crops, just as ideas move between people to enrich cultures.

The athame represents the air element. In the tarot, the suit of swords relates to the element of air. The cards in this suit describe situations involving ideas or communication. In astrology, Gemini, Libra, and Aquarius are the air signs. People born under these signs tend to be mentally oriented, talkative, sociable, changeable, and interested in the realm of ideas.

One of the most widely known legends involving the air element tells of a man who was sent to catch the wind—a tale that has become a metaphor for an impossible task. Another "air" motif is the sacredness of speech, for air is linked with communication. In the biblical version of creation, God's breath created life—the Word was fertile.

Elemental Correspondences

As you become more familiar with the air element and develop a deep, intuitive knowledge of the energy associated with it, you'll just naturally understand which things resonate with this vibration. Following are some things that witches associate with the element of air:

- East
- Yellow
- The numbers five and eleven
- Garnet, zircon, aquamarine, clear quartz, opal
- Ginseng, allspice, clove, honeysuckle, azalea, lily of the valley, apple, mulberry
- Silk, gauze, feathers
- Copper, platinum

Air Magick

Witches often do air magick to stimulate new ideas, improve communication or cooperation between people, or strengthen mental abilities. If, for instance, you want to ace a test, consider performing an air spell. Legal and contractual matters can benefit from air magick, too. Air spells tend to take effect quickly, but the results aren't usually as long-lasting as those of earth spells. Include items from the preceding list when working earth magick.

The wind's direction is important in many types of air magick. For example, always scatter magickal ingredients in a wind moving away from you to carry a message to someone or to take away a problem. Magick for new projects is best worked with the "wind at your back," for good fortune. When trying to quell anger, opening a window to "air out" the negative energy has great symbolic value.

FACT

The ancients believed that the wind was influenced by the direction from which it originated. If wind blew from the south, it represented fire and was said to generate passion, warmth, or vitality for spellcraft. A wind moving from the west included water qualities; from the north, it embodied earth energies; from the east, it doubled the strength of the air element.

Much of air magick involves some type of communication. Reciting words of power, chanting, repeating affirmations, and singing incantations are examples of air magick. Whether you speak these words aloud or write them down, specially chosen words and phrases can help activate your intentions.

Fire

The basic qualities of the fire element are evident in the sun or a hearth fire. Fire's energy is invigorating, active, stimulating, volatile, and hot. You imply these characteristics when you describe someone as having a "fiery" nature. Fire also implies a sense of community and connection: early tribes gathered around the fire to cook, tell stories, and celebrate life.

Although fire's light and warmth brighten lives—indeed, the sun's heat and light are essential for life on earth—fire can quickly rage out of control and shift from a creative to a destructive force. Linked with inspiration, the fire element is also associated with will, for its energy animates matter.

The wand represents the fire element, and the suit of wands in the tarot relates to the element of fire. The cards in this suit describe creative and/or spiritual pursuits, as well as situations involving passion or inspiration. In astrology, Aries, Leo, and Sagittarius are the fire signs. People born under these signs tend to be assertive, impulsive, self-directed, vital, independent, adventurous, and confident.

ALERT!

The great mystic Nostradamus turned to the fire element regularly for his visions. As he explained in one of his writings, "Secrets are revealed by the subtle spirit of fire." Pyromancy (divining by fire) continues to be a favorite means of divination among witches and Wiccans.

Elemental Correspondences

As you become more familiar with the fire element and develop a deep, intuitive knowledge of the energy associated with it, you'll just naturally sense which things resonate with this vibration. Following are some things that witches associate with the element of fire:

- South
- Red
- The numbers one and three
- Topaz, amber, ruby, diamond, bloodstone, tiger-eye
- Cayenne, almond, sandalwood, saffron, sunflower, marigold, ash, maple
- Wool, brocade, lamé
- Gold, iron

Fire Magick

Witches do fire spells to boost courage, stimulate activity, or infuse a situation with passion and vitality. Fire spells can also will an idea into being. If you want to kindle enthusiasm in a romantic relationship or bolster your self-confidence in preparation for a challenge, you could do fire magick.

Fire's volatile nature makes it the most difficult element to control. Although fire spells generate a lot of energy and produce fast results, they are most suitable when your goals are short-term. Include items from the preceding list when working fire magick.

Because fire is associated with purification, magicians employ fire spells to banish negativity and fear. Witches often build ritual fires to burn up unwanted attitudes, conditions, or obstacles. Beltane's fires, however, serve a different purpose: they spark passion, creativity, and fertility. Magicians also use fire for clearing sacred space, enlightenment, and vision quests.

The ancients considered fire to be so powerful that only the gods possessed it. In Greek mythology, Prometheus stole fire from the gods and gave it to humankind. According to the people of the Congo, fire came to earth when an angry god tossed down a burning log. In Finland, the first earthly fire was started by the god Ukko's sword.

Candle magick is the most popular form of fire magick. Candles play a role in all sorts of spells where they activate your intention. In some instances, a candle's flame can be used to focus a witch's mind. Candles may also symbolize the spiritual forces you invite to join in a ritual; or they may represent people, objectives, or situations you wish to influence with your magick.

Water

Think of the ocean's shifting tides and the rain that nourishes plants to understand the qualities of the water element. Water's energy is receptive, cool, quiet, inner-directed, fluid, intuitive, undifferentiated, and creative. Magicians link the water element with the emotions.

ALERT!

The world's legends abound with water deities who protect sailors, as well as mythological creatures, such as sirens, who lure seafarers to their deaths. Reverence for water can be found in many customs and superstitions, from dropping coins into sacred wells (to ask water spirits to grant wishes) to pouring mead into the sea (as an offering) before a voyage.

In a witch's toolbox, the chalice symbolizes the water element. In the tarot, the suit of cups relates to water; the cards in this suit describe emotional conditions and relationships. In astrology, Cancer, Scorpio, and Pisces make up the water signs. People born under these signs tend to be moody, intuitive, imaginative, sensitive, private, and impressionable.

Elemental Correspondences

As you become more familiar with the water element and develop a deep, intuitive knowledge of the energy associated with it, you'll get a feeling for which things resonate with a watery vibration. Following are some things that witches associate with the element of water:

- West
- Blue
- The number two
- Moonstone, pearl, coral, rose quartz, amethyst
- Jasmine, water lily, iris, orchid, raspberry, lotus, ylang-ylang, willow
- Silk, rayon
- Silver

Water Magick

Water magick is often used for healing purposes. If you consider the fact that human bodies are composed largely of water, this idea makes sense. For centuries, the faithful have journeyed to sacred springs and wells, and ailing people have visited spas to "take the waters" in the hope of being healed. The Catholic custom of dotting the forehead with holy water upon entering a church stems from the belief that water possesses special curative powers.

When matters of the heart are at stake, witches often turn to water magick. Water spells usually include some sort of liquid, perhaps a brew or potion that the petitioner must drink. After the magickal concoction has been formulated, it is poured into a ritual chalice while the petitioner mentally projects her intentions into the liquid. Then she and/or her beloved drinks the beverage to make the wish come true.

Many witches bathe before participating in a ritual, in order to wash away unwanted energies and to shift their consciousness from everyday reality to the magickal sphere. The ritual use of essential oils and perfumes is another form of water magick. Water magick can also help you break an unwanted tie—simply toss into the ocean or other body of water a symbol of the person, situation, or thing you wish to release.

Spirit: The Fifth Element

Spirit (also known as ether) isn't an element per se, but it is often included among the magickal elements as the fifth point of the pentagram. It's even harder to define than air. The binding link between the other four, it is the source of magick. Spirit resides within and without, around, above, and below all things. Although you can experience earth, air, fire, and water directly with your temporal senses, Spirit is elusive, and to be witnessed it requires both the witch's faith and metaphysical senses.

Native Americans call this fundamental, life-sustaining energy Grandfather, or Arch of Heaven. In Hindu writing, *atman* is the spiritual essence of creation. Polynesians and the Jains have a similar idea but use the terms *mana* or *jiva* respectively, meaning that which animates all life, or the life principle.

In his book *Modern Magick*, Donald Michael Kraig explains that spirit "is the source of the other four elements. Spirit is the source of all that exists and is the divine light from beyond Keter [the first sephirah of the Tree of Life]."

Because spirit creates everything, abides in everything, and enlivens everything, it is always present. When a witch calls upon a divine being to bless a spell or ritual, she connects with spirit and invites it to participate in her magick. By honoring spirit, she elevates her workings from the physical realm to the divine one.

Elemental Beings

Folklore, legends, and fairy tales are populated by unique beings who are aligned with the different elements. These entities aren't merely products of some storyteller's fertile imagination. Each of these creatures, known as elementals, has a specific function and its personality reflects its particular element. For instance, elves are earth beings who protect nature's sacredness. Most people can't see, hear, or touch them, but if you keep an open heart and open mind—and use your intuition—you can contact them.

In Benin, one elemental is called *aziza* (little people). The aziza live in forests, working magick much like the elves of European lore. Tibetans recognize the *sa-bdag* who bear remarkable similarities to the faery folk of Western stories. The *chinoi* of Malaysia are beings who live in flowers.

Devic beings have agendas, responsibilities, and projects of their own. They're not to be commanded like servants or carelessly invoked without consideration. Witches believe that elemental beings warrant their respect—and if you don't show respect to the elementals, they might not help you.

Magickally speaking, elemental beings are considered more powerful than humans *when in their element*. Although they are specialists in their own realm, they lack understanding of the other elements.

If they so choose, they can be very helpful to witches. Befriend them, and they will serve as devoted assistants in performing magick spells. The processes used to invoke an elemental being and work with it are too lengthy to describe here. If you'd like to examine this subject more closely, read *Dancing with Devas* by Patricia Telesco or *Practical Solitary Magic* by Nancy B. Watson.

Gnomes

Gnomes, whose name means "earth dwellers," dwell in the element of earth. Said to have a great sense of humor and clever minds, they enjoy humans who are kind and honest, and will often help such individuals. At times, however, they can seem gruff or coarse. Sometimes called trolls or leprechauns, these elementals are practical, no-nonsense, "no frills" creatures. They possess a wonderful appreciation for material things and can be valuable aides when you're doing prosperity spells.

Other earth spirits include the dwarves of European faery tales, the *berg-bui* (Teutonic mountain giants), the *kubera* (Hindu guardians of the north), and the *simargl* (Slavic guardians of all plants).

If you wish to work with a gnome, go to a wooded area, call to it, and wait patiently until it reveals itself to you or you sense its presence. Give it a small gift to thank it for its assistance. Gnomes love jewelry—the flashier the better—and quartz crystals. Bury your token in the ground as an offering to the earth spirits.

Sylphs

Sylphs are air elementals who appear as lovely winged beings, a bit like Disney's faery Tinkerbell. The ancients believed that these creatures carry many oracular messages from the gods to human beings. They generally gravitate to intelligent, literary, and analytical people.

In matters concerning communication, sylphs can be great allies—petition them when you're doing spells that involve contracts or negotiations of any kind. If you want to contact someone but can't do it through ordinary channels, a sylph can serve as an intermediary.

Sylphs are also said to interact well with the other elementals. For example, they blend their talents with those of the undines to make snowflakes. Some air spirits from around the world include *ga-oh* (the Seneca spirit of the four winds), *boreas* (the Greek personification of the north wind), and *austri* (a Norse dwarf who rules the air).

If you'd like to commune with a sylph, stand outside in the open air, preferably on a windy day. You can either call out to the sylph and ask it to join you, or whistle to attract its attention. Sylphs are fond of flowers of all kinds. To thank a sylph for its assistance, place fresh blossoms in a sacred spot outdoors as an offering. You can also scatter flower petals in the wind for sylphs to enjoy.

Salamanders

Salamanders look like bright, tiny lizards with tongues of flame. They inhabit the element of fire and are naturally drawn to people who exhibit courage, creativity, and initiative. Other manifestations of the fire spirit include the will-o'-the-wisp described in European and American stories, the *hob* (an English fire-tending faery), Logi (the Teutonic giant who governs wild fire), and Shawnodese (the spirit of the south in some Native American traditions).

Call upon these fire spirits when you do spells that involve action, inspiration, vitality, or passion. Salamanders can serve as liaisons, marshalling the forces of the fire realm to assist you. To contact these elementals, build a small fire or light a candle and gaze into the flame while you request their presence. Remember to thank them for their assistance by burning incense in their honor.

Undines

The undines (or ondines) are water spirits. Sometimes they show themselves to humans as mermaids or sirens, who live and frolic in the waves. Seafarers' folklore abounds with tales of these alluring creatures. Although usually described as quite beautiful, undines can be capricious. Their element—water—governs the emotions, and undines may shift moods unexpectedly. Undines relate best to sensitive, intuitive, and artistic people who don't try to repress their own emotions.

Other water spirits from around the world include Aganippe (a Greek water nymph who lives in the stream that provides poetic inspiration to the Muses), *apo* (Persian water spirits), *gahongan* (Iroquois water spirits), and Nakki (a Finnish water genie whom you can bribe with coins).

Invite the undines to assist you when you're doing love spells. They'll also come to your aid if you seek creative inspiration or want to improve your intuition. Sit quietly beside a body of water and gaze at the surface. Soon you may notice circular spots where the current seems to move more rapidly or bubble—those are the water spirits. Undines are fond of perfume and essential oils. Pour some scent in a stream, lake, or other body of water to thank them for helping you with a spell and they'll continue to serve you.

Tapping Your Own Elemental Power

Every witch has one element to which she most strongly responds; this is her power element. In addition, each witch has a personality element. Your astrological chart will reveal your dominant elements. Your sun sign is important, but you'll want to pay attention to the positions of the moon and planets, as well as your ascendant. Often your power element is the one in which your natal moon is positioned, whereas your personality element corresponds to your sun sign.

Element	Astrological Signs
Fire	Aries, Leo, Sagittarius
Earth	Taurus, Virgo, Capricorn
Air	Gemini, Libra, Aquarius
Water	Cancer, Scorpio, Pisces

Think of yourself as a battery that is charged by the cosmos. By tuning into your dominant elements and connecting to the elemental forces in the universe, you can revitalize yourself and strengthen your magickal abilities.

Your Power Element

How do you determine your power element? By paying attention. Go to places where you can experience each element intimately. Stand in a strong wind, sit by an ocean or waterfall, watch a blazing fire, or walk into a cave or forest. Which location makes you feel the most alive, nurtured, and content? Pay attention to your senses—do they feel more keen or activated in one place than another?

Once you determine which element energizes you, you can find ways to plug into that source of renewable energy any time you need a boost. Here are some ideas to get you started:

- **Earth:** Work in the garden. Sit on the ground while holding brown or black gemstones in your hand. Take long walks in the woods. Keep potted plants in your home and workplace. Eat lots of root vegetables: potatoes, carrots, turnips, beets.

- **Air:** Open the windows. Practice yogic breathing exercises. Go to a windy location and let the breeze embrace you. Watch birds. If you work in a building where you can't open the windows, put an electric fan near your work station.
- **Fire:** Get out in the sunshine. Light candles. Build a fire. Sit next to a heater. Dance to lively music, around a ritual fire if possible. Drink hot beverages and eat spicy foods.
- **Water:** Go swimming. Sit beside a body of water. Take long baths or showers. Play in the rain. Drink lots of spring water.

You can also connect with these elements through meditation. Envision yourself in a setting that corresponds to your power element. Or visualize yourself surrounded by the element in its most fundamental state. As you breathe, imagine you are inhaling that nourishing force into your body where it invigorates you on all levels.

Your Personality Element

Your personality element may or may not be the same as your power element. To discern your personality element, ask yourself the following questions:

- What are your likes and dislikes?
- How do people describe you?
- What hobbies (or art forms) interest you most?
- What's your temperament?

Do any themes appear in your answers? Next, look over the following descriptions of elemental personalities for more insight:

Earth People

You like stability and creature comforts. Usually, you carefully plan out everything and take your time making decisions. People consider you to be dependable, steady, and practical. Your favorite color may be black, brown, or forest green. You enjoy plants and nature. Your hobbies might include gardening, ceramics, woodworking, or other handicrafts.

Air People

The world of ideas appeals most to you and you love learning new things. You engage in long conversations with friends and probably have a large circle of acquaintances. People often describe you as outgoing, independent, and maybe a bit ditsy. Your favorite color may be yellow, pale blue, or white. Reading and/or writing are among your hobbies, and perhaps hang-gliding or flying kites.

Fire People

Passionate and energetic, you enjoy adventure and taking risks. You have no patience with wishy-washy sorts or couch potatoes. Always on the go, you have trouble sitting still. People might describe you as hot-headed or impulsive. Your favorite colors are red and orange. You probably enjoy sports and your hobbies might include dancing, horseback riding, or traveling.

Water People

Your gentle temperament leads you to go with the proverbial flow. Easily influenced by others, your emotions are sensitive and deep. You possess keen intuition and perhaps artistic or musical talent. A natural caretaker, you nurture others and may be a healer. People describe you as shy, reclusive, or moody, and you need quiet time alone. Your favorite color is purple or blue, and your hobbies might include painting, music, fishing, or swimming.

Once you understand your elements, you can focus on the type of magick that suits you best. For instance, air people may have great success with chanting and affirmations. Fire people often gravitate toward candle spells. People with earth personalities tend to be good at herbal magick. Water people can concoct wonderful potions and witches' brews.

If your power element and personality element are different, try to tap both in your magick spells and rituals. For example, a witch whose power element is earth and personality element is air could be an avid communicator who leads group rituals for abundance or healing. Play to your strengths.

CHAPTER 9

The Plant Kingdom

Witchcraft is closely intertwined with the green world. The Green Man, one of the pagan deities, embodies the abundance of nature. The Druids revered trees and believed that the sacred World Tree connected the upper, middle, and lower worlds. A Greek myth explains that the daughters of Hecate (one of the patronesses of witchcraft) taught witches how to use plants for both healing and magick, and throughout history witches have practiced herbalism. Today's Wiccans and witches are continuing to expand humankind's knowledge of the plant kingdom.

Green Witchcraft

For centuries, witches who understood the medicinal and magickal properties of plants served as village healers, concocting remedies for everything from burns to broken hearts. This ancient practice is known today as green witchcraft and is a popular form of magick. This particular version of the Craft focuses on both the biological components and the symbolic qualities of flowers, trees, and herbs.

According to green witchcraft, plants contain spirits. To work effectively with plants, witches communicate with them at a spiritual level, not just a physical one. Every plant is unique, with its own special energies and applications. Rowan, for instance, hung above a doorway protects your home from harm. Mugwort improves psychic awareness. Depending on the nature of the plant and the spell, botanicals are used in amulets and talismans, brews and potions, poultices and potpourris.

Philosophy and Practices

Green witches seek to establish an intimate connection with nature, especially the plants that feed, shelter, warm, and provide for human beings in countless ways. An appreciation of nature and the wonders of creation are part of the green witch's philosophy of life. She strives to work in partnership with her plants and Mother Earth. Her garden is organic, and her lifestyle respects the environment. Green witches consider every tree, herb, flower, leaf, blade of grass—yes, even weeds—sacred, filled with magickal potential.

To practice green magick you must first reconnect with nature. You can't honor something you don't feel an intimate connection with, and you certainly can't call on the energies of plant spirits without spending time with plants. For witches who live in the concrete jungle, this may present some challenges. But even in the heart of the city, you can find parks, botanical gardens, greenhouses, or garden centers where you can commune with plants.

If you choose to become a green witch, plants will play an important role in your life and have many applications. Here are some ways you might choose to work with the magickal properties of plants:

- Watching plant behavior for omens and signs
- Gathering loosened leaves and petals for magick potions
- Using plant matter in amulets and talismans
- Adding plant matter to incense and candles
- Collecting and waxing plants for decorative touches in your Book of Shadows
- Placing live plants in various parts of your home to encourage personal growth and well-being

Green witches do not assume that traditional correspondences for flora are necessarily correct. Instead, they trust in their intuition and personal awareness of the natural world to determine applications. For instance, garlic grown in a particularly wet season may show an energy signature that isn't as fiery as typical garlic. In fact, it may contain a balance of fire and water energy, which is ideal for healing.

The soil in which a plant grows, the amount of sunlight and water it receives, and other conditions affect the plant's magickal energy as well as its outward appearance. So do the thoughts you send to the plant, as Christopher Byrd and Peter Tompkins discovered while researching their bestselling book *The Secret Life of Plants*.

If you have a garden, you might want to keep a journal and list the growing conditions for each plant you intend to use magickally. This becomes your gardening grimoire. Of course, your grimoire will also contain information about the plant magick you do and the results you achieve.

You can also gain insight into a plant's magickal possibilities through meditation. Hold some plant matter—a seed, leaf, or flower—in the palm of your hand, close your eyes, and extend your psychic perception into the plant to intuit its applications. The images or sensations you receive are cues. For example, if the plant feels warm, it could be used to "warm" a cold heart.

Herbal Healing: An Ancient Tradition

Until World War II, herbal medicine predominated in many parts of the Western world (as it still does in most other regions). Today, herbalism is experiencing a revival in the United States and Europe as a natural alternative to potentially dangerous and expensive pharmaceuticals. Green witches, of course, have utilized the healing power of herbs for millennia.

FACT

Since the time of ancient Greece, dandelions were used in medicine. Dandelion juice rubbed on bug bites eases the itching; brewed in a broth and ingested, it soothes fevers. Dandelions are high in vitamins A, B, and C, and contain potassium.

Lore and legend contain a wealth of information—some superstition and some valid—about plant magick. In some cases, what once seemed purely magickal now can be explained scientifically. For example, early healers dressed wounds with mold, long before it was recognized as a source of penicillin.

Holistic physicians today tap the healing powers of plants in homeopathy, flower remedies, and aromatherapy as well as herbal medicine. Some of these modalities rely on a plant's energetic or spiritual body, rather than its physical substance, for healing. Flower remedies, initially developed by Dr. Edward Bach in the 1930s, contain the plant's vibrations, but no actual plant matter. Flowers are placed in water, then allowed to sit in sunshine so that the life force is infused into the water. When a person ingests the water, the plant's energy promotes emotional, mental, and physical healing. Like other holistic healers, witches utilize the spiritual connection between humans and plants to cure ailments.

Divine Flowers and Plants

For witches who honor a specific god or goddess, plants provide a means to please and appease these beings. The mythologies of numerous cultures worldwide link deities with plants. Kama, the Hindu god of love, bears flower-tipped arrows. The plants of the Persian god Haoma offer healing. The Aztec's Xochipilli is known as the flower prince. Zemyna, from the Baltic region, gave birth to all plants. Vidyadhara, from Tibet, teaches how to use the magickal properties of plants.

In some instances, deities temporarily assumed the form of plants, or transformed mortals into plants. When Persephone caught Pluto flirting with a maiden named Minthe, she turned her rival into mint. Similarly, violets are said to be the victims of Venus and Cupid.

Following are the types of plants that appease certain divinities.

Plant	Divine Patron
Apple	Aphrodite, Hera, Odin, Zeus
Basil	Vishnu
Bay	Apollo, Eros
Catnip	Bast
Corn	Demeter, Mithra
Daisy	Freya, Thor
Dandelion	Hecate
Fennel	Prometheus
Garlic	Hecate
Hawthorn	Flora
Heather	Isis
Iris	Isis, Hera
Lavender	Hecate
Lily	Kwan Yin, Juno
Marjoram	Aphrodite, Venus
Mint	Pluto
Mustard	Mars
Parsley	Persephone
Pine	Cybele, Pan, Poseidon

Primrose	Freya
Rose	Venus, Aphrodite, Bacchus, Eros, Isis
Sage	Zeus
Sunflower	Apollo, Demeter
Violet	Io, Zeus
Willow	Ceres, Hera

If you wish to attract the help of a particular god or goddess, you could put plants that are sacred to the deity on your altar. Or incorporate its components into incense, candles, or oils. If the plant is edible, use it in food or beverages.

Petal Portents

Divination by flowers and plants is known as floromancy and botanomancy, respectively. No doubt you're familiar with the belief that finding a four-leaf clover signals good luck. But many other botanicals can provide insights into your future, too. One way to use these lovely oracles is to observe plants in their natural state.

According to those who practice this art, the first blossoming daffodil not only heralds spring, it also foretells financial improvement—and if you see it on a Friday, your prosperity will double. A myrtle plant blooming unexpectedly near your home portends joy and peace. A healthy growing wisteria speaks of sound friendships. And if you wonder when those friends will arrive for a visit, a geranium planted near your door will tell you. Watch it and when the head turns in a different direction, expect guests soon.

FACT

Divining by roses is called Phyllorhodomancy. To use this method, the questioner acquires three freshly cut roses that haven't begun to open yet and places them in a vase of water. Each rose represents a specific answer (yes, no, maybe). Whichever one lasts the longest represents the answer.

A more active approach to divination involves purposefully manipulating the plants. If you can float a candle on a freshly harvested holly leaf, prosperity is forthcoming. If a harvested ivy leaf stays green all night on New Year's Eve, the coming year will be healthy. Tossing flower petals on water and watching their movement is an effective kind of scrying (visioning the future with the help of an object or external source). Burning plant parts and observing the behavior of the fire is a form of pyromancy (divination by fire).

Another technique involves carefully preserving leaves and flowers and fashioning them into a set of runes or cards. Start with a good base medium (stones, wood, or sturdy art paper) and appropriate decoupage covering. Choose leaves or flowers from various plants and affix them to the base material. Each plant possesses a secret, symbolic meaning.

Plants appearing in dreams have special significance for green witches. Blossoming flowers imply fulfillment, hope, and the flowering of new skills (either magickal or mundane). Buttercups represent business success; carnations and roses speak of love; irises predict forthcoming communications from friends or loved ones; and primroses herald new friendships.

Druid Tree Magick

Druids, the spiritual and magickal leaders of the early Celts, considered trees to be sacred. Neo-Druids still do. Trees, they believe, possessed wisdom that could be conveyed to receptive human beings. Druids usually performed their rites and ceremonies in groves of trees. The early Celts often burned the wood of sacred trees in ritual fires—a practice that continues today—especially at Beltane and Yule.

Maya Magee Sutton, Ph.D. and Nicholas R. Mann, authors of *Druid Magic*, explain that in contemporary Irish dictionaries, the word *draiocht* means "magick." Its root, *draoi*, translates as magician, sorcerer, or Druid. This suggests a strong connection between the Druids and the practice of magick.

Each tree has certain characteristics that ancient Druids and today's Neo-Druids utilize. Oaks, which represent strength and endurance, have long been linked with the Druids. Rowan trees afford protection. Hardy holly that can survive harsh winters symbolizes courage. Poplars represent death and rebirth. Willows are associated with intuition; divining rods are often fashioned from their flexible branches.

FACT

Gillian Kemp has created a colorful deck of cards called *Tree Magick*. Based on the mystical meanings of trees, the oracle consists of fifty-two cards illustrated with various trees from around the world. Each tree represents something different. You can do readings with the tree cards, just as you would with tarot cards, to gain information about your future.

The ancient Celts valued trees so highly that they even based their language Ogham (pronounced oh-am) on trees. Each of the twenty letters in the Ogham alphabet corresponds to a different tree. B or Beth, for instance, is linked with the birch; N or Nion represents the ash. The letters are composed of lines, or notches, cut along a central line or stave. A word or phrase written in Ogham looks like a tree limb with branches sprouting from it.

Ogham letters also serve as mystical symbols that can be used in divination. You can inscribe Ogham glyphs on pieces of wood or stone and cast them like Norse runes to answer questions. You can also draw a single Ogham letter on a slip of paper and put it in a magick amulet or talisman. For example, the letter L, which corresponds to the rowan tree, could be included in a protection amulet.

Magickal Herbcraft

Herbs play an important role in the green witch's magick. Although the easiest herbs to come by—especially for city dwellers—are familiar kitchen spices, witches may utilize any part of a plant that is appropriate to their intentions. Here are some ways that Wiccans and witches use herbs and flowers for both magickal and mundane purposes.

- Air fresheners and potpourris
- Altar decorations
- Candles
- Creams and lotions
- Dream pillows
- Headpieces
- Incense
- Oils
- Ritual foods and beverages
- Sachets
- Wreaths

Recite chants, incantations, or prayers over the item while you are making it. This directs positive energy into it, filling the substance with magickal intention, and keeps your mind focused on your goal.

For protection and safety—especially if you're doing healing magick—as well as to enhance its effectiveness, visualize the item being imbued with the white-blue light of Spirit. It's also a good idea to bless each ingredient before you use it.

Many good books provide recipes for green magick workings and kitchen witchery. In time you'll develop an intuitive understanding of the mystical energies in various herbs. As you become familiar with concocting herbal spells and products, you may want to create your own specialties. Magickally prepared items, such as candles and massage oils, make wonderful and very personal gifts, too.

Spellworking with Scent

As early as 1500 B.C.E., healers and priests were employing aromatics for a wide variety of mundane and metaphysical functions. The Babylonians, for example, perfumed construction materials used for building temples. The Egyptians utilized scented oils for everything from seduction to mummification.

In recent years, aromatherapy—healing with scent—has entered the mainstream. The term was coined by the French chemist and perfumer René-Maurice Gattefosse in 1928 when he discovered, quite by accident, that lavender oil helped heal a burn on his hand and prevented scarring. Because scents affect the limbic system of the brain, causing shifts in brain-wave function, they have a wide range of beneficial applications—physical, psychological, and magickal.

Botanical Correspondences and Properties

Aromatherapists employ various scents for therapeutic purposes. Lavender, for example, calms stress and can aid sleep. Peppermint stimulates the mental processes and promotes clarity. Witches pay attention to the magickal uses for aromas as well. Here are some common magickal correspondences for aromatics:

Aromatic	Correspondence
Almond	vitality, energy booster
Amber	protection
Apple	happiness, especially in love
Basil	protection, harmony
Bay	strength, prophetic dreams
Bayberry	money spells
Cedar	prosperity, courage, protection
Cinnamon	career success, wealth, vitality
Clove	healing, prosperity, to increase sexual desire
Eucalyptus	healing, purification

Frankincense	prosperity, protection, psychic awareness
Gardenia	harmony, love
Ginger	cleansing, balance, awareness
Honeysuckle	mental clarity, communication
Jasmine	love spells, passion, to sweeten any situation
Lavender	relaxation, peace of mind, purification
Lilac	psychic awareness
Mint	money spells
Musk	love spells, vitality, to stimulate drive or desire
Narcissus	self-image
Patchouli	love spells, protection, career success
Pine	purification, protection, strength
Rose	love spells, to lift spirits
Rosemary	memory retention, banishing
Sage	cleansing, wisdom
Sandalwood	connection to the higher realms, knowledge, safe travel
Thyme	work with faery folk
Vanilla	increases magickal power
Vervain	money spells, fertility
Violet	attraction
Ylang-ylang	aphrodisiac, love spells, passion, feminine power

Aromagick is one of the loveliest types of spellworking. As you work with scents, consider both their mystical and physical effects. Combine two or more to "customize" your spells.

Concocting Herbal Spells and Potions

The number of possible uses for herbs in spells and potions is limited only by your imagination. Witches frequently include herbs in talismans and amulets. Essential oils are ideal for anointing or charging charms and ritual tools. Incense figures in many spells, as you've already seen—some witches enjoy making their own herbal incense. Burning sage is a common purification technique for cleansing sacred space. Dressing (anointing) candles with essential oils is another popular practice.

Essential oils are extracted from plants, not concocted from synthetic substances like most modern perfumes. When you're working magick, essential oils are preferable to other scents because they contain the life energy of herbs and flowers.

Aromatic sachets, filled with herbs that are appropriate to your intention, can be placed around your home to attract or repel energies. Some witches like to scent their clothing with fragrant herbal mists or perfumes, especially for ceremonies. You can also scent bed linens, carpets, or your car's interior. Many witches add essential oils to bath water. Perhaps you'd enjoy making your own herbal soap, shampoo, lotion, or cosmetics. As you can see, it's easy to bring aromagick into every area of your life.

Herbs and/or essential oils can be combined with other magickal substances to amplify or fine-tune them. For example, you could anoint a piece of aventurine with peppermint oil to double its money-drawing power.

Work during moon signs or phases that support your intentions. If growth or expansion is your goal, do herbal magick while the moon waxes. The waning moon aids spells for banishing or decrease. Prosperity spells are stronger if done when the moon is in Taurus. Choose the most auspicious time of day, too. Work at dawn to inspire hope or launch a new project, at noon to bring hidden issues to light or for public matters, at dusk for closure, and at midnight when you need to rely on your intuition.

Plants and Sacred Space

Many witches include plants in their sacred space, often to mark the four elemental quarters. By choosing a plant with the appropriate elemental association and putting it in the corresponding quarter, you honor the Watchtowers (the elemental guardians of the four quarters that "watch" over the sacred space) and support the energy of the sacred space. The following list contains some common plants and their elemental associations:

- **Earth (north):** Alfalfa sprouts, beets, corn, fern, honeysuckle, magnolia, moss, peas, potatoes, turnips, vervain
- **Air (east):** Anise, clover, dandelions, goldenrod, lavender, lily of the valley, marjoram, mint, parsley, pine
- **Fire (south):** Basil, bay, cactus, chrysanthemum, daylilies, dill, garlic, holly, juniper, marigolds, onions, rosemary, sunflowers
- **Water (west):** Aster, blackberries, catnip, cucumbers, daffodils, gardenias, geranium, iris, lettuce, lotus, roses, water lily, willow

Also consider the time of the year when selecting plants for your sacred space. Certain plants are linked with each zodiac sign.

- **Aries:** Holly, snapdragon, cactus, jonquil
- **Taurus:** Daffodil, clover, lilac, columbine, daisy
- **Gemini:** Azalea, honeysuckle, lily of the valley, heather
- **Cancer:** Iris, jasmine, water lily, white rose, gardenia
- **Leo:** Red rose, poppy, marigold, sunflower, dahlia
- **Virgo:** Lavender, myrtle, aster, fern, heather, daylily
- **Libra:** Cosmos, gardenia, pink rose, violet, hibiscus
- **Scorpio:** Orchid, violet, eucalyptus, foxglove, pinks, wolfsbane
- **Sagittarius:** Paperwhite narcissus, Christmas cactus, red clover, dandelion
- **Capricorn:** Holly, carnation, mistletoe, pansy

- **Aquarius:** Carnation, wild rose, lady slipper
- **Pisces:** Lotus, passion flower, violet, narcissus, wisteria

You can align yourself with cosmic energies by including plants whose energies correspond to the sign in which the sun is positioned at any given month.

Some witches choose plants to honor the gods and goddesses (as discussed earlier). If, for instance, a witch is working with Hera, a bowl of apples and a vase of irises would be suitable—and visually appealing. Of course, there's nothing wrong with surrounding yourself with plants you particularly enjoy, for their fragrance, color, or shape. From the green witch's viewpoint, all plants are sacred and all come from the Goddess.

CHAPTER 10

The Mineral Kingdom

From the witch's viewpoint, everything in nature resonates with energy and life—and everything can be utilized for working magick. Expressions such as *gems of truth, rock solid, clear as crystal,* and *strong as steel* describe metaphorically the value of minerals. These qualities can be especially useful in spellworking. Stones, shells, metals, and other minerals add strength and permanence to a spell. They also ground your thoughts and help your intentions solidify in the physical world.

Mineral Magick

Perhaps you've seen a psychic "read" a person's life story simply by holding her ring in his hand. That's because minerals—stones, shells, crystals, and metals—pick up the vibrations of things they come into contact with and retain those vibrations for a long time. Minerals may appear inert to the untrained eye, but if you try you may be able to sense the subtle emanations given off by stones and metals. Gemstones and crystals, in particular, pulse with their own unique life energy.

Minerals resonate at a slower rate than plants or animals. This quality makes them especially useful in certain types of spells. If you imprint minerals with a magickal intention, they will retain it for months, years, or even longer. Minerals can also be combined with other ingredients to strengthen or lengthen the duration of a spell. In a world of continuous change, minerals remain constant and firm.

Gemstones

Long before gems were prized for their monetary value, they were worn for magickal purposes. The ancients believed gems could heal, protect, inspire fertility, indicate the outcome of battles, and stimulate crop growth. Today, a growing number of witches and other metaphysicians are rediscovering the magick inherent in stones. They realize that crystals and gemstones can be important tools for healing, spellworking, divination, shamanic journeying, meditation, and dowsing.

Gemstones are believed to have their own distinct personalities. According to Nancy Schiffer, author of *The Power of Jewelry*, our ancestors believed gemstones were "capable of human feelings and passions so that they could express jealousy and shock."

Each stone has its own, unique properties and energies that can be tapped for magickal purposes. As a general rule, clear stones are best for working with mental and spiritual issues; translucent or cloudy stones, such as pearls and moonstones, can aid emotional situations; and opaque stones have an affinity with physical matters. Stones of all kinds may be used alone or in combination with other ingredients in spellworking.

Magickal Uses for Gemstones

Witches utilize gemstones in myriad ways, and value them not only for their monetary worth but for their magickal possibilities as well. Here are some of their uses:

- As pendulums, runes, and other divination tools
- For healing and aligning the body's energy centers
- As amulets, talismans, and fetishes
- As ceremonial jewelry
- As components in spells and rituals
- As aids to visualization and meditation
- To adorn magickal tools and augment their powers
- To define sacred space and honor its energies
- As gifts to deities

Some witches believe that dreams about gemstones are significant and can be considered messages from the Divine. Because dreams are symbolic and individualistic, your own interpretation should be given priority. However, in many cases the meaning of a gem in a dream is similar to its magickal correspondences (see the list further on in this chapter).

Dreams of diamonds may mean different things in different cultures. In Europe and the United States, diamonds represent devotion or faithfulness in love. In the Middle East, Persia, and Egypt, they signify good luck. In India, they symbolize victory, success, and zeal.

As you work with gemstones, you'll undoubtedly discover other uses for them, according to your particular intentions and personal style. Trust your intuition and allow the stones themselves to speak to you—they may suggest some unique applications.

Spellworking with Gemstones

Before using gemstones in spells or rituals, it's a good idea to wash them to remove any unwanted vibrations and to prepare them to receive your intentions. Cleanse them in running water with mild soap. Visualize white light permeating the stones and clearing them.

You can combine several stones in a spell to customize it. Let's say, for instance, you are fashioning a talisman to attract wealth. You might include aventurine or tiger-eye, stones typically associated with abundance. But if the person for whom the talisman is being made tends to have trouble holding on to money, you could add a piece of hematite to stabilize finances. Refer to the list of correspondences further on in this chapter to determine which gems are most appropriate for your purposes.

ALERT!

Gems don't necessarily mean the same things in every culture. Therefore, when doing mineral magick, it could be important to consider the nationality or heritage of a person for whom you are working a spell. The person's birth date might also be relevant—it's usually best to work with stones that support his astrological energies.

Once you've chosen a stone to use in your spell, communicate your intentions to it. You can do this by holding the stone to your "third eye" and projecting into it an image of what you want it to do. Or hold the gem to your lips and whisper your objective to it.

If you wish to use gemstones to mark the four directions that define sacred space, place an "air" stone, such as aquamarine, in the east. Choose a "fire" stone, perhaps a carnelian or ruby, for the south. In the west, put a "water" stone, such as pearl or moonstone, and in the north set an onyx, turquoise, or other "earth" stone.

Witches often use gemstones to augment healing. Although this is an art that requires skill and practice to perfect, the properties of some stones are widely accepted and can safely be utilized as subtle healing aids even by novice witches. The gentle vibrations of rose quartz can calm stress; amethysts have been used since ancient times to induce sleep. Remember, however, that gemstones are not a substitute for professional medical care.

Magickal Correspondences and Properties of Stones

Throughout history, people have attributed certain qualities and properties to gemstones. Some stones have been considered lucky, others harbingers of misfortune. The Old Testament of the Bible contains references to amethysts as stones of spiritual power. Soldiers in ancient Rome wore bloodstones for protection. Sometimes the color determines a gem's correspondences. For example, sapphires are associated with the deep blue sea. Other connections stem from long-ago practices involving gems. Jade, which contemporary magicians use in prosperity spells, was traded by the early Egyptians and used as a form of money.

Hebrew legends tell that the emerald was one of the four stones presented to King Solomon (along with lapis, topaz, and carbuncle). These stones represented his authority and wisdom. In Egyptian and Greek mythology (as recounted by Albertus Magnus), emeralds were originally discovered in a griffin's nest.

Much of what modern witches know about the magick of gemstones is rooted in antiquity. As early as four thousand years ago, hieroglyphics described the use of gemstones for medical purposes. The best-known early literature on the subject is *The History of Jewels* by a thirteenth-century philosopher named Albertus Magnus. The following list describes the generally accepted magickal uses for numerous gems.

STONES AND THEIR MAGICAL PROPERTIES

Gemstone	Magickal Uses
Amber	for physical and psychic protection
Amethyst	for meditation, enhancing and remembering dreams, calming emotions, increasing psychic ability; it ranges in color from deep purple to pink
Apache tears	a type of obsidian that many witches carry for luck
Aquamarine	for clarity and mental awareness, encouraging spiritual insight, stimulating creativity
Aventurine	to attract wealth or abundance
Azurite	for dream magick, to promote harmony
Bloodstone	for healing, strength, courage, and physical protection
Carnelian	to stimulate passion, sexual energy, courage, and initiative
Citrine	for clearing vibrations from other stones and crystals, to banish nightmares and improve psychic abilities
Coral	to attract love or increase affectionate feelings; enhances self-esteem, calms emotions
Diamond	to deepen commitment and trust, especially in a love relationship, to absorb and retain energies and vibrations, for strength and victory
Emerald	to aid clairvoyance and divination; to promote healing, growth, mental and emotional balance
Fluorite	to strengthen the conscious mind and mental skills
Garnet	for protection, to deepen kindness, to relieve depression and alleviate fears
Hematite	for grounding, to help stabilize emotions
Jade	for prosperity, longevity; to enhance beauty and health
Jasper	red jasper is good in love spells to stir up passions; brown jasper is excellent for healing purposes; poppy jasper breaks up blockages that prevent energy from circulating through the body
Lapis lazuli	for opening psychic channels, dealing with children, stimulating the upper chakras; ancient Egyptians used it to charge power meridians on the planet

Moldavite	to energize psychic talent, quicken spiritual evolution, open the upper chakras; moldavite is regarded as an extraterrestrial stone because it resulted from a meteor collision with the earth nearly 15 million years ago
Moonstone	to enhance the vividness of dreams and dream recall, to calm emotions
Obsidian	one of the favorite stones for scrying mirrors; sacred to the patroness of witches, Hecate
Onyx	for banishing and absorbing negative energy, grounding, and stabilizing; to help break deeply ingrained habits
Opal	for protection, to encourage psychic ability and visions, to attract love
Pearl	to strengthen self-esteem, for balance in love relationships, to increase femininity, to enhance happiness
Quartz (clear)	to retain information, to amplify the energy of other stones, to transmit ideas and energy, for psychic awareness
Quartz (smoky)	for endurance, to hold problems until you are ready to deal with them
Rose quartz	to attract love and friendship, for emotional healing and balance, to amplify psychic energy
Ruby	to stimulate the emotions, passion, love; to open your heart to divine love; to boost vitality
Sapphire	to increase spiritual knowledge and connection with the Divine, for wisdom, insight, and prophetic vision; star sapphires provide hope and clarity of purpose
Tiger-eye	for abundance, self-confidence, the freedom to follow your own path
Tourmaline	green and black tourmaline are good for cleansing, healing, and absorbing negative vibrations; pink and watermelon tourmaline attract friendship, love, and fulfillment; use them to transmit messages and energy
Turquoise	for protection, healing, prosperity; to ease mental tension and emotional anxiety

Amber isn't really a stone; it's hardened resin. According to lore, amber came from the tears of a setting sun, and as such it's still considered a solar/fire stone. Witches also use it in healing magick, to capture disease in the same way as it once captured insects.

Stones are usually available in a wide range of qualities. A large or gemquality stone isn't necessary for most spells. Use your intuition and let yourself be drawn to choose the right stone for the job.

Magickal Jewelry

Today, of course, most people wear precious and semiprecious gems mainly for adornment. In the metaphysical community, jewelry that combines magick with beauty is highly prized. Many New Age jewelers, who understand the historical and mystical properties of gemstones, now fabricate elegant jewelry for ritual wear, healing, and talismanic purposes.

Gemstones have long been associated with gods and goddesses. In many cultures, gems were considered to be suitable offerings to the deities, and stones were often placed on altars as sacred gifts. In earlier times, only royalty and religious leaders wore gemstones. You can still see vestiges of these ancient beliefs in the practice of kissing the Pope's jeweled ring.

When you wear gemstones, they absorb your personal vibrations. Pearls, in particular, are known to be affected by the emotions of the person who wears them. When you're feeling happy, a pearl will glow with a lustrous sheen, but turns cloudy when you're down in the dumps. If you choose to wear family jewels or antique pieces, be sure to wash them in advance, in order to rid them of any lingering energies from other people.

Amulets and Talismans

The custom of carrying magick amulets and talismans is ancient. The early Egyptians placed good-luck charms in the tombs of royalty to insure safe passage into the world beyond. Ancient Greek soldiers carried amulets into battle to protect them. An amulet or talisman may be a single object that has special meaning for its owner or a combination of several items—gemstones, botanicals, magickal images, etc.—contained in a "charm bag" or "medicine pouch," designed for a specific purpose. The energies of the ingredients plus your belief in their magickal properties give the talisman or amulet its power.

A talisman is designed to attract something you desire: prosperity, love, success, happiness, etc. Gemstones and jewelry have long been favored as talismans. The Chinese, for example, prize jade and wear it to bring health, strength, and good fortune. Amulets are used to repel an undesired energy, condition, or entity. During the Crusades, ladies gave opals to soldiers to keep them safe in battle.

You can fashion amulets or talismans for yourself or for someone else. Once sealed, these magick charms should never be opened. Should a time come when the amulet or talisman is no longer needed, bury it in the ground.

Place the ingredients you've chosen for your amulet or talisman in a cloth or leather pouch and wear or carry it in your pocket. If you prefer, put the items in a wooden box and set it on your altar. It's usually best to fashion a talisman while the moon is waxing; amulets should be made during the waning moon.

Crystals

Quartz crystals are a blend of silica and water formed under certain conditions of pressure, temperature, and energy. These crystals possess amazing abilities to retain information, amplify energy, and transmit vibrations. As a result, they're often used in watches, computers, laser tools, TV and radio equipment, and many other practical implements. In metaphysical applications, crystals' properties make them ideal for healing, storing knowledge, sending energy and thought patterns, and increasing the power of any substance with which they come into contact.

People who work with crystals believe they are actually unique life forms that possess innate intelligence and many diverse powers. Hold one in your hand and see if you can feel it resonate. According to crystal worker, teacher, and healer Dr. Martin Hart, "Crystals can be doorways (gateways) beyond the boundaries of your world, of your universe, into the Possible, the Futures, the Unknown, the Worlds of Other, and to the discovery of their magics. They can be gateways to the new world you are destined to create."

Types of Crystals

Crystals come in many shapes and configurations. Each has its own special properties and uses. Here are some of the most common types of crystals.

- Single-terminated crystals have one point, which can either draw or send energy in a particular direction.
- Double-terminated crystals feature points at both ends that act as poles; these can attract or send energy in two directions.
- Abundance crystals contain greenish specks of chlorite; witches often use them to attract money.
- Creator crystals have smaller crystals or materials growing inside them; these can help you create your desires and manifest them.
- Clusters of crystals contain numerous points, all connected at the base.
- Cathedral crystals contain many spires clustered together and projecting upward from a single base, like buildings in a city.
- Gateway crystals appear to contain small openings or windows within them that can act as portals for journeying into other realms of existence.
- Laser crystals are long and thin, like wands; they are used to project and direct energy.

Crystals can be found in various colors, too, and each possesses unique characteristics. Smoky quartz, which is grayish-brown in color, has grounding properties; it can also store your emotions or thoughts temporarily, until you're ready to deal with them. The gentle vibrations of rose quartz help calm and balance the emotions. Yellowish citrine is good for cleansing other crystals. Amethyst awakens intuition and can aid meditation. Rutilated crystals contain threadlike material (rutiles) that increase the crystals' power.

Magickal Uses for Crystals

Crystals play roles in many spells and rituals, and witches value them for their versatility. Generally speaking, larger crystals are more powerful—as well as more rare and expensive—than smaller ones, but that's not always the case. When choosing crystals, allow yourself to be drawn by the stones instead of simply picking them for their size or beauty. If you listen carefully, you might even hear them speak to you. Here are some ways witches use crystals:

- As pendulums
- For healing and aligning the body's energy centers
- For cleansing and purification
- To direct energy, when used in wands and other magickal tools
- In amulets, talismans, medicine pouches, and fetishes
- To augment the power of other gems
- As components in spells and rituals
- For scrying
- For protection
- To retain information and as memory aids
- To enhance focus and relaxation in meditation
- To define sacred space
- As portals to other worlds of existence

Crystals can also be steeped in water to make a healing crystal elixir. First, charge a crystal with your intention. Place the crystal in a glass of spring water and set it outside in sunlight or moonlight (depending on your purpose). Allow the crystal to imprint the water with its vibrations. Then remove the stone and drink the water.

Your crystals have the ability to communicate with you and with other stones. Carry one with you when you attend a lecture or class; it will absorb the information and help you remember what was discussed.

Spellworking with Crystals

You've probably heard the expression "diamonds are a girl's best friend," but when it comes to doing magick, crystals are a witch's best friend. These complex and versatile stones can be utilized in virtually any spell or ritual, as well as for healing, divination, and other types of energy work.

In *Stone Power*, Dorothee L. Mella recommends trying clear quartz crystal "as an attitude aid, and wear it for draining off any blocked areas that are preventing your dreams from coming true. In a piece of jewelry, this snowy white quartz can help you to use your own inner resources and potentials to alleviate your self-blocks."

Because crystals amplify the energies of other stones, witches often use them in talismans and amulets where they increase the power of the charm. When placed on an altar in the company of other stones, or when combined with other gems on a magick tool, crystals unify and strengthen the various stones' vibrations.

A crystal's ability to focus and direct energy makes it ideal for circle casting. Laser crystals are perfectly shaped for this purpose. If you prefer, affix a crystal to the tip of a magick wand and use it to cast the circle. You can point a wand-shaped crystal (or a wand with a crystal attached) toward the heavens to draw down cosmic energy. Or aim it in a particular direction to send energy where you want it to go.

Many people use crystals for protection. After you've given it this intention, you can carry your crystal in your pocket or purse to keep you safe at all times. You can also keep them in the glove compartment of your car, position several near the doors and windows of your home, and bury one at each of the four corners of your property. When casting a circle, you could place a crystal at each of the four directions or even form a complete circle with crystals; some people bury tiny crystals in the ground to form a permanent circle around a sacred space.

Divining with Crystals

You've probably seen pictures or heard about witches looking into crystal balls to divine the future. This technique is known as crystallomancy, or crystal scrying. To do this, the witch gazes into a crystal—a ball or a large, smooth chunk of clear quartz crystal—and watches for visions to appear within. While doing this, the witch enters a light trancelike state of awareness, allowing messages to seep through from her subconscious, her higher self, and/or Spirit. These messages appear to the witch as images in the stone.

Old magickal texts describe the proper preparation of a crystal before using it for divination. Some called for washing the crystal in special waters, reciting prayers or incantations over it, and waiting for a specific moon phase before making an attempt to solicit the stone's indwelling spirit for help. In some cases, shamans "fed" the stones blood or wine, or slept with them, to improve rapport with the spirit of the crystal.

FACT

According to St. Augustus, Persians were the first to incorporate crystal scrying into their divination practices. Other historians credit the Romans for introducing the art to the rest of Europe. Fifth-century texts mention scrying and recommend using a variety of stones, including quartz, obsidian, and aquamarine.

Find a good-sized crystal that has a nice surface on which to focus your attention. (Gateway crystals are perfect for divination.) Leaded crystal isn't recommended; instead, choose genuine quartz crystal for scrying. Set this crystal on a dark cloth and place it on a table in front of you or on your altar. If you prefer, you can hold it in the palm of your hand. Think of a question while you gaze at the crystal. Don't look at the surface of the stone; look at a point within it. Let your vision blur, breathe deeply, and keep looking. If clouds, colors, or shapes begin to appear, you're doing it right.

Make a mental note of what you see, as well as any ideas that come to you during the process. Continue looking into the crystal until the images stop. Then interpret them according to the following list or follow your own instincts.

- **Black clouds:** A negative omen, dark times ahead
- **Blue clouds:** Joy, hope
- **Green clouds:** Another good omen (a so-called green light)
- **Purple clouds:** Spiritual matters are foremost
- **White clouds:** A good sign, luck or improved conditions
- **Yellow clouds:** Unpleasant news
- **Clouds moving up and to the right:** Yes, or go ahead
- **Clouds moving down and to the left:** No, or stop
- **Swirling clouds:** No definite answer at this time

This divination method is both quick and highly portable. Nonetheless, it has its limits. Most people do not get detailed responses from scrying; thus, it is usually more suited to simple inquiries than ones requiring in-depth information. Be patient with yourself. It takes time and practice to develop this technique.

Crystals in Your Home

According to feng shui, the ancient Chinese art of placement, crystals attract the life force of the universe, known as *chi* or *qi*. Here's a simple feng shui "cure": Place a crystal in a dark corner of your home to make it seem brighter and lift the heaviness that abides in shadows. Feng shui connects each section of your life to a part of your home. If you want to improve conditions in a particular area of your life—relationships, finances, health, etc.—put a crystal in the sector of your home that corresponds it.

Caring for Gemstones and Crystals

It's a good idea to cleanse your gemstones and crystals periodically. Wash them in running water, with mild soap if you like, then let them sit in the sun. This removes any unwanted vibrations as well as dust. You can also purify crystals by gently rubbing them with a piece of citrine. You might clean your crystals before using them in a magick spell or ritual. Also wash them if they've been exposed to any strong emotions or unsettling events.

Some people recommend keeping stones in a velvet or cloth bag, a wooden box, or other protected place when they're not in use. Gems retain ambient vibrations, especially those generated by other people. Don't let anyone handle the stones you use in magical work. Crystal protocol advises that you always ask before you touch someone's crystals or gemstones.

> Crystals like light, so let them sit on a windowsill or other spot where they'll receive the rays from the sun and moon. Hold or touch them frequently—crystals grow dull when you ignore them, but sparkle when you show them love and respect.

The relationship you establish with your stones and crystals will be unique to you. In time, they'll become your good friends. You may choose to designate certain stones for certain purposes. Treat them with respect and they'll gladly assist you.

Metal Magick

Like gemstones, metals were prized by our ancestors for their magickal properties as well as their practical ones. Gold, for instance, was associated with the sun and the various sun gods, such as Ra and Apollo. Silver was linked with the moon and the moon goddesses Diana, Artemis, Isis, etc. When the ancients built temples to honor their gods and goddesses, they often incorporated precious metals in the architecture, decorations, and icons that corresponded to the deities. This practice continues in churches and temples throughout the modern world, although the connections may not be consciously understood today.

Metals resonate with their own, unique vibrations, and these resonances can be tapped for magickal purposes. Magicians often choose to fabricate their ritual tools from metals whose energies are in line with the magician's purposes. A ceremonial chalice, for example, might be made of silver that vibrates with feminine energy. Copper, a metal associated with Venus (goddess and planet of love), could be utilized in a love talisman.

Magickal Properties and Correspondences of Metals

Many of the correspondences for metals and minerals have been handed down from the alchemists. These medieval chemists are best known for supposedly transforming lead into gold, but they discovered many other substances and their properties as well. Alchemists believed that everything on this planet could be broken down into key elemental correspondences. They also understood the connections between heaven and earth, including the energies of the sun, moon, and planets, and coordinated their work to harmonize with celestial movements.

The following list of metals and minerals and their magickal associations derives from various sources, including old magickal texts and mythology. Familiarize yourself with these correspondences and traits before you start applying them in your own spellworking.

Mineral/Metal	Magickal Uses
Boji stone	to inspire symmetry, peacefulness, and a sense of foundation
Brass	a fire-oriented metal that exhibits energy similar to gold but on a gentler scale; popular in healing and prosperity magick
Copper	linked with Venus, copper is used in love spells; the preferred metal for making witching wands, it conducts energy and inspires health, balance, and good foundations
Feldspar	made of aluminum silicate and other minerals, it's associated with love, fertility, and working with the fey
Flint	durability, strength, protection from mischievous faeries
Gold	related to the sun and the God aspect, gold confers strength, leadership, power, authority, and victory to the bearer
Hematite	for grounding and stability

Iron	strength, safety, protection from harmful spirits; some consider iron an antimagick metal, which is why witches prefer not to cut magickal herbs with an iron knife
Lead	for reconnecting to the earth and to encourage practicality; it blocks psychic energies, so don't choose it for a pendulum or wand
Lodestone	the magnetic quality of this stone makes it ideal for attracting good fortune, particularly in love and relationships
Meteorites	because they come from celestial realms, meteorites are good for meditation and spiritual pursuits, astral projection, dreams, and journeying
Pyrite	to protect yourself from being fooled or deceived
Salt	for purification, banishing, and protection
Serpentine	a protective stone, used mostly for health-related purposes
Silver	the metal of the moon and the Goddess, silver inspires insight, dreams, psychic awareness, and creativity
Steel	for protection, especially when made into a ring
Tin	for expansion and traveling; said to be lucky if you put it in your shoe

History and legends from numerous cultures describe myriad magickal practices for various metals. The Greeks inscribed pieces of lead with incantations and used them as amulets to ward against negative charms and spells. Pliny recommended hematite for attracting positive energy. In the East Indies, people put lodestone into the monarch's crown to improve his charm. Alexander the Great gave pieces of lodestone to his armies to protect them from evil influences (particularly genies).

Using Metals in Spells

When working magick, witches use metals alone as well as in combination with gemstones and other materials. Gold and silver, especially, are popular for magickal jewelry. Ritual tools may also be fashioned from these precious metals. Talismans and amulets often contain metals chosen for their magickal properties; a love charm, for instance, might include a piece of copper (Venus's metal). And if you're brewing up a love potion, mix magickal ingredients in a copper pot or pan. Sprinkle salt in the corners of a room for protection or around sacred space to clear it of unwanted energies. Place herbs associated with Sagittarius in a tin box and carry it along when you travel to insure a safe, happy journey.

In feng shui, a type of magick that originated thousands of years ago in China, metal helps provide strength, structure, and permanence. If you're having trouble holding on to money, for example, a feng shui practitioner might recommend placing a metal object in the section of your home that corresponds to wealth.

As you become familiar with the characteristics of different metals and minerals, you'll no doubt devise your own, personal ways for using them in spells and rituals.

Shells, Fossils, and Rocks

Shells and fossils also have their place in magickal work. Since ancient times, they have served as units of monetary as well as mystical value. As physical records of earlier geological periods and long-ago life forms, shells and fossils symbolize endurance and the cyclical nature of earthly existence. These natural objects carry specific energy imprints that witches today can activate and direct for specific purposes.

Stone casting is a divination method that uses shells, stones, or other minerals to provide guidance and answers to questions. Take a collection of stones (shells, etc.) and toss them on a surface. The way each stone lands, the overall pattern, and the symbolic value of the stones, are all interpreted. Runes are also carved on stones, bone, and shells, then used for divination.

Rings of standing stones, such as those at Stonehenge and nearby Avebury, define sacred space. Individual stones often mark the four directions in a ritual circle. Stones imprinted with natural circles offer protection. In sweat lodge ceremonies, red-hot rocks fuel the purification process that aids spiritual growth. In feng shui, heavy stones hold down chi and provide stability.

Clearly, stones of all kinds have long held a sense of magick for humankind—who hasn't reached down and picked up a pretty pebble and kept it as a touchstone? Perhaps their very ancientness, their role as witnesses to history, provides a sense of connection and continuity. As repositories of experience, the mysteries they contain make them an unparalleled source of knowledge that we have yet to fully grasp.

Substance	Uses
Amber	fossilized resin, sometimes containing insects, it's worn for protection
Bone	to provide strength and structure; for longevity
Coral	to attract love, to enhance intuition and creativity; red and pink coral are the preferred types for protecting children
Cross stone	sometimes called a faery cross, it honors the four quarters and their corresponding elements
Geode	to create a natural womb for energy; for mental or physical fertility; an ideal Goddess emblem
Hag stone	also known as a holey stone, it's a plain rock with a hole through it that's found near water; stimulates health, luck, and blessings, and is considered the gift of the sea goddess
Jet	a fossilized bit of wood, it provides strength and courage, particularly in difficult situations
Lava	born of fire, lava burns away sickness and negativity
Petrified wood	if you can determine the tree from which it comes, its energies will be connected to that type of tree; generically, petrified wood helps you honor cycles in your life and supports longevity
Pumice	carry a piece of pumice to ease your burdens and make the road ahead less difficult
Round stone	for good fortune; to encourage wholeness and unity; it also represents the Sacred Circle
Sand dollar	a gift from the sea, the sand dollar provides protective energy, especially of your personal resources and energies (note the natural pentagram design)
Shells	to connect with your intuition, enhance feminine qualities, improve divinatory ability; for relaxation
Stalagmites and stalactites	once carried for protection and male fertility, stalagmites produce upward moving energy, while stalactites direct it downward; for increasing or banishing power, respectively
White stone	among the Celts, a white stone found adjacent to a holy well could help the bearer see faeries

Stone casting is a divination method that uses shells, stones, or other minerals to provide guidance and answers to questions. Take a collection of stones (shells, etc.) and toss them on a surface. The way each stone lands, the overall pattern, and the symbolic value of the stones, are all interpreted. Runes are also carved on stones, bone, and shells, then used for divination.

Rings of standing stones, such as those at Stonehenge and nearby Avebury, define sacred space. Individual stones often mark the four directions in a ritual circle. Stones imprinted with natural circles offer protection. In sweat lodge ceremonies, red-hot rocks fuel the purification process that aids spiritual growth. In feng shui, heavy stones hold down chi and provide stability.

Clearly, stones of all kinds have long held a sense of magick for humankind—who hasn't reached down and picked up a pretty pebble and kept it as a touchstone? Perhaps their very ancientness, their role as witnesses to history, provides a sense of connection and continuity. As repositories of experience, the mysteries they contain make them an unparalleled source of knowledge that we have yet to fully grasp.

CHAPTER 11

The Animal Kingdom

Since ancient times, animals and people have joined forces in myriad ways for magickal purposes. Mythology contains countless stories of humans and deities merging with animals to form mysterious creatures such as the centaur. The pagan Horned God is often depicted with the legs and horns of a goat; the Egyptian god Anubis has a jackal's head and human body. Shamans call upon totem animals to guide them on their journeys. Witches often seek the assistance of animal companions—the best-known being black cats—called "familiars."

Human-Animal Relationships

Although many people consider animals lesser beings, witches know that animals can teach humans a great deal. In earlier days, people observed animals in order to understand natural events such as weather conditions and earthquakes. Animals could lead humans to water or shelter. Animals weren't viewed as separate from human beings—some people even knew the language of the animals. Priests and shamans enacted rituals, sometimes wearing animal pelts or feathers, to honor the animals and petition their assistance.

From a practical perspective, human beings are deeply indebted to the animal kingdom. For millennia, animals have provided humans with food, clothing, tools, and other essentials. They've enabled people to perform tasks that would have been impossible otherwise. Elephants in southeast Asia haul huge trees out of the jungles and dogs pull sleds across the Arctic regions. Cats rid barns of rodents. Seeing Eye dogs aid the blind. In nursing homes, animal companions help elderly patients enjoy happier, healthier lives.

From a magickal perspective, animals can enrich a witch's life and work in numerous ways. Observing animals can help you establish a better connection with the natural world. Adopting their traits and abilities can expand your own powers. Animals can also serve as guides into nonordinary realms of being and as harbingers of things to come.

Familiars

Many witches choose to share their lives with familiars—spiritually attuned creatures to whom the witch turns for insights into nature's lessons, and for help in working magick. Black cats, of course, are commonly associated with witches, but dogs, birds, rabbits, and, yes, even toads can fulfill the role of familiar. In the Harry Potter stories, Harry purchases an owl as his familiar while his poorer friend must be satisfied with a rat. In actuality, the witch doesn't necessarily choose his familiar, so much as the animal and the witch seem to discover and bond with each other.

No matter what kind of creature it might be, the familiar is no mere pet. Rather, the animal is a respected partner and companion, who reveals truths and offers the characteristics inherent to its nature to the witch for magickal purposes. Birds, for instance, often carry messages between humans or between the earth and the spirit world.

According to global lore, nearly any creature can become a familiar. In Lapp, Finnish, and Norwegian stories, for example, flies are familiars. Amphibians—specifically, sea snakes—similarly show up in New Hebrides stories. And among the Zulu, familiars can be made from reactivated animal corpses.

If a witch seeks a familiar, he usually puts out a call through a spell or ritual. This ritual typically takes place outdoors, near the home. The witch begins by creating sacred space, then he meditates, prays, and places the request in the hands of nature. During the meditation the witch visualizes his own living space, so the right creature can easily find its way to the door.

Cats, for instance, are notorious for showing up unexpectedly. But sometimes you might have to seek out your familiar. One witch tells how her feline familiar called to her psychically—she actually heard the words "Come to the animal shelter." The command was so clear and insistent that she immediately drove to the local shelter where the cat was waiting for her. Trust your intuition. You'll know your familiar instantly when you encounter him or her.

Because animals tend to be more sensitive than humans in many ways, your familiar can provide signals and guidance, especially regarding other people. Observe your pet's reactions to visitors and friends—Fluffy or Fido could give you information you might not have picked up on your own. Animals are demonstrably good at predicting earth and weather changes, too, and they often sense impending danger long before a human could. They can also see things people can't, including nonphysical beings such as faeries and ghosts.

Spirit Animals, Power Animals, and Totems

Spirit animals are similar to angelic guardians. These noncorporal beings guide, protect, and assist witches in both the physical and the nonphysical worlds. Some people believe spirit animals once existed in physical bodies, but have now passed over to the spirit realm where they continue to aid human beings.

The Kahunas of Hawaii and Polynesia say that the spirits of animals live inside people. These spirit creatures endow human beings with special talents or skills that are in line with the animals' characteristics. For example, someone who has a spirit eagle inside him might possess keen eyesight. A graceful dancer might embody the spirit of a gazelle.

Everyone has at least one spirit animal who acts as a guide and guardian throughout the person's life. (The term "animal" in this case is used to refer to birds, reptiles, and insects as well as mammals.) This lifelong spiritual companion is often called a totem animal. At times, additional spirit animals may show up to help in certain circumstances. These creatures, frequently referred to as power animals, lend their special energies or qualities to you temporarily. If you must overcome a formidable obstacle, for instance, an elephant might come to you to offer its strength and tenacity.

Remain open to nature's voice and avoid anticipating what animal might be your own totem. In some cases, your totem may possess qualities similar to your own. A busy, hardworking witch might have a bee or ant as a totem. In other cases, your totem might display traits you've repressed or rejected, and need to reawaken within yourself.

Connecting with Your Animal Guides

Meeting a power animal or totem often takes place in a ritual setting. Or the animal spirit may reveal itself to you through a seemingly chance encounter with its physical counterpart. If you notice an animal you've never seen in your area before or in an unusual situation, it's probably significant. Sometimes a spirit animal will come to you in a dream, or through repeated sightings in a variety of media. If you are fiercely protecting and nourishing a pet project, for instance, you might suddenly start seeing pictures of bears in magazines, on television, and so on.

An animal's symbolism corresponds to the whole creature, both its positive and negative aspects. The otter, for example, is playful, but it can also get nippy. A witch with an otter totem, therefore, might have a biting sense of humor or take frolicking a bit too far.

You can also choose to meet spirit animals through a process called journeying. This visualization technique usually involves going into a light meditative trance and imagining you are tunneling into the earth, perhaps by entering a cave or following a tree's roots down deep into the ground. As you journey, mentally ask animal helpers to present themselves to you.

When an animal appears, ask it what it wants to tell you or offer to you. A deer might advise you to be gentle with yourself and others. A lion may bring you courage. Try to become one with the spirit animal and feel what it's like to be that animal. The more you can involve your senses, the better. Remember to thank the animal for its friendship and help, before saying goodbye and returning to your ordinary awareness.

Adopting Animal Powers

Once you've met your spirit animal, you can begin to incorporate its powers into yourself. To better acquaint yourself with the animal's characteristics, you could watch nature programs on television, visit a zoo or farm, or read books or magazine articles about the animal. Some people like to display images of their spirit animals on their altars or in prominent places in their homes. Others carry small tokens in the shapes of their animal helpers. You can purchase clothing, jewelry, and accessories decorated with animal images from organizations that protect wildlife, or you could even get a tattoo of your totem animal.

Practice behaving like your spirit animal. Arch your back and stretch like a cat. Stand tall like a giraffe. Swim and dive gracefully like a porpoise. Roar like a lion. Notice how you feel doing this. A number of yoga postures are named for animals, and you might benefit from trying these.

Show gratitude to your spirit animal for assisting you. Thank it for being in your life. Leave food outside for its earthly representatives. Donate money to organizations that help animals. Express kindness and consideration for all animals.

Animal Messengers

Our ancestors' lives depended on interpreting nature's signs accurately. Early human beings were well-versed in reading weather patterns, the ocean's tides, animal behavior, and so on. Today, most people have lost this ability. If you pay attention, however, you'll soon notice that the universe regularly sends you signs to help guide you along your path in life—it's a bit like relying on road signs along the highway.

One way your higher self speaks to you is through animal appearances. Whether you see a physical animal in the wild (or in an unlikely spot), come across an unexpected image of one, or meet one in a dream, consider the visitation a message. The more alert you are to animal messengers, the more likely they are to show up to aid you and the better your communication with your higher self will become.

Signs and Symbols in Nature

Diviners from all over the world have observed animal movements and behaviors when trying to predict the future. Today happenstance encounters with most wild animals are becoming increasingly unlikely. Thus, a modern witch who sees images of a lion on a business card, the side of a bus, and in a newspaper ad might consider that a sign. The following list shows signs and omens that correspond to various animals:

Animal	Signs and Omens
Ant	work, diligence; biting predicts a quarrel
Beetle	good fortune; the larger the beetle, the better your luck
Butterfly	transformation, change for the better
Camel	good luck
Cat	meeting a black cat brings improved fortune and freedom from troubles
Cricket	domestic bliss
Dog	something new on the horizon (unless it's a black dog, which predicts misfortune)
Donkey	unexpected burdens (a lot on your proverbial plate)
Eagle	examine a situation closely; keep your eyes open
Fox	beginnings that get off on the wrong foot; a need for cleverness or craftiness
Frog	matters of love or health (the condition of the frog will tell you more)
Gazelle	grace or speed is needed in a situation
Goat	fortunes can be improved, but hard work and determination are necessary
Hare	be cautious
Heron	act or think independently
Horse	good news, perhaps involving travel, is forthcoming
Lamb	peace and harmony
Lizard	disappointment or lack of closure
Mouse	difficulties, often of a financial nature
Mole	dig beneath the surface to find the truth
Mule	business interests taking a downturn, perhaps due to stubbornness
Pig	worries; insensitivity
Snake	treachery and betrayal, or jealousy
Spider	creating something of beauty, perhaps a home
Toad	the death of this creature portends increased tension
Weasel	deceit; be alert and wary

You might choose to keep a journal of animal sightings and your impressions regarding them. Date the entries. Record what happens after the animal's appearance, to see if the future unfolded as foretold.

Elemental Correspondences

Witches associate animals with the four elements: earth, air, fire, and water. It's easy to see that fish correspond to the water element and birds to the element of air. However, some creatures have two common connections: a seagull, for instance, is at home in both the air and the ocean. The following list shows the links between animals and the elements/directions:

Element	Animal
Earth (North)	bear, cow, deer, cat, dog, gopher, mole, mouse, rabbit
Air (East)	bat, most birds, butterfly, dragonfly, ladybug
Fire (South)	desert creatures, lion, lizard, scorpion, rattlesnake
Water (West)	crab, fish, sea horse, dolphin, whale
Water/Air	dolphin, flying fish, seagull, swan, crane, heron, duck
Water/Fire	electric eel, stingray, jellyfish
Fire/Air	bee, wasp, other stinging insects
Earth/Water	amphibians, beaver, otter, seal

You can use animal symbolism to mark sacred space. Place animal images that relate to the element of a particular direction in that quarter.

Animals in Dreams

Animals often wander into a witch's dreams, and these nocturnal visits are likely to be significant. A creature that appears to you in a dream could be your power animal or totem trying to help with a specific situation. In some cases, the animal's symbolic value could have bearing on a personal or spiritual matter.

FACT

According to the Ainu, bats were created by the god of the world; they are courageous and wise, and they battle disease. In China, five bats seen together represent joy, prosperity, longevity, happiness, and contentment. Conversely, in Japanese Buddhist tradition, bats signify sadness and restlessness. For the Maori of New Zealand, spotting a bat is an omen of bad luck.

Any personal feelings you have toward the animal should be considered part of the dream's interpretive value. For example, if you're afraid of dogs and you see a dog with someone you've recently met, there might be a reason to be cautious about that person (especially if you felt ill at ease when you met this person in waking life). If you really adore birds and see a friend with one in your dream, it might be time to call that friend or visit with him. Here is a brief list of animal harbingers and meanings in dreams:

Animal	Meaning
Bat	making your way through an uncertain situation successfully; alternatively, improved luck and happiness
Bear	forbearance, protectiveness, fearlessness, and possibly the need to rest or retreat
Birds	symbolic value changes according to the specific bird; generally birds represent liberation, movement, and the ability to distance oneself from a situation. A bird that's singing happily foretells success.
Bull	masculine energy, stubbornness, fertility, leadership skills, the ego/self (especially for men); moving forward too quickly and doing damage in the process
Camel	prepare for a time of scarce resources
Cat	playfulness, quick reactions, independence, feminine energy, mystery
Chameleon	transformation, adaptability, knowing when to remain quiet and out of sight
Crab	moodiness or misdirection; situations that seem to lead nowhere; overprotectiveness

Crow	wisdom, hidden knowledge, magick
Crocodile	lies or misrepresentation
Deer	swiftness, gentleness
Dog	steadfast friends or companions
Dolphin	rapid movement and decision-making; messages that require attention
Dragonfly	improved health or fortune; balancing head and heart
Eagle	clarity (or a need for it), freedom, difficult goals, authority
Elephant	memory, strength, overcoming obstacles
Fish	abundance, fertility, the potential for miracles (note the specific type of fish and its condition for more insight)
Fox	cunning, charm, craftiness
Frog	renewal (particularly in health-related matters)
Giraffe	stretching yourself or being more open-minded; seeing things from a broader perspective
Goose	good news is forthcoming, possibly combined with improved communication or a creative endeavor
Horse	movement/travel, freedom, transition, ambition, personal power/self-confidence
Hummingbird	something from the past (possibly a former lover) is about to appear
Insects	small aggravations (the meaning relates to the type of insect that appears and the dream's overall context)
Lion	authority, courage, ferocity (when necessary to defend something you love)
Lizard	the ability to break away from the old and begin anew
Monkey	playfulness or flattery (not always with good results)
Mouse	frugality through innovation
Otter	frisky behavior that causes you to overlook something important
Owl	wisdom, messages, and news; pay attention to your inner voice in reacting to these missives
Peacock	pride, being egotistical (a showoff)
Pig	insensitivity, indulgence
Porcupine	be on guard; a prickly situation that requires great care
Rabbit	abundance, creativity, fertility, good luck
Raven	a warning of some sort
Sheep	passiveness that can lead to undoing
Snake	a new life or opportunity, transformation, shedding something old

Spider	fate's hand at work in something, creativity; you may be caught in a web of your own making
Tiger	courage, competence, tenacity
Vulture	a predator nearby
Whale	a literal or spiritual journey that aids enlightenment; regeneration
Woodpecker	a change in literal or figurative weather on the horizon

Aggressive animals warn either of danger in your life or that you feel threatened. If an animal is killed in your dream, some type of literal or figurative death is going on around you. If a scary animal is chasing you, it may represent something in yourself that you are avoiding. Because animals are often associated with instincts and primal nature, dreaming of an animal being tamed warns you to control your "animal" behavior (for instance, curb exuberant physical passion).

Animal Imagery in Magick

When witches, shamans, and other magicians include animal imagery in their spells and rituals, they're enacting a form of sympathetic magick. This means that the action or instrument used in the spell bears a similarity to the desired result. The animal images on the cave walls of Lascaux, France, which date back 15,000 years, for instance, may have been painted by early magicians to insure success in the hunt.

If you wish, you can include an animal image in your sacred space to represent the theme of a spell or ritual. A spell for protection could benefit from bear magick; a horse might symbolize travel. Place a figurine or picture of the animal in the space where you do your workings to call upon the animal's energy and to awaken its traits in yourself.

Animal Art

Because the subconscious responds better to images than words, pictures can often be very effective aids to spellworking. Some Native American tribes carved totem poles depicting their animal helpers, to petition those animals' assistance. You might enjoy drawing, painting, or sculpting representations of your spirit animal. Creative endeavors in themselves are a powerful form of magick—magick, after all, is the act of consciously creating circumstances through visualizing the results you desire.

Magicians sometimes incorporate animal images—in a stylized form—into sigils. The word *sigil* comes from the Latin *sigillum*, meaning "sign." Sigils are meaningful diagrams made up of words, phrases, pictures, numbers, and other symbols encoded into a pattern that only the designer can comprehend. For example, if you are doing a spell to help you handle a delicate matter with grace, you might fashion a sigil using the word *grace*. Write the letters on a piece of paper, configuring them into a design that appeals to you. Then add a simplified illustration of a swan, perhaps only a few curved lines to indicate the neck and body.

Fetishes

Anyone who's read Shakespeare's *Macbeth* is familiar with the idea of using animal parts in magick: "Eye of newt and toe of frog / Wool of bat and tongue of dog . . ." Early humans trusted animal spirits for their powers. A magus who needed courage looked to nature's blueprint and found a lion, whose heart could be carried or otherwise used in a spell. When a witch needed stealth, it made sense to use the chameleon's skin as a spell component. To enhance perspective, a shaman might choose a bird's eye as a talisman.

A fetish is an object believed to possess magickal power. A witch might carry or wear the fetish, or keep it near her for a specific purpose such as protection. Sometime fetishes contain items that relate symbolically to their intentions. For example, you might incorporate bits of antler into an amulet to prevent you from hitting deer while driving.

ALERT!

Use precautions when working with animal components. All animal parts should be cleaned properly to avoid the potential for disease. Furthermore, there are laws governing what is legal to have in your home in terms of animal parts. Be prudent and cautious, and check with local authorities if you're uncertain.

Most witches and magicians no longer sacrifice animals in rituals, nor do they "harvest" animals for spells. Modern Wiccans and witches honor nature and all her creatures. However, animal components that have been found naturally can be utilized in contemporary witchcraft. As mentioned earlier, feathers you come across unexpectedly could augment vision and communication. Tufts of rabbit fur found on a prickly bush would be good to put in a fertility talisman.

Shapeshifting

Mythology, fairy tales, and legends contain many tales of humans and deities assuming the bodies of animals temporarily. Zeus, for instance, changed himself into a swan in order to seduce Leda. Merlin instructed the young King Arthur in the art of shapeshifting, teaching him to take on the forms of a badger, hawk, and bird.

Shapeshifting means changing your form into something else—an animal or another human being—for a particular purpose. Shamans often shapeshift in order to acquire the powers of an animal during a journey. Witches might choose to shapeshift in order to explore, gain knowledge, or see things from a different perspective, or for healing purposes, or to conceal their true identities.

Shamans and witches sometimes take on the shapes of animals or other creatures in order to become invisible and protect themselves. Authors Caitlin and John Matthews write in their book *The Encyclopedia of Celtic Wisdom*, "Enchantment into a non-human shape has the effect of preventing a person from being recognized." In Celtic terminology, this is called *Fith-Fath* (pronounced fee-fah), which means "guise."

When you shapeshift, you don't actually turn into an animal; you experience its energy as strongly as you can so you become *like* the animal. If you wish to practice this art, begin by meeting your power animal or totem during meditation. Ask permission to enter it briefly, to learn what it can teach you. Envision yourself entering into the animal's body and becoming one with it. Try to see the world through the animal's eyes. Feel yourself existing within its form; sense the world as the animal does. You may wish to actually move about in a manner that's characteristic of the animal. When you've learned what you sought to learn, thank the animal and return to your usual human form.

Some people like to don animal masks or costumes as part of their shapeshifting practices. Others enjoy observing animals in their wild habitat. As you watch birds and animals in nature, try to communicate with them and listen to what they "say" to you. If you keep your heart and mind open, you can learn a great deal from the animal kingdom that will help you—and them—in the practice of magick and the process of evolution.

CHAPTER 12

Magickal Symbolism

Symbols are images that encapsulate the essence of whatever they represent. When you see one, you instantly understand something fundamental about what the symbol stands for. Historically, witches and occultists have also used symbols to protect secret knowledge from people who aren't ready to receive it. Therefore, many spells and rituals employ a variety of symbolic gestures, patterns, objects, colors, etc. Symbols speak directly to the subconscious, which understands pictures better than words, even if your rational mind doesn't.

Color

You may not be aware of it, but you are constantly affected by the colors in your environment. Psychological studies have shown that human responses to color can actually be measured physically—red stimulates respiration and heart rate, blue lowers body temperature and pulse.

Colors contain myriad symbolic associations. Blue, for instance, reminds you of the sky; green suggests foliage, grass, and healthy crops; orange is the color of fire and the sun. Among Druids, blue was a sacred color that denoted someone who'd achieved the rank of bard (a formally trained story-teller entrusted with the oral history of a group). Christians associated blue with peace and compassion, which is why the Virgin Mary is often depicted wearing blue. So deeply rooted are these connections that witches can use color to influence the mind and produce magickal results.

Color	Correspondences
Red	passion, anger, heat, energy, daring
Orange	confidence, activity, warmth, enthusiasm
Yellow	happiness, creativity, optimism, ideas, communication
Green	health, fertility, growth, wealth
Light blue	peace, clarity, hope
Royal blue	independence, insight, imagination, truth
Indigo	intuition, serenity, mental power
Purple	wisdom, spirituality, connection with higher realms
Pink	love, friendship, sociability
White	purity, clarity, protection
Black	power, wisdom
Brown	stability, practicality, grounding in the physical world

Black, a color witches frequently wear, has many negative connotations to the general public, including death and mourning. To witches, however, black is a color of power, for it contains all the colors of the rainbow. It's also reminiscent of the night, the time when witches often gather to work magick, and of mystery. In spellworking, black is associated with the planet Saturn and used for banishing, endings, and forbearance.

FACT

The body's energy systems—the chakras—are usually linked with the seven colors of the visible spectrum. Red is associated with the root chakra, at the base of the spine; orange with the sacral chakra; yellow with the solar plexus chakra; green with the heart chakra; blue with the throat chakra; indigo with the third eye; and purple with the crown chakra at the top of the head.

The intensity of a color corresponds to its intensity in spellworking. Bright yellow, for example, brings to mind the sun and fire; therefore it can activate and invigorate a spell. Pastel yellow has a gentler vibration that's usually associated with the air element and ideas.

Astrological Color Correspondences

Witches also tap the astrological associations with colors for magickal work. Each of the four elements, the zodiac signs, and the heavenly bodies in our solar system can be linked with one or more colors.

Zodiac Sign	Color Correspondences
Aries	red
Taurus	green, brown
Gemini	light yellow, pale blue
Cancer	silver, white, teal
Leo	bright yellow, gold, orange
Virgo	olive green, tan
Libra	pink, peach, lavender
Scorpio	black, reddish brown
Sagittarius	orange, gold
Capricorn	black, gray, navy blue
Aquarius	cobalt blue, sky blue
Pisces	purple, indigo, aqua

When circle-casting and delineating sacred space, witches often draw on the elemental connections with colors. As discussed earlier, each of the four compass directions is aligned with one of the four elements. These colors are placed at the quarters to symbolize the forces present there. (Note that some cultures and spiritual traditions, including Native American tribes, associate different colors with the directions.)

Element	Direction	Color Correspondence
Fire	South	Red
Earth	North	Green
Air	East	Yellow
Water	West	Blue

Each of the days of the week is named for a planet. Because each color relates to a planet, the day that is linked with that planet is also linked with its color.

Day of the Week	Planetary Ruler	Color Correspondences
Sunday	Sun	gold, orange
Monday	Moon	silver, white
Tuesday	Mars	red
Wednesday	Mercury	yellow, light blue
Thursday	Jupiter	orange, purple
Friday	Venus	pink, green
Saturday	Saturn	dark blue, black

You may wish to experiment with wearing colors on the days of the week that are associated with them. Or use the appropriate colors to attract the planetary energies you desire for spellworking.

Spellworking with Color

Colors lend their vibrations to spells and rituals, enabling you to augment your magickal work with their energies. Let's say, for example, you want to fabricate a love talisman. You could sew a pink pouch and fill it with love-drawing ingredients. If you're creating a prosperity affirmation, you can increase its benefit by writing it on green paper. Many witches burn colorful candles in spells and rituals, as you'll soon see. You might also want to drape your altar with colors that suit your intentions or that correspond to the time of the year. If you do magickal artwork, keep color symbolism in mind.

When you dress, wear various colors *not* just because they're your favorites or because they look good on you. Try wearing the color that's associated with your birth sign to see how that affects you. Or wear other birth signs' colors to attract specific attributes associated with that sign. You might like to wear white or silver during lunar rituals, yellow or gold during celebrations to honor the sun.

Colorful Candle Magick

The term *candle* comes from *candere*, a Latin word meaning "to shine." Symbolically, candles represent hope, a light in the darkness, a beacon that shows the way to safety. Five thousand years ago, the Egyptians formed beeswax into candles and placed them in the tombs of Egyptian rulers to light their journey into the realm beyond.

Candles play a role in nearly all religious, secular, and magickal ceremonies. Some candle spells are simple and widely used, such as blowing out candles on a birthday cake or lighting a novena candle when making a request. Others involve complex rituals that require you to position numerous candles in special formations and move them repeatedly over a period of days or weeks. Many witches set candles on their altars to represent the fire element, to symbolize goals or intentions, to honor deities, or to create an ambiance that shifts them out of their ordinary existence.

Some witches use candles as a scrying tool. The flickering flame has a relaxing effect on the conscious mind and allows your intuition to come to the fore. Light a candle, set it on a table or altar at eye level, and gaze into the flame. Soon you may see visions forming in the flame or in the smoke rising from the candle.

Because candle magick is one of the most popular forms of spellworking, witches usually keep a collection of candles on hand, in a range of colors. Refer to the preceding lists and select colors that are appropriate to your intentions. In some cases, however, tradition and Craft lore recommend using colors other than those already discussed for certain spells and purposes. You can combine candles of different colors to fine-tune your spells. Here are some suggestions:

- Black candles can help you determine the truth of a matter and get to the bottom of things.
- Brown candles ground energy and provide foundations for your intentions.
- Burn dark blue candles to connect with your instincts and dreams.
- Sky blue candles encourage safe travel and spiritual awareness.
- Gold candles improve mental clarity and attract good fortune.
- When you're working on money matters, burn green candles.
- Pink candles encourage affection, love, and friendship.
- Burn purple candles when you need to compose yourself, use power wisely, or demonstrate authority.
- Red candles add passion and excitement to love spells.
- Silver candles emphasize occult learning and intuition.
- White candles represent purity and protection; light them to establish sacred space.
- Burn light yellow candles when you feel your self-assurance waning or you need an attitude boost.

To strengthen the power of a candle spell, carve a symbol that represents your goal into the wax. As the candle burns, your intentions will be released into the universe. Many witches "dress" candles with aromatic oils that correspond to their objectives. (See Chapter 9.) Pour a little oil in your palm, then rub it over the entire surface of the candle until you've coated everything except the wick.

If you are doing a spell to promote growth or increase, light candles during a waxing moon. If you're doing a spell for endings, banishing, or decrease, light candles while the moon is waning.

Some spells call for lighting a candle each day and letting it burn for a period of time, over a span of several days or weeks. After each burning session, snuff out the flame; then relight the candle the next day (or according to the dictates of your spell). Never leave burning candles unattended.

Fabric and Materials

Do you consider yourself a "touchy-feely" person? You can use your sense of touch to enhance your magick. Remember, the more you engage your senses and your imagination, the more power you put behind a spell. Witches often wear special clothing when performing rituals: rich velvet or tapestry robes, long flowing dresses, or Renaissance garb, for example. Dressing for the occasion separates the event from everyday activities and sets the tone for magickal workings, just as dressing up in evening clothes makes you feel different than wearing jeans or a business suit. Notice how you feel when you don various types of clothing and the sensations you experience when different fabrics touch your skin.

Some witches practice skyclad (naked), others prefer to wear robes, masks, and various accouterments. Some covens use special markings or colors to indicate different things, such as the season, the purpose of the ritual, or a person's level of achievement in that group.

In some rituals, members of the group may be chosen to represent the guardians of the four directions or to invoke these guardians. These individuals might wear clothing in the colors associated with the quarters. The person who marks the south dons red garb, the person at the north dresses in green, the person in the west wears blue, and the person at the east wears yellow.

Costumes and masks play roles in sympathetic magick, too, whereby a person "becomes" what the costume represents in the sacred space.

Consider the medicine man who puts on the mask of an honored tribal spirit before going to a healing ritual. Participants no longer see a friend or family member; they see the face of a spirit. Thus, robes and costumes provide an extrasensory dimension in ritual practice.

Astrological Correspondences

Just as colors are connected with the four elements and the astrological signs, so are fabrics. Some of the correspondences in the following list are obvious; leather, for instance, relates to Taurus, the bull. Others are based on the similarities between the characteristics of the material and those of the sign. Virgo is a practical, unassuming sign and those qualities also pertain to canvas cloth.

Astrological Sign	Related Fabrics
Aries	lamb's wool
Taurus	leather
Gemini	gauze, chiffon, voile
Cancer	flannel
Leo	lamé, brocade, velvet
Virgo	cotton, canvas, chintz
Libra	silk, satin
Scorpio	snakeskin
Sagittarius	spandex, lycra
Capricorn	mohair, cashmere, hemp
Aquarius	feathers, metallic fabrics
Pisces	rayon, nylon, watermarked taffeta

When celebrating a ritual, you might choose to wear fabrics associated with the prevailing zodiac energies in order to attune yourself to the time. Yule, for instance, is the perfect time to don a mohair cape. Or dress in materials that either emphasize or complement your own astrological attributes.

Magickal Décor, and More

Take a few moments to notice the fabrics that occupy your sacred space. Are they the same as those in your home and workspace? Or are they specially chosen to convey a sense of magick and mysticism? The ambiance you create will have a profound impact on your mental state when you are performing spells and rituals.

Your altar cloth, in particular, should be of a material and color(s) that evoke feelings of reverence, peace, power, joy, mystery, and/or other emotions you associate with your magickal life. Perhaps you'll want to change it periodically, to reflect the changing seasons, your magickal intentions, or developments in your spiritual path. Pay attention to the rug or floor underfoot, which provides your sense of stability and foundation. You might also want to include an upholstered chair or cushion for meditation; if so, make sure its fabric inspires comfort and serenity. If you serve food or drink in your sacred space, you might enjoy using special table linens for ritual meals.

Witches also consider the materials from which they fashion mojo bags. You could make a love talisman from red silk, a prosperity talisman from green velvet, or a protection amulet from black hemp. You can combine different materials and colors to represent the unique nature of your intentions. For example, add permanence to the green velvet prosperity talisman by tying it with a leather cord. The more you can involve your imagination and your senses in the process, the more successful your magick will be.

Shapes as Symbols

Magick utilizes patterns, which are forms of energy. Each pattern is like a fingerprint, indicating where the magick came from and where its intended designation lies. Witches often say, "As within, so without; as above, so below." This adage may help you understand that all things on the spiritual plane have some kind of representation in the here-and-now. Shape is the manner in which metaphysical patterns manifest themselves in the mundane world.

Any shape can have meaning (just look at ink blots!). Intricate shapes strengthen concentration and your ability to perceive detail, beauty, and complexity. Simple shapes free the mind to imagine what lies beyond the pattern. Two patterns that are gaining popularity in contemporary Western spiritual traditions, the mandala and the labyrinth, can be either elaborate or simple.

Artists frequently include symbols in their work in order to present ideas. For example, the medieval artisans who fabricated stained glass windows for Europe's great cathedrals chose images that portrayed religious concepts to the masses, who at that time were largely illiterate.

Numbers, letters, and geometric shapes are common symbols you see around you every day, usually without giving them a second thought. The average person only recognizes the obvious meanings of these familiar images, but to someone versed in occult knowledge they reveal something deeper.

The Shape of Things

Geometric shapes contain symbolism that transcends time and place. The cross, for example, isn't unique to Christian belief; it existed it in ancient Celtic, Egyptian, and Native American cultures, too. This simple yet powerful image represents the union of the archetypal male energy or heaven (the vertical line) with female energy or earth (the horizontal line).

"Nature is a temple in which living columns sometimes emit confused words. Man approaches it through forests of symbols, which observe him with familiar glances."
            —Charles Pierre Baudelaire (1821–1867), French writer

The star is a common symbol of hope, the circle a well-known symbol of wholeness. Spirals represent life energy in many cultures. Triangles signify trinities, whether Father-Son-Holy Spirit, maiden-mother-crone, past-present-future, or some other threefold concept. The following list gives the symbolic meanings of basic geometric shapes:

Shape	Meanings
Arrow	warrior energy, direction, movement, hitting the mark
Circle	union, wholeness, life's cycles, the full moon
Circle with a slash	refusal or banishing
Cross	intersection of male and female/heaven and earth/spirit and matter, the four corners of creation
Square	foundations, stability, permanence, truth and rightness
Star	hope, wishes and dreams, protection
Six-pointed star	intersection of male and female/fire and water
Triangle (point down)	feminine energy, water
Triangle (point up)	masculine energy, fire
Spiral	life energy, the spiritual path that leads inward and outward

According to green witches, the shape of a natural item provides a blue-print for how it should be used magickally. If you find a heart-shaped stone or leaf, for example, apply it to spells that involve matters of the heart. You see a heart, you think love—and that thought produces positive energy to support the witch's intention.

Magick Numbers

The Greek mathematician and philosopher, Pythagoras, who lived in the sixth century B.C.E., is usually credited with having developed the system of numerology that's still used today. The study of numbers, known as *germatria*, is also based in esoteric Judaism and the Kabbalah. This practice attaches a number equivalent to each letter in a word. Viewed in this way, every word contains a secret meaning based on the number values of its letters, as well as its outer meaning.

Additionally, each number possesses certain characteristics or resonances, as the following list explains:

Number	Meanings
0	wholeness, all and nothing
1	beginnings, individuality, initiative
2	polarity, partnership, duality, balance
3	creativity, self-expression, expansion
4	form, stability, permanence, order
5	change, instability, communication
6	give-and-take, cooperation, beauty, harmony
7	retreat, introspection, rest, spirituality
8	material mastery, manifestation, responsibility, sincerity, practical matters
9	transition, completion, fulfillment, abundance
11	humanitarianism, higher knowledge, insight
22	spiritual power, wisdom, mastery beyond the physical realm

You can tap the qualities inherent in numbers to enhance, activate, bind, or otherwise influence a spell. Witches often use the number three, in particular, to complete a spell. Because three points are necessary to form a plane, this number signifies bringing an intention into the physical realm, literally making it three-dimensional.

Shapes and Numbers in Spells and Rituals

Once you understand the symbolism inherent in shapes and numbers, you can utilize them in spells and rituals to emphasize specific energies or intentions. You might wish to add a heart to a love talisman, for example. In Texas, many people display the "Texas star" (which is actually a pentagram) on their homes—although most of them don't realize its connection with protection—and the Texas Rangers have worn badges shaped like pentagrams since the 1800s.

Witches sometimes carve symbols on candles. As the candle burns, the intention signified by the symbols is released into the universe. If you were doing a prosperity spell, for instance, you could engrave a dollar sign on a candle.

Numeric symbolism can also be incorporated into spells, charms, and rituals. Let's say you want to do a candle spell to attract a romantic partner.

Because two is the number of partnership, you'd light two candles to represent you and your prospective partner. If you're fashioning a prosperity talisman, you could place eight items in the mojo pouch. Or seal the pouch with a ribbon into which you've tied eight knots. The date when you perform a spell or ritual could be significant, too. The first day of the month, for example, might be a good time to do a spell to launch a new venture.

You can mix and match symbols to customize a spell. Inscribe two pink candles with hearts for your love spell. The important thing is to get your imagination involved. What symbols speak to you? The most powerful images have poignant, personal significance and stimulate a resonance in your mind. Remember, visualization precedes manifestation.

Sigils: Secret Magickal Symbols

Have you ever wished you could write in secret code? You can. In fact, magicians often design uniquely personal sigils to produce a desired result. No one else can interpret the symbols—they are encrypted spells that hold meaning only for the person who creates them. And because these magick symbols are strictly personal, they're also very powerful.

Although there are various techniques for designing sigils, the easiest one involves weaving an image from letters. Start by writing a word or a short affirmation that states your intention. Delete any letters that are repeated. Entwine the remaining letters to form a design. You can use uppercase and/or lowercase letters, block or script. Position them right-side up, upside down, forward, or backward. The finished image depicts your objective in a graphic manner that your subconscious understands.

Both creating the sigil and applying it are magickal acts. You can draw a sigil on a piece of paper and slip it into a talisman or amulet. Display a sigil on your altar to remind you of your intention. Carve one on a candle, then burn the candle to activate your objective. Some people have even had sigils tattooed on their bodies. Give your imagination free rein. There's no limit to how many sigils you can draw or how many ways you can use them.

Dream Symbols

No one knows exactly why people dream, yet researchers and psychotherapists generally agree that your dreams are trying to tell you something that can help you in your waking life. Usually dream messages are presented in symbolic rather than literal form, so understanding the meanings behind dream symbols is important.

Some symbols appear in many people's dreams; others are unique to the individual dreamer. Over time, general interpretations have been attached to the most common dream symbols. The following list includes a number of familiar symbols that turn up in dreams, along with their generally accepted meanings.

Image	Interpretation
House	you and your life; the basement represents your unconscious, the main floor shows your daily living situation, the attic or upper floors describe your mental or spiritual side
Car	your body and your passage through life; the driver represents who's controlling your life; the car's condition reveals health and physical matters
Water	emotions; the type of water (deep, murky, cold, turbulent, etc.) indicates the quality of your feelings
Sex	merging your masculine and feminine sides, or incorporating another person's qualities into yourself
Death	a transition or change; something is moving out of your life
Birth	a new direction, perspective, or endeavor; creativity; opportunity
School	learning lessons; taking an exam represents being tested in an area of life
Monsters	things you fear or parts of yourself you haven't integrated

Images that turn up repeatedly in your dreams are especially significant. If you experience recurring dreams, your subconscious may be trying hard to convey something to you. Pay attention. Sometimes dreams reveal the future. A dream that lets you see in advance what's coming may help you to prepare yourself or avoid a problem altogether.

Learning to interpret your dreams opens a door to greater understanding in all areas of your life. Many witches find that their dreams provide insights and information that they can use in their magickal work.

CHAPTER 13

The Witch's Tool Kit

All fields of knowledge and all trades employ special tools. The tools of the Craft speak to the subconscious mind in forms that help support magickal work. A tool's shape, material, and other features provide clues to its symbolism and thus its role in magick. Although some of the items in a witch's tool kit may look familiar, their magickal purposes differ significantly from their roles in the mundane world. Some of the tools witches favor are used by magicians of other stripes as well.

The Role of Tools in Magick

Witches and Wiccans will tell you that tools are good helpmates to magick, but they are not necessary to the success of any spell or ritual. Even the most elegant tool is only a centering device, something to focus your mind on your magickal work. Without the witch's will and directed energy, the potential in any tool will remain dormant. For example, a witch might talk about quartz crystals as having energy-enhancing power, but until a crystal is charged and activated, that ability "sleeps" within the stone. The magician is the enabler, the catalyst. A focused will is all that any effective witch needs to perform magick. Everything else just makes the job easier.

Symbolism and Significances

As you've already seen, witches often use symbols to embody ideas. The primary tools witches employ in rituals—the wand, chalice, athame, and pentagram—symbolize the four elements. The wand represents the element of fire, the chalice signifies the water element, the athame symbolizes air, and the pentagram represents earth.

Notice that the shapes of these tools correspond to the human body. The wand and the athame, which symbolize masculine power, look distinctly phallic. The chalice (and cauldron) depict feminine energy and the womb. The five points of the pentagram stand for the five "points" of the body: head, arms, and legs.

If a magical tool isn't available, find something else with appropriate symbolic value. If you don't have an athame, a butter knife will do (especially for kitchen witches), as will a dirk (Scottish witchcraft), a sword (commonly used in high magick), or even your finger.

You can see the four main tools illustrated in the tarot, too. Each suit in the deck is named for one of these tools: wands (sometimes called rods or staves), swords (or daggers, meaning athames), cups (or chalices), and pentacles (or pentagrams, sometimes called coins or disks). As such, they describe fundamental life energies and ways of interacting with the world.

Charging Magickal Tools

It doesn't matter whether you make your own tools or purchase them ready-made. What's important is that you "charge" them before you use them for magickal work. Until you charge your chalice, it's just a goblet. The practice of charging it imbues it with your own energy and consecrates it for magickal purposes.

A charging ritual may be very simple or very complex—it's your choice. One easy and popular technique for charging your tools calls upon the four elements, again in symbolic form. First, wash the tool to cleanse it of any ambient vibrations. Next, hold your tool in front of you and visualize your energy flowing into it.

Sprinkle the tool with saltwater and say aloud: "I charge you with water and earth." Then hold it for a few moments in the smoke of burning incense while saying "I charge you with fire and air."

Some witches design rituals that involve the element to which the individual tool corresponds. You could charge your chalice by submerging it in a sacred pool of water for nine days. Similarly, you could bury a pentagram in the ground beneath a venerable tree or place your wand in the sunshine to let the sun's rays charge it. If you wish, you can include music, crystals, or essential oils in the ritual. Be creative—engage your imagination and your emotions in the process.

Caring for Magickal Tools

Although some witches display their tools on their altars, most people recommend storing tools in a safe place, such as a trunk or chest, when you're not using them. Wrap them in silk to protect them from dust, dirt, and ambient vibrations. If you drink wine or another beverage from your chalice during a ritual, of course you'll want to wash it before putting it away. However, there's no need to wash your other tools after using them—the more you handle them and do magick with them, the more you imprint them with your energy.

ALERT!

Don't use your magick tools for mundane purposes. Use a regular kitchen knife, not your athame, for cutting food and herbs; drink everyday beverages from an ordinary glass, not your ritual chalice. Reserve these tools for spellworking and ceremonial occasions.

It's usually not a good idea to allow anyone else to handle your magick tools. If you work regularly with a magickal partner, however, you might make an exception for that person.

Wand

Contrary to popular opinion, witches don't tap people with magick wands to turn them into toads or make them invisible. Witches use wands to direct energy. You can either attract or send energy with your wand. Aim it at the heavens to draw down cosmic power. Point it toward a person, place, or thing to project energy toward your goal. Some magicians define sacred space by tracing a protective circle around a designated area with a wand.

FACT

In the first of the Harry Potter tales, young Harry goes shopping for a magick wand and, in an amusing scene, the wand chooses him. In the real world of magick, that's not how it happens. The witch or wizard selects the wand, not the other way around.

Traditionally, wands were made from wood (the Druids preferred hazel or yew), but a wand can be fabricated from any material. Because the wand is a fire tool, you might prefer one that's made of brass, iron, bronze, or gold—metals that correspond to the fire signs Aries, Leo, and Sagittarius. A gold, orange, or red-colored glass rod will work, too. A wand should be at least 6 inches long, but only as long and thick as you find comfortable to handle.

You might like to decorate your wand with gemstones and/or crystals (refer to the lists in Chapter 10). Some magicians also engrave magick symbols or words of power on their wands. Paint it fiery colors, adorn it with red or gold ribbons, anoint it with cinnamon, sandalwood, clove, musk, or almond essential oils—whatever appeals to you and imprints the wand with your energy.

Pentagram

The pentagram is a five-pointed star with a circle around it. Many Wiccans and witches wear this symbol as a protection amulet. You might choose to display one on the door to your home or on your altar. In circle-casting, witches often trace pentagrams in the air at the four directions to insure safety. Sometimes they also make this mark on their foreheads with essential oils or decorate their clothing with pentagrams.

Pentagrams can be added to any protection spell. If you're doing a candle spell, carve a pentagram into the candle's wax. If you're making an amulet, embroider a pentagram on a pouch or draw one on a piece of paper and slip it inside a mojo bag.

The pentagram represents the earth element and is linked with the feminine force. Consequently, you might like to have a pentagram made of silver, a feminine metal ruled by the moon, or copper, which is ruled by Venus. Perhaps you'd like to decorate your pentagram with crystals or gemstones that relate to the element of earth (see Chapter 10 for ideas). As part of the charging process, some witches anoint their pentagrams with essential oil of mint, pine, patchouli, amber, or basil.

Athame

The origins of the word *athame* have been lost to history. Some speculate that it may have come from *The Clavicle of Solomon* (published in 1572), which refers to the knife as the *Arthana* (*athame* may be a subverted form of this term). Another theory proposes that athame comes from the Arabic word *al-dhamme* (blood-letter), a sacred knife in the Moorish tradition. In either case, magickal manuscripts dating back to the 1200s imply the use of ritual knives in magick (and special knives were certainly used in ancient offerings).

This ritual dagger is usually a double-edged knife about 4 to 6 inches long. Wiccans, however, sometime prefer crescent-shaped athames that represent the moon. The athame's main purpose is to symbolically clear negative energies from a space you'll use in spellworking. It can also be utilized to slice through obstacles, again symbolically. Some Wiccans and witches like to cast a circle with an athame instead of a wand.

ALERT!

If you decide to purchase a vintage dagger for your magick work, make sure it hasn't drawn blood in the past. Some magicians believe that an athame used to physically harm another will never again be functional in magick, although in ancient times witches often "fed" special knives with blood.

Because you won't actually cut anything physical with your athame, it needn't be sharp. This tool represents the air element and the mind; it corresponds to the zodiac signs Gemini, Libra, and Aquarius. Therefore, you might like to decorate it with feathers, crystals, or gemstones that are associated with the element of air (see Chapter 10), and perhaps anoint it with carnation, lavender, or ginger essential oil.

Chalice

Some people say the Holy Grail was actually a magick chalice. In rituals and rites, witches often drink a ceremonial beverage from a chalice. Many chalices feature long stems so they can be passed easily from hand to hand. Sharing the cup with coven members signifies connectedness and unity of purpose. You may choose to drink magick potions you've concocted from your chalice, too.

FACT

The Chalice Well in Glastonbury, England, is a sacred site for Celts and followers of goddess religions. Many people believe it is the final resting place of the Holy Grail. For 2,000 years this well has been in constant use and has never been known to run dry. A symbol of the life force, the well is revered as a gift from Mother Earth to her children.

The chalice is associated with the water element and the astrological signs Cancer, Scorpio, and Pisces. To charge it, you could sprinkle it with "holy" water from a well, spring, or lake that is special to you. A symbol of the feminine force, the chalice's shape clearly suggests the womb. Therefore silver, because it's ruled by the moon, is a good material for your magick chalice. Some people prefer crystal, colored glass, or ceramic chalices—the choice is entirely yours.

Cauldron

According to Norse mythology, the god Odin received wisdom and intuitiveness from a cauldron. Celtic legend mentions a cauldron as a tool of regeneration for the gods. Stories such as these give us clues as to where our modern symbolic value for the cauldron originates. Specifically, witches see the cauldron as an emblem of the womb from which all life flows. The three-legged cauldron represents the threefold human and divine nature.

The cauldron performs both symbolic and practical functions for Wiccans. Witches may use a cauldron to cook magickal or ritual foods and to hold beverages. Additionally, the cauldron can be filled with fire, water, flowers, or other items at a ceremony or rite. If you like, you can build a fire inside your cauldron and drop wishes written on paper into the flames—the cauldron's creative qualities nurture your requests and bring them to fruition. Although usually iron, a cauldron can be made of any fireproof material including copper, steel, or terra cotta.

A good alternative for a cauldron is a brazier. *Brazier* comes from a French term meaning "live coals." A brazier is a fire-safe container that can hold a small flame or burning incense. Braziers are ideal for indoor rituals and spells where fire is a key component of the rite.

Broom (Besom)

The besom is a long-handled tool with a bundle at one end that was once made from the broom plant, which grows on European heaths and pastures. Broom is characterized by yellow flowers and angular branches ideal for bundling. Thus, the instrument made of this plant came to be known as a broom.

Since Roman times, the broom has been associated with feminine power and magick. Prior to childbirth, women used a broom to sweep the threshold of a house both for protection and to prepare the way for the new spirit to enter. Gypsy marriage rituals included jumping over a broomstick to ensure the couple's fertility; this ritual neatly marked the line between single and married life. The broom appears in the folklore of various countries and cultures, such as these:

- In some parts of the Western world, a broom propped up outside a house identified it as a house of prostitution.
- In Madagascar, women danced with brooms while their men were at war in order to sweep away the enemy.
- In China, the broom represents wisdom and insight because it brushes away worries.
- In Japan, brooms are used during spring rituals to purify the ceremonial space.
- In Victorian-age America, a new broom would never be bought in May, "lest you sweep the family away."

No, witches don't fly on brooms—that's just a colorful misconception. Instead, they use them to sweep away unwanted energies from sacred space.

Candles and Incense

Candles are probably the most popular tool in a witch's tool kit, used in a wide range of spells and rituals. (Chapter 12 covers some aspects of candle magick.) The concept of illumination carries both a practical meaning— visible light that enables you to conduct your daily tasks—and an esoteric one—an inspiration or awakening that enlivens mundane existence and expands understanding. The flame represents the element of fire, inspiration, passion, activity, energy, and cleansing.

Some witches like to make their own candles, blending the wax with herbs, essential oils, and dyes that represent the witch's intentions. You can even shape the wax into a human form to create what's known as a "poppet." Typically, poppets are created to represent a specific person to whom the witch wishes to send magickal energy, usually at a distance. Poppets may also be fashioned to represent a creature or situation, and actions done to the poppet symbolize the actions done to whatever or whomever the poppet represents. For instance, if you were to make a poppet of a beloved pet and carefully wrap it in white cloth to protect it, the animal would receive the benefit of that protection. This practice is known as sympathetic magick.

Poppets can be made of various materials other than wax. Witches sometimes use corn or wheat to create poppets that represent the "spirit" of the grain. Traditionally, these were displayed in the home where they ensured luck, a bountiful harvest, and ongoing protection.

Incense is another popular and versatile magick tool. In Latin, *incense* means "to make sacred." For centuries, churches and temples have used incense to clear the air and to honor deities. In Buddhist belief, burning an offering of incense invokes the Buddha into a statue of the holy being.

Witches purify sacred space with incense. Sage is the most frequently used herb for this purpose, but you can burn pine, frankincense, or eucalyptus if you prefer. You can also charge talismans, amulets, and other magickal tools with incense by holding the object in the smoke for a few moments.

Burning incense combines the elements of fire and air. Incense often serves as a vehicle for conveying prayers to the deities—as the smoke rises, it carries your requests along with it. Choose a scent that matches your intentions. The best incense is blended from pure gums and resins, without synthetic binders. You can even make your own by grinding up aromatic wood or resin and adding finely powdered kitchen herbs or dried flowers.

Knots

In spellcraft, knots offer a simple way to contain or loosen energy. The obvious symbolism of tying a knot indicates an intention to bind something or someone. If, for example, you wanted to prevent an enemy from harming you, you could create a poppet (see preceding section) to represent your enemy and bind his hands and feet with string. If a witch perceives unwanted energies in a space—especially while performing a spell—she can tie a knot in a piece of clothing or the altar cloth to trap that energy until after the magickal working.

FACT

Knot magick most likely originated with the arts of weaving, sewing, and fishing, which involve knotting in one form or another. A woman weaving her husband a scarf would bind a little magick into every strand to protect his health. A fisherman would tie knots in his fishing net to attract a better catch.

You can tie energy of any kind into a knot. Witches sometimes tie a line of knots on a long cord, placing thoughts, emotions, incantations, etc. into the knots. These lines are sometimes called a witch's Ladder. Untying a knot at a later date frees the energy bound therein.

You can use knot symbolism in the following types of spells:

- Bindings and banishings (especially illness and negative energy)
- Channeling energy into a specific location (the energy can be captured in the knot, and then released when it's most needed)

- Securing relationships (hence the term "tying the knot" to refer to marriage)
- "Tying up the loose ends" of a situation

You can tie intentions into knots, too. Let's say you want to stabilize your finances. The best number for this purpose is four. You could make a money charm and secure the pouch with a gold ribbon. Tie four knots in the ribbon and concentrate on your goal each time you tie a knot. Or tie a ribbon around your bills, using four knots to limit the outflow of money.

Other Tools

Just as a carpenter generally adds new tools to his collection, you might wish to add a few other items to your witch's toolbox. Bells are tools that magicians ring to signal the different steps in a ritual. The lovely sound can also clear sacred space because it dispels stagnant vibrations in the air. Chimes, gongs, and singing bowls can also serve these purposes.

The sword, a larger version of the athame, is generally used to banish unwanted energies from a ritual space. Like the dagger, it can also let you symbolically cut through obstacles in your path, but it's never wielded as a weapon. Witches sometimes use swords to cut an energy pathway into and out of the sacred space once a circle has been cast.

The staff is a larger version of the wand and like the wand its main purpose is directing energy. A staff may also be used like a sword to open energy pathways.

A double-headed ax called a *labyrs* serves as a holy symbol for some witches, particularly those who choose to follow Artemis or Rhea. The image of a labrys is also suitable for anyone following Greek magickal traditions, sometimes in combination with or as a substitute for the pentagram.

An asperger sprinkles water in and around a sacred space. In Scotland, a freshly picked branch of heather may be dipped in water and used in this way, symbolically cleansing and adding a lovely aroma to the space. Feathers, flowers, leaves, and brooms can also be used for asperging.

Witches who practice a Norse or Germanic tradition sometimes choose a horn as an alternative to a cup or goblet. Additionally, a horn can be used as a symbolic item. Place it on the altar during times of need to invoke the spirits of plenty. Musical horns can also be played to call the quarters or to signal the release of a spell.

Keeping a Grimoire

Also known as a Book of Shadows, a grimoire is a witch's secret journal of magickal and occult knowledge. Here's where you keep a record of the spells and rituals you perform, the ingredients and tools you use, the potions, formulae, charms, and incantations you create—and of course, the results you generate. It's a bit like a cook's personal collection of favorite recipes.

It doesn't matter whether you choose a large leather-bound journal or a simple loose-leaf notebook to chronicle your magickal workings—no one but you will see this secret compilation, so what's convenient for you is all that matters. Date your entries. If you like, include moon phases and/or other relevant astrological data. Write down your intention for doing the spell. Be sure to describe your results and reactions, along with any thoughts, feelings, or experiences you deem important.

You'll probably do your favorite spells many times, so it's a good idea to add comments each time you repeat them. If you vary a spell at any time, note that, too. Some spells take a while to materialize; if possible, keep track of results that develop over time.

Always store your grimoire (and all magickal tools) in a safe place. Remember, your Book of Shadows is your very private and personal magick log. You don't want this information to accidentally fall into the wrong hands.

CHAPTER 14

The Art of Spell-Casting

Just as there's an art to baking a cake, there's an art to casting a spell. When a witch performs a magick spell, she designs a series of thoughts and actions that will bring about a condition in the visible world. A spell might include images, words, movements, and/or objects, but the most important "ingredient" is the witch's will. When you cast a spell, you connect with the creative force that abides in the universe. You serve as a conduit for that force. You're the catalyst that produces a result.

14

Ethical Spell-Casting

Whether simple or complex, all spells involve focusing the power of intention to produce outcomes. Your intention not only provides the fuel that energizes a spell, it also colors the spell. As discussed in Chapter 1, your motive for doing a spell determines whether it's "white" or "black" magick, or somewhere in between.

There's nothing wrong with doing "gray" spells—most spells, in fact, fit into this category. It's not incorrect or selfish to use your magickal talents to improve your lot in life. However, a wise witch always examines her reasons for casting a spell before she takes any action. Sometimes the only difference between a gray and black spell is your intention. Let's say, for example, you want a certain job. It's logical to do a spell to improve your chances of landing the position you desire. But if your spell intentionally causes someone else to lose the job so you can take over, that's black magick.

Black magick doesn't always involve the ritual of casting a spell. Many people perform black magick without even realizing it. If, in the heat of the moment, you curse someone or wish something bad to happen to him, you're doing black magick.

It's also important to feel good about the spells you do. Witches have different opinions and preferences when it comes to working magick, and although certain practices may not be wrong, they might not be right for you. For instance, some witches engage in sex magick, but it's not for everyone. Stay within your own comfort zone.

Witches subscribe to a few general guidelines that constitute morally responsible spells. Here are the basic spellcraft "don'ts."

- Don't design a spell that might harm another person or interfere with his free will.
- Don't cast a spell that includes components or methods that violate your own personal taboos or ethics.

- Don't work with languages or symbolic items that you don't fully understand.
- Don't do spells if you are ill, angry, or otherwise off-center, as this can affect the outcome dramatically.

If you follow these simple guidelines, you'll avoid the problems, pitfalls, and unpleasant ramifications that can sometimes accompany spell-casting.

Sympathetic Magick and the Law of Similars

To understand how spells work, it is necessary to understand the concept of "sympathy" and what's known as the Law of Similars. Sympathy, in a magickal sense, means that a designated item, when properly used, has the power to affect something or someone because of the symbolic relationship between the item and the target of the spell.

Candle magick often makes use of sympathy. A love spell, for instance, might utilize two candles to represent a couple. To heal a rift between the two individuals, a witch might move the candles a little closer together each day over a period of time until the candles are touching. Poppets (discussed in Chapter 13) embody the concept of sympathy and the Law of Similars. The early Egyptians utilized poppets in spellcraft, carefully forming and dressing the dolls, and adding incantations that described the poppet's desired effect on the person it represented.

FACT

Little did our ancestors know that scientists who study subliminal perception would confirm their magickal practices. Today, figurative representations play a part in everything from advertising to religion, affecting the subconscious in specific ways.

The Law of Similars states that there is a divine fingerprint in nature that gives clues to an item's spiritual function. For example, red plants can be used in magickal cures for blood problems. A heart-shaped leaf might be a component of a love spell. A phallus-shaped stone could be utilized in a spell for male virility.

Like their predecessors, contemporary witches still consider an item's shape, color, and other physical attributes as indicators of its magickal significance. In this manner, witches believe they are giving greater dimension to the energy of a spell, therefore an outcome will manifest more satisfactorily.

Forming Your Intention

The purpose of a spell is to manifest something you need or desire. That need or desire (or both) compose your intention. When you cast a spell, your intent is as vital to your success as your beliefs. Focusing attention on what you want puts energy behind your objective, enabling your mind to consciously create the circumstances you desire.

"A spell involves words and actions chosen to achieve a certain goal or desire, and is driven by the will of the person performing it. Words, symbols, and tools are combined to produce a ritual. Power is raised and directed out to the Universe to do its work."
—Debbie Michaud, *The Healing Traditions & Spiritual Practices of Wicca*

As you design a spell, ask yourself a few basic questions. What is your reason for doing a spell? What outcome are you seeking? How passionately do you want what you're trying to achieve or accomplish? Are you ready and willing to accept the outcome?

Be very clear and specific when asking for what you want. Remember the old saying "Be careful what you wish for." Ambiguous statements tend to yield confusing and sometimes unwanted results. Bear in mind that just like a computer, spells do what you tell them to do. So if you perform a spell to find a perfect companion and get a wonderful dog, your magick certainly has manifested—exactly as you asked but not exactly as you'd hoped. Spells always take the easiest and most direct route to manifestation, so if you don't state exactly what you intend, the outcomes can be interesting—to say the least.

It's not necessary to envision how all the events leading up to the outcome will unfold. However, you must be able to clearly imagine the end result you seek. In fact, *seeing from the end* is essential. Hold firmly to your vision of the outcome you desire and trust that it will manifest.

Keep it Simple

Multitasking has become the norm in our busy modern world, but it's not the best way to do magick. When your attention is diffused in several directions, its creative power becomes dissipated.

ALERT!

Magick doesn't have to be complicated to work. Complexity doesn't imply power, nor does simplicity mean weak magickal results. In many instances, the simpler a spell the better. Simplicity allows you to focus your mind and spirit completely on the task at hand.

Limit a spell to a single objective or desire. Don't design a spell to find the perfect partner and improve your finances (although if you attract a wealthy partner, both goals might be accomplished simultaneously). If you want to create more than one condition, cast a different spell for each intention, preferably on a different day. Some magicians suggest waiting until one spell has manifested before doing another. By focusing on a single goal and putting all your energy behind that objective, you improve your chances of bringing your goal to fruition and avoid confusion.

Spoken Spells

In Old English, the word *spell* meant "story or narrative." The noun form referred to a recitation or the act of speaking aloud. The verb *spellen* meant "to read something letter by letter." Spoken spells were probably the earliest form of spell-casting, dating back to a time when few people could read or write.

Verbal spells, also called charms, make use of the power of sound and vibration. (See Chapter 6 for more about sacred sound, affirmations, and words of power.) The word *charm* comes from a Latin term *carmen*, which means "incantation." Many spoken spells rhyme or have a distinct rhythm in their delivery, making it easier for the witch to commit them to memory. Recitation and repetition have the additional benefit of forming impressions in the brain, providing a channel for your thoughts to flow through to manifest your intention.

A witch might wait until the first night of a full moon to recite the charm, then recite it thrice each night thereafter for a designated period of time. The full moon represents completion and coming to manifestation. The number three represents the body-mind-spirit connection. In this manner, the witch combines lyrical verse with other symbolic systems to improve the results of the spell.

Charms are a simple, no-frills sort of magick, considered by some people as a "low" form of spellcraft (as opposed to the highly ritualized magick performed by ceremonial magicians). Originally, verbal spells probably dealt with mundane matters rather than exalted ones. Prayers, however, also fall into the category of spoken spells. Don't be misled by their lack of complexity; verbal spells can be quite powerful and fast-acting.

Written Spells

In earlier times, written spells were the province of a few wise men and women who were more literate than the majority of the populace. In many cultures, the written word was revered as a gift of the gods, especially among the Egyptians and Greeks. For this reason, written spells came to be considered more potent than verbal ones.

One of the oldest and best-known written spells is the word *Abracadabra*, customarily used to banish sickness. In ancient Chaldean texts, Abracadabra translates as "to perish like the word." The letters in Abracadabra were written in the form of a descending triangle on parchment, which was then laid on the inflicted body part. Then the paper was removed and stuck in the cleft of a tree. As time and the elements destroyed the paper, the magick would begin to work. This whole process is an example of magickal symbolism, sympathy, and similars—the word disappears into nothingness; the paper disappears into nothingness; and, therefore, the disease or illness takes the hint and follows suit.

FACT

When you write with a pen or pencil, you activate the acupressure points in the thumb and fingertips. These points induce relaxation and strengthen the connection to the subconscious mind. Thus, writing contributes to the power of a spell because it helps to center your mind and engages your imagination.

Written words, affirmations, incantations, and sigils are often included in contemporary spells. A written intention might be slipped into a talisman or amulet. Spells are sometimes written on paper, then burned to release the intention into the universe. Witches might write a spell a set number of times—the number corresponds to the spell's objective (e.g., six times for joint endeavors, eight times to attract financial security). The color of the ink, the shape of the paper, even the addition of aromatics to the ink or paper may contribute to the overall effect of the spell.

Why go through all this fuss? Because witches believe that the more dimensions magick has (with sensual dimensions being especially significant), the better the results will be.

Choosing Components for Spells

It is reasonably safe to say that there is not a stone, plant, animal, or other natural object that hasn't been used at one time or another for magickal purposes. This book has already discussed the importance of symbolism and imagery in spellcraft, and how witches use sympathy and similars to work magick. As you concoct your own spells, pay attention to the images and symbols you include and notice how you react to them. Choosing and combining the right ingredients is essential to spellworking.

If you think of a spell as a magickal recipe, you'll understand why the components (that is, the ingredients) are so important. If the components are not measured correctly, if they are not added to the mix at the right time, if you don't give them enough time to "bake" properly, the magick goes awry.

ALERT!

A good spell component is anything that's essential to the recipe, something that builds the energy until it's just right. Each component should resonate with the nature of your intention. All the ingredients must blend on a metaphysical level. Their energies should complement one another and contribute to the outcome. Of course, the witch herself is the key component of any spell.

To illustrate this point, following are some possible components for a prosperity spell. Chapters 9 through 12 contain lots of information about various spell components and their associations.

- Animal symbolism: rabbits (known for their prolificacy)
- Gemstones: aventurine, tiger-eye, turquoise
- Color symbolism: gold or silver (the color of coins)
- Herbs: saffron (the herb of kings), mint
- Numeric symbolism: four or eight
- Timing: during the waxing moon (to inspire growth)

You might wish to compile a list of appropriate components, then design a spell that combines the ones you like best or have access to. Putting such a list together provides numerous options for a witch. He could burn a gold candle, put mint leaves and a piece of aventurine in a talisman, tie eight knots in a cord and wear it for eight days, or carry a gold coin in his pocket.

A good working knowledge of components is essential to effective spellcraft; over time, you'll know by heart which items to use, just as an experienced cook knows what to put into a soup or pie. Let your intuition and imagination guide you as you choose and combine ingredients.

Adapting Spells

Today, you'll find many books on spellcraft that contain instructions for casting spells. You can also purchase ready-made kits that include all the ingredients necessary for a spell. Nonetheless, if those instructions or ingredients don't make sense to you or break your personal ethics, the spell will not work.

The best spells are those you create yourself or adapt to suit your own purposes. The process of collecting ingredients, preparing them, and designing the steps of your spell focuses your mind on your intention and adds energy to the spell. Sometimes you must adapt a tried-and-true spell because you can't get the designated components. For example, if you lived in New England and used ash leaves or bark in protection spells but then moved to Texas, you would not be able to find such plant life; you could then compensate by substituting another ingredient, such as basil.

One of the beauties of spellcraft is its versatility. Spellcraft, of course, isn't a fixed, rigid dogma; it's a living, growing body of knowledge and experience that continues to expand as the number of witches working magick grows.

With the previous example in mind, it's easy to see that there will be many times when a witch or Wiccan will want to adapt a spell or devise one of her own. How do you begin the process? Adapting a spell is far easier than creating one, so let's start there. When a witch examines a spell, she looks for continuity and comprehensiveness.

- Does the spell target your goal through its words, actions, and components?
- Does it do so on a multisensual level (involving your hearing, sight, touch, taste, and smell)?
- Does every part of the spell make sense and excite your higher sentiments?

If the answer to any of these questions is no, try to find a substitute. To illustrate, many old love spells call for blood as a component. But modern awareness of disease (or squeamishness) might make blood inappropriate. Instead a witch could use red wine. The red juice from crushed raspberries, strawberries, or passion fruit (fruits associated with love) would also work well. In this manner, she can still follow the basic spell while relying on components that are safe and support her ethics.

Creating Spells from Scratch

People who are new to magick often ask if it's okay for them to create their own spells. The answer is a resounding yes. Think of it this way: someone, somewhere had to come up with the idea for the first spell, and the hundreds of thousands of spells after that. Personally created spells are often considered a very important step in the witch's training and adeptness.

Once you've become familiar with casting spells and adapting existing spells for your individual purposes, you're ready to design your own, original spells from scratch. Other than your fundamental knowledge of magick, you no longer have a construct to work from. You must devise all the actions, symbols, timing, wording, and other components of the spell yourself—that's what makes creating original spells so exciting. It's like being the composer of a piece of music and the performer as well.

Combining Components

The components you include in a spell should support, strengthen, balance, and harmonize with one another. They should also be items you feel comfortable using. Some witches enjoy working with flowers, herbs, and other botanicals. Others have a fondness for gemstones and crystals. No one type of ingredient is inherently better than another, but your feelings will certainly influence a spell's outcome.

Keep your objective in mind at all times as you select ingredients. For instance, if you are making a love talisman, you might want to include pairs of ingredients: two rose petals, two pieces of rose quartz, etc. Consider the symbolism of each component and how well it aligns with your intention. A ring is a powerful symbol to put in a love talisman; a coin clearly symbolizes an intention to attract wealth.

Choosing your own ingredients, rather than following a prescribed formula, allows you to fine-tune a spell to your specific needs. Let's say you're doing a prosperity spell to help you (1) attract money and (2) hold on to it. To achieve both objectives, you could combine a piece of aventurine with a piece of hematite. Once you understand the basic natures and symbolism of various components, you can mix-and-match them to create exactly the right combination of energies.

Designing Steps and Procedures

In cooking, it's necessary to follow certain steps and procedures in a particular order. The same is true in spell-casting. Following these steps will help you create spells that are just as effective as those you learn from a book or from another magician.

1. Boil down the purpose of the spell to a word or short phrase.
2. Find the ingredients suited to your goal (by using correspondence lists in this and/or other resource books).
3. Determine the best possible timing for the spell (see Chapter 18).
4. Decide if you want to include an affirmation or incantation. If so, write it so that it describes your components and your goal.
5. Cleanse and bless all the items you will be using as part of the spell (this rids them of unwanted energies).
6. Consider any actions that might help support the magick and where best to insert them in the spell-casting process (for example, lighting a candle at the outset to illustrate your intention).
7. Prepare yourself and the space where you'll cast the spell, as described further along in this chapter.
8. Focus your will to raise energy and guide it mentally toward your objective, then release it and trust in the outcome.
9. Keep a journal (or grimoire) of your results for future reference.

It's not necessary to always follow every step of this process. There will be moments when you can't conduct a spell at "just the right time," or when you don't have perfectly suitable components. Some spells don't require numerous ingredients or actions—a visualization or simple statement of intent may be all that's necessary. Your thoughts and your will are the most important components of any spell; the rest are optional.

Creating a Magickal Environment

When you dine in a restaurant, the setting and ambience contribute greatly to the overall experience. The same is true of spellworking. Knowing this, witches attempt to create an environment that's conducive to magickal activities, that transports them from their everyday existence—at least in imagination—into a place of power and mystery. Think of how you feel when you enter a great cathedral: reverent, peaceful, attentive, outside ordinary time and space. That's how you want to feel within the magickal environment where you cast your spells.

"In Witchcraft, we define a new space and a new time whenever we cast a circle to begin a ritual. The circle exists on the boundaries of ordinary space and time; it is 'between the worlds' of the seen and unseen . . . a space in which alternate realities meet, in which the past and future are open to us."
—Starhawk, *The Spiral Dance*

Some witches choose to work indoors, setting aside a room or corner in their homes for spellcraft. Others prefer to practice outside, in a garden, a wooded grove, or near a lake or stream. Any place can be transformed into a sanctuary—your intentions and actions are the catalysts that change ordinary space into sacred space.

Preparing Yourself for Spell-Casting

Effective spell-casting requires mental and emotional clarity, as well as concentration, relaxation, and sincerity. If your mind is still entangled in daily affairs, if you are distracted or upset, you may not be able to produce the outcomes you desire. Therefore, it's important to prepare yourself for magickal work, just as you might prepare yourself to give a concert.

To achieve the correct state of mind, witches often engage in personal cleansing and centering rituals before casting a spell. Many witches meditate before spellworking, and some do yoga or engage in other relaxation practices. Taking a ritual bath is a popular—and enjoyable—custom. Bathing for purification and health is a time-honored tradition with spiritual dimensions as well as physical ones. Because water represents the emotions, the unconscious, and feminine creative power, bathing shifts your focus from left-brain to right-brain, from logical thinking to intuition. When you take a ritual bath, you symbolically cleanse yourself of earthly attachments and concerns, and prepare yourself to receive divine guidance.

Pour a few drops of essential oil of pine, sandalwood, citrus, peppermint, or eucalyptus into your bathwater. Or brew an herbal tea with botanicals that relate to your intention (see Chapter 9) and add it to the water. Turn off electric lights and burn candles. Play relaxing music to help you get in the mood for magick. Clearing your mind in this way lets you put the cares of the day behind you so they don't distract you from your objective.

To facilitate the transition from a mundane to a magickal environment, some witches like to wear special ritual clothing. Loose-fitting garments that won't constrict your movements are usually best. Choose colors and fabrics that correspond to your objectives, or ones that make you feel comfortable and powerful. Many witches also don jewelry with symbolic and magickal associations before spellworking. The very act of dressing for the occasion helps to shift your awareness and sharpen your sense of purpose.

Preparing Sacred Space

Before you begin a magick spell, you'll want to remove any unwanted energies from the space where you'll be working. One of the best ways to do this is to light a sage wand (a bundle of dried sage leaves, tied together) or stick of sage incense; allow the smoke to waft about the space, until the air is purified. Witches often sweep the area clean with a broom—not just the floor, but the air as well. You might choose to ring a bell, drum, or sound a gong to chase inharmonious vibrations and entities from your sacred space.

Remember to bring all the ingredients and tools you'll need for your spell into the area before you cast the circle. Once inside, you should not leave the circle until you've completed the spell.

If you wish, you can use an athame or sword to disperse negative energies. Hold your tool parallel to the ground with the point facing out while you walk in a clockwise direction around the space you are sanctifying. Casting a circle around the area where spellworking will take place is usually recommended, both to contain magickal power and to prevent unwanted energies from interfering. (Refer to Chapter 7 for more information.) When the circle is in place, you are ready to begin casting your spell.

Letting Go

Once you've finished casting a spell, let it go. Do it right, then give the universe a chance to manifest your intention. Mentally holding on to your objective keeps it from materializing. Don't second-guess yourself or wonder if your spell will succeed. Doubt interferes with the creative process. Doubt is to magick as water is to fire.

"Doubt exhausts our inner resources. . . . If we doubt that our goal can be attained . . . the dark force operates and the light force is blocked. . . . When we have doubts about succeeding . . . we lose our path."
—Carol K. Anthony, *A Guide to the I Ching*

Some spells involve a series of steps that are enacted over a period of days. Some call for repeating the spell a number of times—say, once each day between the new moon and the full moon. For the most part, however, when you cast a spell you set the wheels in motion. You needn't redo the spell or reinforce it—just trust that your magick will work in the proper time and the proper way.

Gratitude

Gratitude is the final step in casting a spell. Always end every spell by showing gratitude to the Goddess, your guides, your higher self—whomever you see as the creative power in the universe. An expression of gratitude may be as simple as saying "thank you" at the close of a spell. Some witches say thank you three times, then close the spell with "so mote it be." Others like to make an offering of some kind. Others demonstrate gratitude for the help they've received by giving aid to someone else.

Gratitude has two purposes in magickal work. It indicates that you fully believe your intention will be manifested, and acknowledges the help you receive from unseen forces outside yourself, without whose assistance manifestation in the visible world would be impossible.

CHAPTER 15

Portable Magick Spells

In today's highly mobile society, witches on the go make good use of "portable" magick spells. Taking a lucky charm on a trip, however, is hardly a new idea. Ancient mariners believed wearing an emerald around the neck would protect against perils at sea. The Crusaders carried ladies' kerchiefs with them to the Holy Land as good-luck tokens. Charms, amulets, talismans, and fetishes can be taken along wherever a witch may journey.

Choosing and Combining Ingredients

Consider this scenario: You're enjoying a peaceful walk at a place that has special meaning for you, when you spot a pretty pebble lying on the ground. You pick it up, study its markings for a moment, rub its smooth surface, then slip it into your pocket. From time to time, throughout the day, you touch the stone fondly. Back home, you place the stone on the mantel or coffee table, where it continues to engender pleasant thoughts. Perhaps you carry it with you on future sojourns.

This token, which you've imbued with positive energy, has all the makings of a lucky charm. In fact, many simple talismans are nothing more than ordinary objects that have been infused with meaning by their owners—the good feelings and thoughts associated with such objects are what give them their power.

Objects found in this manner, and especially those that come from sacred sites, are ideal ingredients to use in magick spells. So are mementos of spiritual experiences.

When choosing ingredients for magick spells, pay attention to both the purpose of the spell and your own associations with the objects themselves. The very nature of portable magick spells dictates their components, to some extent. Small, lightweight ingredients are essential, so that you can easily tuck the finished product into a pocket, purse, briefcase, or suitcase. If you plan to wear an amulet or talisman, you'll need to design it with comfort, convenience, and beauty in mind.

Symbols, Images, and Sigils

Symbols, pictures, and sigils drawn on paper are ideal to use in portable magick spells. First of all, they weigh practically nothing and can be rendered small enough to slip into a wallet or pocket. Secondly, visual images make a stronger impression on the subconscious than words.

To increase the sensory impact of a magickal image, add color. Draw a symbol on paper of a color that relates to your intention: pink for love, green or gold for wealth, etc. Use colored pens or markers, too. Cut the paper into a shape that supports your goal, such as a circle to encourage harmony or a square for stability. When you've finished, dot the paper with an appropriate essential oil (see Chapter 9 for suggestions).

If you prefer, draw a temporary symbol or other image directly on your body with nontoxic, washable ink or paint. Some people have permanent spells tattooed on their skin. These truly portable magick spells take up no room, won't get lost in transit, and can be placed where they will have the most meaning for you.

Natural Ingredients

Gemstones, crystals, botanicals, essential oils, and other natural ingredients can be used alone or in combination with other spell components. For millennia, people in all parts of the world have worn gems for magickal purposes. Indeed, jewelry set with gemstones is the perfect portable spell. Choose a single stone that corresponds to your intention or combine several that complement one another, energetically as well as aesthetically.

"When you wear certain gems on your left side you can consciously control and modify stresses from your environment . . . . [W]hen you wear gems on your right side, your gems can aid your productivity."
—Dorothee L. Mella, *Stone Power*

Small amounts of dried, powdered herbs and flowers can be added to talismans or amulets. Some essential oils can be dabbed on the skin and worn as quick-and-easy, fragrant magick spells. Try a little amber oil for protection or jasmine oil to attract love.

Traditionally, witches have also used body parts in magick spells. Countless women throughout the ages have tucked bits of their lovers' hair in lockets and worn them around their necks. If you want to keep a lover from straying, stitch one of your hairs into an article of his clothing. Hair and fingernail clippings are sometimes included in talismans, too.

Affirmations and Incantations

The most portable of all spells are affirmations and incantations (see Chapter 6). All a witch need do is say one of these spells to activate it. Some witches repeat an affirmation or incantation three times to "fix" it or the number of times that corresponds to their intentions.

Effective affirmations and incantations may be combined with visualizations. Or add a sensory element to increase their impact. Saying a rosary, for example, combines the sense of touch with spoken prayers.

The acupressure point known as "Middle of the Person," located between the upper lip and the bottom of your nose, aids memory and concentration. Gently press this point while you recite an affirmation or incantation in order to increase its effectiveness.

If you prefer, write an affirmation or incantation on a slip of paper and add it to a talisman or amulet. Or write down a favorite magickal statement and carry it in your wallet.

Charms

Charms were probably the original form of portable magick (see Chapter 14 for more about charms in spellcraft). The word *charm* comes from the Latin *carmen*, which means "incantation" or "song." This would imply that, at least at the outset, charms were sacred words uttered with intention. Later on, the term was also applied to small symbolic items that a person carried to encourage good fortune or avert evil.

Charms play an important role in various magickal traditions. In many tribal cultures, a person could not claim the title of Shaman until she knew how to contrive dozens of traditional charms.

Usually charms are relatively simple and straightforward. Charms can be created in three ways: spoken, written, and physical. Once devised, a charm's energy remains active (unless the witch intended otherwise) for a period of time, typically no more than a year.

Verbal Charms

Verbal charms are the easiest and most convenient, because they require nothing more than some clever phrasing and your vocal cords. A charm is like a poem, or in some cases a prayer. Many charms, both ancient and modern, rhyme or have a poetic rhythm that helps a witch commit them to memory. The following example is a simple verbal charm from Europe:

Leaf of ash,
I do thee pluck
To bring to me
A day of luck.

This little ditty isn't a literary masterpiece, and yours doesn't have to be either. What's important is that the charm expresses your wish or goal and is easy to remember. That way, you can repeat it whenever it comes to mind, giving the original charm energy to manifest your objective.

FACT

Verbal charms can also be set to music. The Greek mathematician Pythagoras, who lived in the sixth century B.C.E., used music in his spells for foresight and healing. The notes of the musical scale correspond to the body's chakras, and some contemporary sound healers combine chants with music to facilitate well-being.

It's quite common for charms to be repeated a specific number of times. This repetition utilizes the mystical value of numbers (see Chapter 12). A witch might repeat a phrase eight times (the manifestation number) or perhaps twelve times (the number that represents cycles coming to fruition).

Written Charms

Even in ancient times magi, Druids, and other wisdom-keepers were often literate. Therefore, it's not surprising that they eventually came to express their magick on paper. This medium provided the practitioner with even more options for symbolic value. Now the color of the ink, the color of the paper, the pattern created by the paper, or the words themselves could support the spell.

You can write a spell on a ribbon, then wear it in your hair or around your waist. Written spells may also be placed in an amulet or talisman. Buddhists hang prayer flags that contain written blessings outside their homes and temples; when the wind blows the flags the prayers are carried around the world.

Written charms involve more than the words themselves. Of course, the words must reflect the witch's intention, but that's only part of the spell. How the words are written—not only their meaning—is also important. For instance, if you're trying to banish a habit, you might write the name of that habit backward on paper. What happens to the affirmation or incantation after it's written adds another dimension to the charm. Many spells are written on paper and then burned to release the energy of the charm. In a spell to banish an old habit, burning symbolizes the destruction of the habit.

Physical Charms

Physical charms involve actions or objects, sometimes in conjunction with spoken or written spell components. The little ditty used earlier to illustrate a verbal charm can be followed by a physical charm. As the witch says the word "pluck," he takes a leaf from the ash tree and carries it all day to inspire good fortune. Many physical charms are derived from nature; a four-leaf clover and a rabbit's foot are familiar examples.

You can make your own lucky charm for prosperity—all you need is a coin minted in the year of your birth (or in a year that has special significance for you). If this is a coin with a high silver content, all the better. Empower the coin for luck by repeating the following incantation:

> *By word, will, and this silver coin,*
> *Magick and good fortune herein join!*

Carry the coin in your wallet or purse. Or place it on your altar. If you know feng shui, put the lucky coin in your home's Wealth gua.

FACT

During the nineteenth century, man-made charms became popular, specifically in the form of charm bracelets, which were often given as presents. Each charm contained symbolic meaning and its own special blessings for the recipient. An anchor represented strong foundations; a heart was the gift of love; a dove brought peace.

Amulets

Many people use the words *charm, amulet,* and *talisman* interchangeably. However, these three types of portable magick are not the same. Each has its own, distinct purpose and application. The components that make up these spells will also be different. Both amulets and talismans can make use of written statements, physical objects, spoken words, actions, natural materials, and various symbolic associations.

Since prehistoric times, human beings have respected the power of amulets and talismans. Archaeologists have discovered these physical charms among the remains of ancient cultures around the world. Stone Age people carved axe-shaped talismans as symbols of power. The ancient Egyptians wore head ornaments shaped like serpents to signify wisdom and energy. Solomon's Seal, commonly viewed as the Jewish star, actually predates the Jewish religion and was worn as a talisman in numerous cultures. The Christian cross, the pentagram, the Sanskrit letter for OM (or AUM), the Egyptian ankh, and eye amulets are all familiar examples of early talismans and amulets.

The word *amulet* comes from Latin *amuletum*, which means "a charm"—so it's no wonder people still confuse one with the other. The Greeks called amulets *amylon*, or "food." This definition implies that people used food offerings to ask gods and goddesses for protection. They may have even eaten or carried a small bit of that food as an amuletic token.

ALERT!

The Greeks drank peony tea and carried a leaf with Athena's name written on it to safeguard themselves from hexes. The Japanese carried double walnuts to fend off the evil eye. The Romans affixed garlic to doorways to keep away harmful entities.

An amulet's main purpose is protection. It wards off danger and guards the owner from all manner of harm: illness, assault, accident or injury, theft, natural disasters, evil intent, or black magick. Until something external creates a need for their energy, amulets remain passive. Consequently, an amulet's power might remain latent—but still present—for a very long time.

Creating Amulets

Amulets may be fashioned from all sorts of materials: stone, metal, animal parts, or bundled plant matter. Gemstone amulets are perennial favorites—our ancestors prized them, just as people still do today.

The ancient magi gave precise instructions on how to make amulets. The base components had to be organized and measured precisely, and any carvings had to be done in an exact order. Say, for example, a witch wanted to create a health amulet for a sickly person. Copper would be a good base material. An emblem for recovery would be applied to the copper base first, because that was the primary objective. Afterward, a symbol for ongoing protection from sickness would be added.

It is customary for the magician to recite verbal spells over the amulet during its creation. In most cases, amulets should be created during the waning moon. You could also consider making an amulet when the sun and/or moon is in Capricorn, or when Saturn is in an auspicious place.

Nearly every plant has been used at one time or another. Some botanical amulets contain herbs valued for their healing or cleansing properties; others rely on the Law of Similars (see Chapter 14). In amulets made of stone and metal, the more precious the base material, the stronger the amulet. When animal parts are involved, the animal is chosen for qualities that can aid the bearer of the amulet. For example, an amulet formed of lion skin would give the person wearing it courage in battle.

Frequently amulets are worn by the person who seeks protection, but they don't always have to be carried. They can be placed with valued items, hung in windows, planted in gardens, or put anywhere else their protective and safeguarding energy is desired. You can place a travel amulet in your car's glove compartment or in a suitcase. Attach one to your pet's collar to keep him safe. Amulets to protect the home are often hung on, above, or just inside the front door. Eye amulets, which symbolize the eye of God watching and guarding a person or premises, are often displayed this way.

Talismans

Talismans serve as active participants in magick. Unlike amulets, which remain inactive until an outside force stimulates their protective energy, talismans instigate conditions. The witch's wand is a good example of how a talisman operates; it directs energy and aids in casting spells. Today the word *talisman* refers to any token that has been created specifically to attract or activate a desired result.

Many old stories tell that spirits dwelled in talismans and could be commanded by the magician to do specific tasks. Aladdin's lamp was a kind of talisman. The lamp held a jinni, which is a very powerful spirit constrained to obey its owner.

Talismans can be worn, especially if their purpose is to confer strength, health, courage, or other personal traits. However, you can also place a talisman elsewhere to attract a desired outcome. For example, you could put a wealth talisman in the cash register of your business or a drawer in your desk. If you know feng shui, put a talisman in the section of your home that corresponds to your goal.

Unlike amulets, talismans can influence conditions from a distance. A talisman needn't be in the right place at the right time. For example, a love talisman can attract a partner on the other side of the world. A talisman designed to produce fame might be created when a child is born even though years may pass before the intention manifests.

Like amulets, talismans must include materials appropriate to their functions. For example, when making a love talisman you could use rose quartz, rose petals, small heart-shaped tokens, or other components that symbolize love. An effective talisman could be as simple as a single gemstone or quite complex, including numerous carefully chosen ingredients. (Refer to Chapters 9 and 10 for lists of correspondences.)

It is especially important to create a talisman at an auspicious time, when astrological factors will support its purpose. In most cases, talismans should be made or acquired while the moon is waxing. Consider the position of Venus when fashioning love talismans. Jupiter's placement will influence a talisman for success or abundance.

Although talismans are more potent than either charms or amulets—at least in terms of how far their energy extends—their power tends to get used up rather rapidly. As you recall, Aladdin only got three wishes. When designing talismans, keep the following in mind:

- Choose personally meaningful base components that support your magickal goals.
- Determine whether the talisman's use will be long-term, short-term, or one-time only.
- Pattern the magick so it can be activated or turned off as needed.

As you fashion a talisman, recite affirmations or incantations over it, instructing it to bring forth your intentions. You may wish to charge a talisman by sprinkling it with saltwater and holding it in the smoke of burning incense.

Fetishes

The word *fetish* probably comes from Latin *facticius* (artificial), by way of Portuguese *feitico* and French *fétiche*. A fetish can be any object. The important point is that the person who carries it must either have a strong emotional connection to the object or regard it as representing a higher authority (such as a nature spirit or the Divine).

FACT

The cross of the Christian church is, by all definitions, a fetish. It represents a higher power (Jesus), and many people wear small crosses as items of protection and blessing. The rosary comes under this heading as well, representing the Virgin Mary, to whom prayers are directed for assistance.

These conditions distinguish a fetish from an amulet or talisman. In some cases, though, you'll find some overlap. For example, a pagan police officer might use his badge as a fetish because it represents a power (albeit mundane) and because he has it with him constantly.

A fetish represents only one objective—you wouldn't carry a single fetish for love, protection, *and* success. Many fetishes serve as "one shot" magick spells—you need a different one for each instance when help is sought. A witch might make up a bunch of fetishes at the same time, all of them designed for the same purpose. For example, she might fabricate a number of fetishes to stimulate artistic endeavors, wrapping bay leaves (to represent the sun god Apollo) in pieces of yellow cloth (the color of creativity) and empowering those bundles with an incantation. Then whenever she hits a dry spell and needs a little inspiration, she can use one of the bundles.

You activate the energy of single-use fetishes by carrying them, burning them, burying them, or floating them on moving water. Burning releases your wishes to the heavens and disperses the energy. Burying helps the energy grow. Floating in water helps transport the energy where it's desired.

Knots and Numbers

Earlier this book discussed the power of numbers and their significance in magickal work. Knots, too, as you've already seen, can be tied to hold energy and intentions. When fashioning amulets and talismans, you can combine magick numbers and knots to add power to your spell.

Many amulets, talismans, and fetishes are composed of ingredients placed in a container such as a drawstring pouch or mojo bag. Herbal charms might consist of leaves or pieces of bark bound with twine. The string that holds these components together can become an active part of the spell, sealing and charging it. Here's how:

1. Determine which number best corresponds to your objective (see Chapter 12).
2. Design an affirmation or incantation that clearly describes your intention.
3. Visualize your goal manifesting, and energize it with emotion.
4. As you tie each knot, repeat your affirmation or incantation aloud and project your will into the knot.

Ribbons and cords may also be tied with magick knots and used themselves as amulets or talismans. Follow the preceding steps to knot your intention into the ribbon or cord. Wear the knotted cord to attract your desires, affix it to a doorknob to safeguard your home, put it around your pet's neck to protect him. If you prefer, burn or bury it to work its magick.

Travel Magick

The average American drives about 12,000 miles each year. On top of that, air travel worldwide totals about 1,900 billion passenger miles annually. That's a lot of traveling, enough to prompt a mobile witch to cast a few travel spells. Considering the risks involved while en route, it's no surprise that protection spells are the most popular travel spells.

Travel spells cover more territory than protection, however. Before embarking on a trip, you might do a spell to prevent delays or obstacles. Or you could do a spell to meet interesting people. Spells to keep your luggage from getting lost are useful, too. One of the simplest and most popular spells helps you get a parking space—envision an empty space waiting for you near your destination, then ask the parking goddess Barbara for assistance. You could also recite this catchy incantation as well:

> *Parking goddess full of grace*
> *Help me find a parking space.*

Travel Spell Components

Travel spells should contain symbolic images that represent your objective and hold meaning for you. If you'll be flying, include a picture of a plane or a feather; if you're journeying by sea, choose a tiny boat as a charm. Photos of your destination, maps of towns or countries, or miniature replicas of sites you plan to visit—the Eiffel Tower or the Statue of Liberty, for example—can also be components of a travel spell. If your trip involves a goal such as getting a job or finding a new home, include symbols that describe your objective: a Monopoly house, a token of your profession, etc.

As with any charm, the components of a travel amulet or talisman must correspond to the nature of the spell. Here are some suggestions:

- For protection: amber, quartz crystal, pentagram, basil, ash bark
- For a smooth trip: topaz, aquamarine (sea voyage), citrine, sage, sandalwood, maple bark
- For pleasant company: rose quartz, garnet, red clover, copper
- For a productive business trip: aventurine, jade, mint, silver coins

Many witches like to take a spell kit with them when they travel. This kit might contain a few simple magick tools, perhaps a candle, some essential oils, a crystal, a miniature wand. (Some jewelry companies make beautiful wearable travel wands.) If you're traveling by air, however, you won't be able to take matches or an athame on the plane, and only small amounts of liquids can be carried on board. Before you leave home, check travel restrictions to verify what's allowed and what isn't.

Portable Altars

Being in a strange place can be unsettling, even to veteran travelers. A portable altar can help ease the awkwardness of an unfamiliar locale, the sterility of a motel room, or the loneliness of being away from home.

A mini travel altar can be a simple cardboard box filled with objects that are significant to you. Include incense, a travel candle in a covered tin, a favorite crystal, perhaps a small statue of a beloved deity, whatever items you wish to take along. You might like to decorate your portable altar with colorful magickal imagery. Or pack a silk scarf in the box and use it as an altar cloth. You shall have magick wherever you go!

CHAPTER 16

Rituals

Rituals play important roles in both sacred and secular life. The way you prepare for your day is a ritual. The way you travel to work is a ritual. Holiday celebrations are rituals. Rituals serve as links between past, present, and future, providing a sense of order and continuity. Wiccan rituals take you out of the mundane realm and bring you into the magickal one. The steps of a ritual build energy and enable you to release it toward your goal.

The Purpose of Ritual

Human beings are creatures of habit. Rituals make people comfortable and provide a kind of continuity—something regular and dependable—that gives them a sense of security. They help control life's hectic pace and let you recognize your place in the cycle of earthly existence. Rituals also contain a great deal of information about historical and cultural traditions, as well as the beliefs of social groups and individuals. Just watch a family at Christmas—what you're seeing is a ritual that describes each person's place within the ritual, the family, and the greater society.

A ritual is like a spiritual instruction book, complete with blueprints. Ritual participants express a desire or goal to the universe. The environment, words, movements, and objects involved in the ritual raise energy and direct it toward that desire or goal. In effect, each participant becomes part of the magick.

Rituals celebrate all sorts of things. Some rituals offer reverence and gratitude to divine figures (usually on his or her sacred day). Others honor historic events of a particular community, nation, or culture. Since ancient times, rituals have marked the seasons of the year, the progression of the moon's cycles, equinoxes, solstices, and so on. The most significant rituals mark the stages of human life: birth, marriage, death, and all the minor events in between.

A ritual can have a specific purpose for any one, or all, of the people assembled to perform it, such as a rite of healing or a ritual focused on helping crops to grow. The energy raised during a ritual holds the potential to touch the needs, feelings, and thoughts that lie at the heart of each participant and to extend into the world as a whole.

The Wiccan Ritual

For a Wiccan, ritual is ultimately about fulfillment—fulfillment of everything it is to be a witch or a Wiccan, or a human, for that matter. During ritual, the eternal and the temporal dance on the same stage. Human spirits can become one with the Divine, their energies merged with each other and the energy of the world. Ritual brings the unseen, timeless realm to your doorstep and allows you to freely explore it. It also provides a construct through which to build more energy than spells provide and direct it outward to a need or goal.

"As a magician, you use ritual in order to create within yourself a mental state that allows you to give clear and direct instructions to your unconscious mind . . . . Ritual is a means to an end, not an end in itself."
—Nancy B. Watson, *Practical Solitary Magic*

Ritual is both personal and communal. It can evoke deep individual experiences and perceptions, or initiate incredible meaning for a group. In a group setting, someone trained as a priest or priestess may facilitate the ritual, bringing every member of the group into the pattern. In some cases, each member takes a turn or plays a role in the ritual. Solitary practitioners enact rituals alone, following the steps devised by other priests and priestesses before them and/or designing their own procedures.

Not all witches or Wiccans work ritual frequently, and many do not follow the exact processes described in this chapter. Each ritual, and each group enacting a ritual, is likely to have its own flavor and form, as unique as the people at that gathering. That is how it should be, for among witches human diversity is considered a strength, not a weakness.

Key Features of a Ritual

Wiccan rituals fit together a variety of tried-and-true magickal methods to form a congruous whole, rather like a spiritual jigsaw puzzle. Dancing around a ritual fire, singing, chanting, meditating, communicating with deities, casting spells, crafting charms, making wishes, pouring libations, asperging the participants or the sacred space—every part of a ritual has purpose and meaning in relation to the whole.

In Wiccan rituals, great care is taken to make sure there are no meaningless words or actions. A ritual without meaning becomes a liturgy to which the participants have no connection, and therefore cannot effect magick.

Not every ritual you create or attend will contain all of the following elements. However, any of these features applied in meaningful combinations will help generate similarly meaningful results.

Location

Where a ritual transpires has a tremendous effect on the participants and the resulting magick. Many witches enjoy enacting rituals outdoors. This allows participants to connect with nature and to recognize their place in the universe. If you're a solitary witch, you have more options than a group of thirty people might. If you live in a heavily populated city, you may not have as many sites to choose from as rural witches do.

Accept your limitations and plan with the goals of the ritual in mind. Make sure that your space, whether indoors or outside, can comfortably hold all the people participating in the ritual and allow for the process to take place. If you're going to do a spiral dance, you need a lot of room. Sitting and meditating, by comparison, requires far less space.

Ambiance

The right environment for your ritual is essential. Ideally, the place where you perform ritual should be a sacred space dedicated to this purpose. You don't want anything to distract, interrupt, or otherwise take you away from the ritual at an important juncture—it should go without saying that ritual space is a cell-phone-free zone. Set the right mood by using appropriate decorations, aromatics, altar configuration, and so on. All of these components should reflect the ritual's purpose.

Seasonal rituals usually include decorative and symbolic touches that reflect the cycle being commemorated. Fresh blossoms might grace an Ostara ritual; evergreen boughs compliment a Yule celebration.

Well-chosen music, incense, and thematic items can make a big difference in the ambiance of a ritual. These touches affect your senses, which in turn influence both the conscious and subconscious mind.

Personal Preparation

Everyone in attendance should be in the right frame of mind, for their combined thoughts and emotions generate the ritual's energy. When you participate in a ritual, you set aside daily concerns and mundane thoughts to focus on the goal of the ritual.

FACT

Before beginning a ceremony, many witches take ritual baths to cleanse themselves in body and mind. Salt is usually added to the bathwater (symbolizing purification) and sometimes essential oils. Ideally, you should bathe in a stream, lake, or the ocean; however, most ritual baths take place in an ordinary indoor tub.

Witches gather in circles to demonstrate visually and spatially each participant's equal responsibility and relevance in the ritual. Everyone who chooses to participate should feel wholly comfortable with the ritual and its components. They should understand the ritual's significance, its goals, and the steps involved, and be ready to contribute mentally and physically to the ritual's purpose.

For the good of all, anyone who cannot fulfill these conditions is better off not participating. One person's lower energies or distractions become a weak link in the circle of the power of creation and the direction of magickal energy.

Tools and Components

Do you need a complete altar setup? Do you want to wear costumes? What about a special altar cloth? A ritual might require any of the following tools:

- Asperger
- Athame
- Broom
- Candles
- Cauldron
- Chalice
- Circumference-marking material (such as chalk)
- Crystals or stones
- Drum or other musical instruments
- Essential oils
- Feather or fan
- Foods or beverages
- Incense
- Incense burner
- Masks (or other props)
- Objects representing the four elements
- Offerings
- Pentagram
- Plants or flowers
- Salt
- Smudge wand
- Statuary
- Sword
- Wand

Everything that will be used in the ritual should be cleansed in advance. In addition, each ritual object should be charged for its task in the ritual. (Refer to the cleansing and charging methods described in Chapter 13.) Bring all the items you'll need for the ritual into the area where you'll be working *before* you cast a circle.

Progression

A ritual follows a logical progression, like a play. The ritual's progression creates the pattern—the actions and words that become tradition.

Each ritual should have a defined beginning, such as creating sacred space. The beginning of a ritual sets the tone for everything to follow. In particular, it transports the participants to that place between the worlds and unifies their hearts and spirits, directing them toward the ritual's goal. A typical beginning in a group setting might include breathing in unison, holding hands, and calling the Watchtowers. Practitioners of solitary rituals might take a moment for prayer or meditation, followed by invoking the circle.

After the ritual space reaches this juncture, what happens varies dramatically, depending on the ritual and its goals. As mentioned previously, this middle portion might involve weaving spells, dancing, singing, drumming, meditations, visualization, divination, enactments, and so on. Whatever takes place should be congruent with the beginning of the ritual.

As is the case with spellcraft, the more sensual aspects you include, the more energy a ritual is likely to raise. As participants work their way through the ritual, everything perceived through their senses helps them maintain focus and direct energy. When the members of the circle are raising energy, drumming might get faster or chanting might grow louder, for example. Each cue communicates the goals of the ritual to the individual's awareness and to the Divine, and therefore nourishes the magick.

"I think the highest purpose of ritual or magickal work is to seek our gods, to commune with the cosmic 'mirror' and the spirits of nature in order to learn more of the divinity within ourselves and reach evermore toward personal growth in its highest expression."
—Maria Kay Simms, *A Time for Magick*

Human beings like closure; solid endings also bring the participants' attention back to mundane matters. A ritual without a defined ending is like omitting the last chapter in a book; it leaves both the participants and the energy hanging. It's also important to thank and release the Watchtowers who have been present during the ritual. Furthermore, participants need this time to gear down a bit (or ground out, as witches say). End the ritual by deconstructing the circle, saying a closing prayer, or stating a parting wish. Some circles end with a chant:

The circle is open, but unbroken
May the peace of the Goddess be forever in your heart.
Merry meet and merry part
And merry meet again.

The Seasons of the Witch

The Wheel of the Year is the Wiccan model of the annual calendar, which is viewed as a circle. Eight major observances or sabbats are important to Wiccans, pagans, and many witches (see Chapter 4 for more information). Every season has specific meaning and symbolic value, and within each season there are other celebrations that mark the Wheel of Time's motion.

For Wiccans, the rituals that mark the following sabbats are most significant:

- **Samhain** (All Hallows' Eve or Halloween): October 31
- **Winter Solstice or Yule:** Late December (around the 21st)
- **Imbolc, Brigid's Day, or Candlemas:** February 1 (some celebate around February 5)
- **Spring Equinox or Ostara:** Late March (around the 21st)
- **Beltane:** May 1 (although some mark this holiday around May 5)
- **Summer Solstice or Midsummer:** Late June (around the 21st)
- **Lughnassadh or Lammas:** August 1 (or as some choose to celebrate it, about August 5)
- **Autumn Equinox or Mabon:** Late September (around the 22nd)

The Wheel of the Year depicts the journey of the Sun King, who rides his chariot through the sky. At Yule, the longest night of the year, he is reborn out of the darkness of winter and begins his annual ascent into the heavens. The sabbats describe the cycle of his growth, maturity, decline, and death.

Samhain

Samhain (pronounced SOW-een) is the most sacred and solemn of the sabbats. Rituals honor ancestors and loved ones who have passed out of the visible world into the world of spirit. Celebrated on October 31, Samhain is the witch's New Year's Eve, the end of the old and the beginning of the new cycle.

The ritual of wearing costumes on Halloween stems from the custom of making wishes on the new year. Dressing up as the person you'd like to be in the coming year is actually a colorful magick spell.

Winter Solstice or Yule

Yule celebrates the sun's return and the renewed cycle of life. Commemorating ties to family and tribe, as well as nature, are also part of this sabbat's rituals.

Many witches exchange gifts and gather with loved ones at Yule. Burning a Yule log (typically oak) in a ritual fire is a favorite custom, and decorating the home with evergreen boughs symbolizes the eternal nature of the spirit.

Imbolc, Brigid's Day, or Candlemas

The word Imbolc means "in the belly" and this holiday honors fertility in all forms. Brigid, the beloved Celtic goddess of the hearth, healing, and smithcraft, is also known as "Lady of the Flame." Consequently, fire (the element of inspiration) is featured in the rituals held on this sabbat, where candles are lit in her honor.

Imbolc is also a time to work magick for the land and the welfare of young animals. Some witches like to do health and healing rituals on this day. Spells, affirmations, and meditations that nurture creativity are appropriate now, too.

Spring Equinox or Ostara

During this season of hope the earth blossoms and new life of all kinds appears after the cold winter months. Spring rites focus on fertility and abundance.

The Spring Equinox is an ideal day to cast spells to launch new projects and creative ventures so that they get off on the right foot.

QUOTE

"This is the time of spring's return, the joyful time, the seed time, when life bursts forth from the earth and the chains of winter are broken. Light and dark are equal: It is a time of balance, when all the elements within us must be brought into a new harmony."
—from an Ostara ritual in *The Spiral Dance*, by Starhawk

Beltane

Another fertility holiday, Beltane coincides with a period of fruitfulness. The Maypole, around which young females dance, is an obvious phallic symbol; the ribbons represent the weaving of fate's threads in the coming year.

Fire, which symbolizes the sun's increasing strength, is a key element of Beltane rituals. Modern witches toss wishes into the "balefire" or jump the fires to encourage fertility of the body or mind. Beltane is said to be a favorite holiday of the faeries—leave them an offering of sweet bread and cream to make them happy.

Summer Solstice or Midsummer

This joyful holiday marks a time of plenty, when crops are ripening and the sun is at its highest point in the heavens. Midsummer rituals are celebrated with feasting and revelry in thanksgiving for the earth's bounty.

Traditionally, witches harvest magickal herbs on the Summer Solstice for greatest potency. They also make good-luck charms, especially those designed to attract abundance, health, and power.

Lughnassadh or Lammas

This is the first of the harvest celebrations. Lammas means "loaf mass"; traditionally, this is when loaves were baked from the first harvest of wheat. Contemporary Wiccan rituals still involve baking and breaking bread together.

Lughnassadh (pronounced LOO-na-saad) honors the Lugh, the Celtic god of craftspeople. Therefore, this is the time to honor your craft and to symbolically harvest the magick that you've nurtured up to this point in the year.

Autumn Equinox or Mabon

The second harvest festival, this sabbat represents a time of balance and harmony as well as thanksgiving. The days begin to grow shorter and the harvest is gathered in abundance. However, the gathered food must last a long time, so one of the themes for this celebration is frugality.

Mabon is also a good time to express gratitude for the blessings bestowed. Rituals might involve feasting, putting up food for the winter, and giving back to the earth by making offerings.

Lunar Rituals

Legends and witching lore say that witches gain power from the moon. Where did this adage originate? Perhaps it came from ancient Greece, where Hecate (goddess of the moon) also taught and protected witches. And at least part of the tale may have stemmed from the witches themselves who gathered beneath the moon to work their magick and conduct rituals.

FACT

Scottish lore advises a woman who's searching for physical beauty to bathe in heather water beneath a full moon. This folk spell relies on the connection between the moon and water, both of which express the feminine force in heaven and earth.

The tradition of using the moon's monthly cycle and its symbolism to empower spells, charms, and rituals continues in modern times. Many Wiccans and witches still celebrate Esbats (full or new moon rituals), or plan their magick according to the phases of the moon.

Lunar Phases

The crescent moon represents the youthful or maiden aspect of the Goddess. This is a time to plant symbolic seeds and do spells for increase and expansion—as the moon's light grows, so will your seeds. Weave magick directed toward slow, steady improvements while the moon is waxing. Rituals focus on enhancing insight and creating opportunities.

The full moon represents the mature or mother aspect of the Goddess. Rituals embrace wisdom, maturity, nourishment, creativity, and fertility. The full moon is the best time to weave any type of positive, creative, or abundance magick, because it marks a fullness of metaphysical power.

The waning moon represents the Goddess in her crone stage. The Crone knows life's mysteries and has grown content with who and what she is. This time of the lunar cycle supports any magick aimed toward endings, decreasing, or banishing. Rituals focus on releasing and letting go, ridding yourself of negative thought forms and habits that you've outgrown.

The dark moon is like a three-day death (followed by rebirth with the next crescent). Witches use this time for introspection and contemplation. Rituals may involve leaving behind anything from the past that has bound you and preparing to initiate new growth in the coming cycle.

Moon Names

In many cultures, every full moon throughout the year has at least one descriptive name. Here are some of the names for the full moons:

Month	Shamanic	Celtic	Neo-Pagan
January	Frost moon	Quiet moon	Ice moon
February	Starving moon	Moon of ice	Snow moon
March	Storm moon	Moon of winds	Death moon
April	Water moon	Growing moon	Awakening moon
May	Corn-planting moon	Bright moon	Grass moon
June	Honey moon	Moon of horses	Planting moon
July	Raspberry moon	Moon of claiming	Rose moon
August	Gathering moon	Dispute moon	Lightning moon
September	Spider-web moon	Singing moon	Harvest moon
October	Leaf-falling moon	Harvest moon	Blood moon
November	New snow moon	Dark moon	Tree moon
December	Long night moon	Cold moon	Long night moon

When a month contains two full moons, the second is called a "blue moon." When two new moons occur in one month, the second is known as a "black moon."

Rites of Passage

Rites of passage are rituals that mark important moments in the wheel of human life. The birth of a child, coming of age, the death of a loved one, marriage, and eldership are five rites of passage that immediately come to mind. At the birth of a child, Wiccans welcome his spirit into the world. This process often includes an introduction to all the elements and a blessing.

When that child comes of age, he has the right to become a fully recognized adult member of the community and begin participating fully in ritual (if he so wishes). The coming-of-age ceremonies vary from culture to culture but generally include elements of learning, initiation, and social affirmation. At this time, magickal tools are often presented as gifts and he is now expected to be responsible for them.

The marriage (or handfasting) ceremony allows the community to witness and support the adult's choice of a life partner and links two spirits into a harmonious one (in which neither individual is lost). A magickal marriage often includes jumping over a broomstick or sword at the end of the ritual. This rite marks passage into a new life together and also fosters fertility.

Eldership honors a person's wisdom and contributions to the community. Croning ceremonies are usually celebrated when the witch has completed her second Saturn Return (at the age of about fifty-eight to sixty). Some things do get better with age, and magick is certainly one of them. The Neo-Pagan community does not view old age as a detriment; it is respected and the insights that old witches offer are gratefully accepted.

At the end of a witch's life, her spirit is ushered on to its next form of existence. This ritual is typically called a Summerland rite. At this gathering, people open the circle for the spirit of that individual to join them in one last dance and song, and to say their farewells. In this way, the circle provides peace and closure, trusting that everyone will meet again in another life.

Designing Your Own Rituals

The Wheel of Time has many more special moments than are outlined in the eight-spoke festival calendar. In the center of this wheel resides the individual witch and her own personal events, experiences, customs, and choices. Witches and Wiccans may enact their personally meaningful rituals alone, with a magickal partner, with their covens, or with friends.

Many witches celebrate rites of initiation. You might wish to hold a ritual to ask for healing or to express thanks for recovery. Birthday festivities, new job celebrations, retirement observances, forgiveness rituals, new-home blessings, and earth-healing gatherings are some examples of personal rituals. Realistically, you can create and enact a ritual for anything that has deep meaning to you.

"We must get back into relation, vivid and nourishing relation to the cosmos and the universe. The way is through daily ritual, and is an affair of the individual and the household, a ritual of dawn and noon and sunset, the ritual of the kindling fire and pouring water, the ritual of the first breath, and the last."
—D.H. Lawrence

As you design your own rituals, consider the points outlined in this chapter. Refer to earlier chapters to determine which tools, ingredients, symbols, sensory components, and other features you wish to include. Invite those who'll participate with you to offer suggestions. Read other books for ideas, such as Starhawk's *The Spiral Dance*, which provides lots of rituals to follow or adapt.

These additional rituals bring the magick home to your heart. In personally chosen rituals, you are no longer celebrating a cycle of the earth, a phase of the moon, or an event designated by society as worthy of note— you are celebrating your humanity and important occurrences in your own life. All too often we don't pause at these junctures and give them their due attention, but we should, and you can.

CHAPTER 17

Divination and Oracles

What will tomorrow bring? Since ancient times, people throughout the world have sought answers to this question by consulting oracles: seers, shamans, and divination devices. Thousands of years ago, the Greeks petitioned the Oracle at Delphi for advice. Chinese court astrologers of the Zhou dynasty interpreted upcoming events in the stars, clouds, rain, and wind. The rulers of ancient Sumeria and Babylonia looked to diviner priests to reveal the future. To understand today's confusing world, many witches still turn to oracles for insight and guidance.

What Is Divination?

Divination is the art of predicting the future. The word literally means to "let the divine realm manifest." An oracle may be a person with special abilities to see beyond the limits of the visible world—a psychic, astrologer, or shaman. Physical tools such as tarot cards and runes are also called oracles.

FACT

Celtic oracles known as *frithirs* served as prognosticators for the Scots. Four times a year, on the first Monday of each quarter, the frithir would fast, then step outside blindfolded just before sunrise. Upon removing her blindfold, the frithir opened her eyes and interpreted the significance of the first thing she saw.

Oracles connect you with your subconscious or inner knowing. They also serve as a link to Divine Wisdom or higher mind. In theory, some part of you already knows the answer to your question. Additionally, the answer lies embedded in the cosmic web that weaves together the seen and unseen worlds. Oracles give you access to information that you aren't able to perceive through ordinary means.

In some cases, information about the future comes to people unbidden. Many people receive visions or images in dreams that foretell upcoming situations. Religious texts as well as books about dream interpretation contain a plethora of examples of this type of divination. In this sense, a dream can also be considered an oracle.

Choosing Divination Devices

In recent years, increased interest in oracles has led to the production of many original and beautiful divination devices. There are literally thousands of different card decks on the market to choose from. You can even purchase computer programs for doing readings. No device is inherently better than another. The important thing is that you feel comfortable using it.

Let your intuition guide you. Hold a pendulum in your hand and sense its vibrations. Finger runestones to see if they speak to you. Stores often keep sample decks of tarot cards for you to peruse before selecting one. Many witches own more than one oracle, perhaps one to do readings for others and another for personal use. You might even enjoy designing your own oracle.

Using Divination Devices

All oracles operate on the principle that symbols trigger your intuition. When you shuffle tarot cards, cast runes, or use any other oracle, you open your consciousness to receive information from your higher mind. Oracles let you see situations from a different perspective and serve as conduits between heaven and earth.

Your willingness to receive guidance from a source other than your everyday, rational thinking processes will affect your ability to gain clear, meaningful insights. If you are skeptical about the possibility of seeing into the future or doubt the answers you receive, you block the flow of information.

What happens if you don't understand the oracle's response? Instead of asking the question again, try rewording it or ask an additional question about the same issue. Perhaps the initial question was too broad or not specific enough. Or simply request further illumination. Keep it simple—ask only one thing at a time. But if you just don't like the answer you received, don't keep querying the oracle hoping the next reading will be better. Wait a few days before asking again—the situation or your perspective may change, thereby influencing the outcome.

The I Ching

For three thousand years, the *I Ching* (pronounced ee-ching) or *Book of Changes* has been used in China and the East. This ancient oracle, which deals with the relationships between individuals, society, and the Divine, is thought to have been created by Confucius. Some researchers believe it is based on a method that dates back five millennia that involved reading meaning in cracks in the shell of a tortoise.

FACT

In 1950, an English translation of the *I Ching*, published by Princeton University Press, introduced Westerners to this Chinese oracle. Compiled by Richard Wilhelm and Cary F. Baynes, this edition is still the most popular version of the *I Ching* and has sold more than a million copies.

Presented in book form, the *I Ching* consists of sixty-four hexagrams (patterns made up of six lines) composed of solid and broken lines. Each hexagram has a specific meaning, conveyed in symbolic language. As Carol K. Anthony explains in her book *A Guide to the I Ching*, "When we correctly understand the meanings of the hexagrams, they bring a sense of enlightenment and release from the tensions that come from misunderstanding the meaning of life."

Consulting the I Ching

To consult the *I Ching*, most people today contemplate a question then toss three coins together six times; each coin toss corresponds to a line in a hexagram. Heads equate with solid lines, tails with broken lines. When a toss results in three heads or three tails, you have what's called a "changing line." Changing lines show the development of the matter at hand.

After completing the six coin tosses to form a hexagram, you look up the pattern and read its meaning. If any changing lines appeared, you read additional information relating to that line. Next, you reverse *only* the changing lines—a broken line becomes a solid line and vice versa—and look up the meaning of the new hexagram that's evolved from the first. The combination of initial hexagram, changing lines, and second hexagram provide insight into the current situation, advice about how to handle it, and predictions for the future.

The early Chinese used yarrow sticks to determine which hexagrams answered their questions. Some of the new *I Ching* kits use cards, marbles, or other methods to produce an answer. Barbara Walker suggests that you can turn an ordinary chessboard into a tool for querying the *I Ching*. Label each of the sixty-four squares with a particular hexagram, then toss a die onto the board. Whichever square the die lands on is your answer.

> "Like many other systems of divination, the *I Ching* was founded on the theory that random mixing of the system's units would imitate the constant mixing of the elements in the cosmos, to bring the incomprehensible future and the secret plans of the gods into human understanding."
> —Barbara G. Walker, *The I Ching of the Goddess*

Other Magickal Ways to Use the I Ching

Hexagrams may be included in talismans, amulets, or other spells. Examine the sixty-four hexagrams to determine which one best relates to your intention, then draw it on a piece of paper and place it in a charm bag with other ingredients. If you prefer, lay a hexagram such as Peace or Joy face up on a windowsill, then set a glass of spring water on the pattern. Leave it overnight in the moonlight. In the morning, drink the water that has been imprinted with the hexagram's vibration to incorporate its energy into yourself.

You can also display the image in a spot where you'll see it often; each time you look at it your intention is impressed on your subconscious. If you know feng shui, put a drawing of the hexagram you've chosen in the appropriate gua in your home. For example, if you'd like to increase the joy in a primary partnership, draw hexagram fifty-eight (Tui) on a piece of paper and place it in your home's relationship gua. By combining these two magickal systems—feng shui and the *I Ching*—you can create some very powerful spells.

The Tarot

No one really knows when or where the tarot came into being. What we do know is that decks similar to modern ones were used during the Renaissance in both Italy and France. The earliest known tarot deck still in existence dates back to the early 1840s. The first entire deck still extant was painted by the Italian artist Bonifacio Bembo for the Duke of Milan.

During the Middle Ages, people who used divination devices risked punishment if caught. Therefore, wise men and women may have taken the tarot to other parts of the world to protect it from being destroyed. Some researchers believe gypsies were responsible for bringing tarot cards from the Middle East back to Europe, where they gained popularity during the Renaissance.

Most contemporary tarot decks contain seventy-eight cards. Twenty-two of these make up what's known as the major arcana, which researchers believe composed the original tarot. These are the most powerful cards in the deck. Tarot readers generally agree that they indicate energies operating on many levels beyond the mundane.

The other fifty-six cards are called the minor arcana. Most likely, these were added at a later date and may have developed from an early Italian card game called *tarrochi*. Notice the similarities between the minor arcana cards and a regular poker deck. Both contain four suits of ten numbered cards each, and both feature "court cards." However, most tarot decks include four court cards per suit—king, queen, knight, and page—whereas poker decks only have three. Some authorities say the Joker is a reinterpretation of The Fool card from the major arcana.

Consulting the Tarot

When you consult the tarot, you usually start by shuffling the cards while contemplating a question or situation you want to know more about. Then you lay out a certain number of cards in a prescribed pattern known as a "spread." Each position in the spread signifies something different: the past, present, future, other people, obstacles to overcome, beneficent forces, and so on. To get an answer, you interpret the meanings of the individual cards along with their positions in the spread.

- Major arcana represent divine wisdom, spiritual forces, or fate.
- Minor arcana cards depict everyday events and activities.

- Court cards often describe the people around you: kings refer to mature men, queens to mature women, knights to young or immature people, and pages to children.
- Numbers on the minor arcana cards have special meanings. Refer to Chapter 12 for information about the symbolism and significance of numbers.

When many major arcana cards appear in a reading, the indication is that situations in your life are being influenced by circumstances outside your control. Minor arcana cards describe areas in life over which you have control.

The most popular tarot deck today is known as the Rider-Waite deck, created in 1909 by Pamela Colman Smith in collaboration with Arthur Edward Waite and published by William Rider and Son. Many recent decks incorporate cultural, philosophical, or spiritual themes—including Wicca—into their designs. Others base their images on a specific motif, such as angels, dragons, or crystals.

The four suits of the tarot are important, too. They symbolize the four elements: fire, earth, air, and water. Notice that the suits depict the four primary tools used by witches and other magicians: the wand, pentacle, athame (or sword), and chalice (or cup). The suits in a regular deck of playing cards also correspond to the four elements.

Tarot Suit	Poker Deck Suit	Element	Magick Tool
Wands	Clubs	Fire	Wand
Pentacles	Diamonds	Earth	Pentagram
Swords	Spades	Air	Athame
Cups	Hearts	Water	Chalice

These connections are intentional, not coincidental. A reading that includes many pentacles indicates that money, material concerns, and/or practical matters are of primary interest to the person for whom the reading is being done. If many cups appear in a reading, the question involves a relationship or an emotional situation.

Other Magickal Ways to Use Tarot Cards

The vivid imagery on tarot cards makes them ideal for spellworking—and many witches use them for this purpose. One of the easiest and most popular methods is to choose a card that symbolizes your intention. Then place the card on your altar or display it where you'll see it often to remind you of your goal. If you know feng shui, put the card in the appropriate gua of your home to blend the magick of both systems.

Tarot cards and candles combine nicely, too. Select a card that symbolizes your intention and place it in front of a candle. Then light the candle and gaze at the card, projecting your will toward your goal. If you prefer, lay a card of your choice on your altar, face up, and set a crystal on top of the card. The crystal's point directs the imagery on the card outward to fulfill your intention.

ALERT!

Tarot cards are wonderful aids to meditation and contemplation. Choose a card that represents a situation or condition you seek, such as Temperance or Strength. Gaze at the image on the card and allow your mind to reflect upon its meaning. The card's symbolism will influence your subconscious.

Tarot cards also can be added to amulets and talismans. Select a card (from a deck you don't ordinarily use for readings) and slip it into a mojo bag, where it will complement the other ingredients. If you want to attract prosperity, for example, choose the nine or ten of pentacles. Or carry the card in your wallet or purse to draw money your way.

The Runes

Norse mythology tells us that the god Odin (or Woden) brought the runes to human beings. Used for two thousand years in Northern Europe and

Scandinavia, the runes were brought to the British Isles by Viking and Saxon invaders. Centuries later, J.R.R. Tolkien's trilogy *The Lord of the Rings* introduced many readers in the United States to the runes and Ralph Blum's bestselling *Book of Runes* taught them how to use the oracle.

The word *rune* means "secret" or "mystery." It also refers to things that are whispered, to knowledge that's revealed to us during moments of stillness and contemplation, which suggests that meditating on the runes can help you understand their meanings.

FACT

Early runes were carved on stones, wood, and bone. Germanic peoples engraved them on swords, tools, jewelry, drinking cups, leather goods, boats, and standing stones along the roadways of Scandinavia. They were used to increase fertility, influence weather, encourage love and healing, and provide protection against evil.

The most popular version of the runes comes from an old Teutonic alphabet, the Elder Futhark, which contains twenty-four letters. Each rune is a letter. Unlike the letters in modern alphabets, however, these ancient glyphs aren't just components of words, they convey deeper meanings as well.

Each rune is named for an animal, object, condition, or deity. The rune Berkana, which looks like a B, corresponds to the birch tree; it represents birth and growth. Ehwaz refers to a horse and signifies movement or progress.

Although most people think of the runes only in terms of the letters in one of the old Norse alphabets, other alphabets can be used for divination and spellworking, too. One such alphabet is Ogham, the Irish language that links each letter with a tree.

Consulting the Runes

You can do quick-and-easy rune readings by spreading out all the runestones in your set and mixing them with your hands while you contemplate a question or situation about which you seek information. Select one rune; its meaning provides insight into your question. More complex rune readings involve casting several runes onto a cloth and interpreting their positions.

You can also lay out runes in patterns or spreads, in the same manner as you would lay out tarot cards in a reading—you can even use your favorite tarot spreads for rune readings. The positions of the runes within the overall pattern, as well as their individual meanings, become significant when interpreting the result.

Other Magickal Ways to Use the Runes

Just as the ancient Norse did, you can include runes in amulets and talismans for love, protection, health, prosperity, and other blessings. You might like to decorate your magickal tools with relevant runes. Or engrave a meaningful rune on a piece of jewelry and wear it to attract what you desire.

Perhaps the most familiar rune is Gifu, which means "gift." It looks like an X, a popular symbol for a kiss. In the old Norse alphabet, this rune is linked with love, so it's perfect to include in love spells. Draw an X on paper and add it to a talisman, along with rose petals and other ingredients that correspond to love and romance. Or carve Gifu on a candle and light it; as the candle burns, it releases your intention into the universe.

The Pendulum

When you use a pendulum, you're doing a form of dowsing. Most people think of dowsing as a way of searching for water that's hidden underground, but that's only one method. When you use a pendulum for the purpose of divination, you're searching for answers hidden within yourself.

A pendulum usually consists of a small weight—a crystal or some other stone, for instance—hung from a short chain. You hold the chain, letting the pendulum dangle at the end of it, while you ask a simple question. The pendulum responds by swinging in a direction predetermined to mean either yes or no.

Consulting a Pendulum

A pendulum isn't capable of handling complex questions, but it can be used to answer virtually any yes-or-no question. Most of the time, a pendulum will swing from side to side to let you know that the answer to your question is no. A backward-and-forward movement generally means the answer is yes. However, it's a good idea to ask your pendulum aloud which direction will indicate yes and which will indicate no.

Try not to influence the pendulum's movement—allow it to swing of its own accord. Rest your elbow on a table or other surface, and either grasp the chain between your thumb and index finger or drape the chain over your fingers. Don't get impatient—it may take a few moments for the pendulum to respond.

Sometimes the pendulum swings in a diagonal line. This can mean the matter is uncertain or that your question can't be answered at this time. You might want to try asking again at a later date. If the pendulum doesn't move, try asking a different question or phrase the question in a different manner. If your pendulum circles in a clockwise direction, it usually means the situation you're asking about is favorable. If the pendulum moves in a counter-clockwise circle, conditions seem unfavorable.

Other Magickal Ways to Use a Pendulum

You can use a pendulum to dowse for just about anything, from buried treasure to the best spot to drill a well. You can dowse an area to find a lost object. You can dowse a house or apartment to see if it's right for you. Or dowse the land to determine the best place to build a home, business, shrine, garden, etc.

You can even dowse a map. This technique is great if you're thinking about taking a trip or looking for a new place to live. Hold the pendulum over a map of an area that interests you and ask, "Is this the place?" If the response is no, try another area. Keep at it until the pendulum says yes.

Scrying

Scrying means looking into a smooth, reflective surface to see images of things that lie outside your ordinary range of vision. Many witches use crystal balls, dark mirrors, or pools of water for scrying, but you can gaze into anything that appeals to you. The shiny surface merely stimulates your intuition. What you see is your own thoughts projected there and reflected back to you.

The famous sixteenth-century seer Nostradamus gazed into a bowl of water for hours at a time, watching visions of the future appear before him. Scrying in this manner enabled him to predict events that would occur centuries later.

A genuine crystal ball or large piece of quartz crystal is ideal for scrying because it contains all sorts of natural irregularities that help spark the imagination. Turn it in different directions and you'll see different scenarios. If you prefer, gaze into a candle flame or incense smoke (use frankincense or another scent that enhances intuition). Or just lie on your back and watch the clouds as they drift by—what do their changing shapes reveal to you?

The key to effective scrying is being able to still your mind. Allow impressions to bubble up from your subconscious. Don't try to analyze what you see too closely, just observe the images that present themselves to you. Trust your impressions, even if they don't make sense right away. Pay attention to your feelings, too, and anything else that pops into your head. It's probably best not to scry when you're upset or just not into it. And if you start to feel tired, stop—you can always try again another day.

Other Methods of Divination

Every time you flip a coin before making a decision, you're consulting an oracle. When you look at a wooly caterpillar's coloring to determine whether the coming winter will be harsh or mild, you're divining the future. Signs that might be omens are around you all the time, everywhere, if you choose to see them.

Some people randomly open a favorite book or religious text and consider the first passage they read to be inspired guidance. Others turn on the radio and listen for meaning in the first song that plays. Many witches and shamans see significance in sightings of animals and birds. Anything can be an oracle.

Don't discount a form of divination because it seems too simple—those daisy petals you plucked when you were a kid to find out if the person you had a crush on loved you could be as reliable as the runes. The oracular device is merely an aid to help you access your own inner knowing.

Pay attention to events, experiences, and impressions, especially those that repeat themselves. Soon you'll sense that something or someone seems to be communicating with you. That's what divination is all about: receiving guidance for the future from a source other than ordinary logic.

Caring for Oracles and Other Divination Tools

It's a good idea to cleanse your divination tools before consulting them. Stone runes, pendulums, crystals, *I Ching* coins, and magick mirrors can be washed with mild soap and water. To clean tarot cards, light a sage wand or stick of incense and hold the deck in the rising smoke for a few moments. If you prefer, place your tools on a windowsill and let the sunlight remove any unwanted vibrations.

Quartz crystals and especially citrine can be used to purify other tools. Set a crystal on top of a deck of tarot cards overnight or place a crystal in a pouch along with your runes. Lightly stroke a crystal ball with a piece of citrine to clear it. Or set the citrine beside a divining crystal so the two are touching; the citrine will cleanse the other crystal.

When not in use, store your tools in a safe place. Many witches recommend wrapping them in silk cloth to protect them from ambient vibrations and dust. You may wish to place them in individual pouches or wooden boxes. Treat oracles with respect and care, as you would dear friends, and they'll serve you for many years to come.

CHAPTER 18

Astrology and Numerology

You don't need to be an expert in astrology and numerology to work magick, but a general understanding certainly helps. These predictive systems enable you to time events and foresee the future, in order to perform rituals and spells most effectively. More importantly, they reveal the pattern that is the Divine order of the universe, thereby providing a context within which to see your place in the cosmos and the never-ending cycle of existence.

As Above, So Below

Perhaps you've heard the saying "As above, so below." What does this mean? Basically, this phrase, common among witches, reminds you that everything in this world is part of a pattern that's reflected elsewhere in the universe and the astral plane. And, vice versa, everything in the rest of the universe and the astral plane has some shadowy symbology in the here-and-now. This point is very important to spiritual seekers; it allows for the possibility that there is something magickal but substantive "out there" that may be seen and interpreted. It also provides some measure of hope that those mysteries, which have been around for a very long time, will slowly be revealed and understood.

Astrology's Roots

Since the beginning of time, human beings have gazed up at the sky and marveled at the celestial patterns they saw. But astrology as a branch of natural omen interpretation originated in approximately 2000 B.C.E. in Babylon. Written accounts dating to 1700 B.C.E. explain how divine beings move the stars around the sky to warn people of forthcoming events. A complete collection of astrological omens and signs developed from this concept. Not long thereafter, Mesopotamian priests came to see the connection between celestial objects and the order of the universe, including the pattern of the future. It was from this hub that ideas about astrology spread into Greece, Egypt, Syria, and India.

FACT

The earliest surviving horoscope dates to about 400 B.C.E. It appeared in the Cylinder of Gudea (Babylon), which recounts the author's dream of the Goddess reviewing a map of stars and then providing people with predictions based on what she saw there.

Aristotle developed an ideology and methodology for astrology in about 300 B.C.E. His efforts were later supported by the Greek physician Galen, who was a strong advocate of celestial omen and sign reading. Nonetheless, early astrology bore little resemblance to what is presently popular. In the ancient world, astrology was linked with astronomy and served as a calendar and road map. By watching the stars, people knew when to plant, harvest, and travel.

Birth Signs

Around 4 C.E., a Greek astronomer by the name of Eudoxus introduced the idea of natal astrology as a kind of celestial code for determining a person's characteristics and fate. Although birth charts were cast for royalty and other important individuals, ordinary people didn't begin to concern themselves with such things until the early 1900s, when the first published horoscope appeared in a widely circulated newspaper. At around the same time, the *Farmer's Almanac* became quite popular. This publication included sections of advice for sowing, planting, and even cutting hair according to various astrological cycles.

ALERT!

The word "horoscope" comes from the Greek *horoskopos*, meaning "observer of hours or seasons." In the Islamic tradition, specially trained astrologers taught children how to find their true star, the one that governs their destiny. Once it was found, the astrologer tracked the star's behavior with other celestial objects and made predictions accordingly.

Of course, what appears in the horoscope section of newspapers today is an overly simplified and highly generic version of a very complicated art, to be read more for fun than guidance. Most people prefer to have a professional or a good computer program construct a detailed birth chart that considers the numerous astrological influences in their lives. These influences include the positions of the sun, moon, and planets as well as their relationships to each other and to the earth. Fixed stars, asteroids, sensitive points, and other features can also be interpreted in a person's natal chart.

Celestial Influences on Earthly Affairs

It's obvious that the sun's position (relative to earth) brings about the changing seasons, and the moon's phases influence the tides. But the movements of the planets profoundly affect events on earth, too. From an astrological perspective, each heavenly body generates distinct energies that impact human beings, social and political situations, weather patterns, and earth changes. As they move through the sky, the planets cause conditions commensurate with their energies. For example, Mars—named for the Roman war god—stimulates action, tension, and conflict. Its cycles produce increased stress that may lead to aggressive behavior, in the personal lives of individuals and even between nations.

Around the time Uranus, the planet of change and upheaval, was discovered in 1781, the French and American Revolutions took place. These uprisings expressed many Uranian themes, most notably independence from authority, and brought about democracy in these nations.

Witches watch the movements of the planets and time magickal workings to take advantage of auspicious astrological patterns. The positions of the sun, moon, and planets in the various signs of the zodiac produce certain cosmic energies that can impact the outcome of a spell. For best results, it's also a good idea to notice how planetary cycles affect your own birth chart.

The Birth Chart

Your birth chart is a blueprint of you, revealing your personality, innate abilities, interests and proclivities, challenges and limitations, approach to life, and much more. An astrologer can look at your chart and instantly see a great deal about you: what sort of career suits you, what types of people you're attracted to, and what things you enjoy doing.

"Astrology is astronomy brought to Earth and applied to the affairs of men."

—Ralph Waldo Emerson

A birth, or natal, chart is calculated for the date, time, and place of a person's birth. It takes into consideration the positions of the sun, moon, planets, and other heavenly bodies relative to earth. The chart looks like a pie cut into twelve pieces. Each piece is known as a house and each house corresponds to a different facet of life. The second house, for instance, describes your physical resources and potential for earning money.

When a planet is situated in a house, it activates circumstances related to the areas of life governed by that house in a way that's in keeping with the planet's nature. If Mars is in your second house, you might aggressively pursue wealth or earn money from a job that involves conflict (sports, the military, etc.). Additionally, your chart shows the relationships between the heavenly bodies and how they interact with one another. Some of these relationships, called aspects, are harmonious, others are stressful.

"[Astrology shows us] that there is a rhythm to the universe and that man's own life partakes of this rhythm."

—Henry Miller

Your birth chart, like your genetic makeup, remains in effect for your entire earthly existence. However, due to the continuous movements of the celestial spheres, the circumstances in your life keep changing. As the planets shift in the sky, they influence factors in your birth chart—and your life. Astrologers examine these cycles, known as transits and progressions, to determine what the future will bring.

Magickal Talents of Each Birth Sign

Some witches examine their birth charts when planning important magickal events such as an initiation or eldership rite. They might also consider how their charts relate to the charts of other members in a spiritual group they wish to join. Each natal chart is unique, with special strengths and weaknesses that affect the individual's magickal life as well as his mundane life.

Many good books exist that explain the personality traits of the twelve sun signs. The following paragraphs describe some magickal proclivities of people born under each sign. Look for your birth sign and read the generalized description. Does it ring true?

Aries

These independent people often become spiritual leaders and pioneers, seeking enlightenment in their own way rather than following established traditions. They may devise new magickal approaches or explore uncharted territory.

Taurus

People born under this sign love earth-oriented magick and make excellent druids. They also have a knack for expressing magickal ideas through art, food preparation, herbalism, gardening, and healing.

Gemini

These individuals may take an eclectic approach to witchcraft. Their quick minds and communication skills enable them to learn magick quickly and teach it to others. Chanting, incantations, and affirmations are among their favorite magickal practices.

Cancer

Intuitive Cancers frequently possess divination and dowsing skills. Many excel as kitchen witches and healers, for they enjoy nurturing and caring for other people.

Leo

People born under this sign have a strong sense of drama. These natural leaders enjoy performing rituals and may gravitate toward ceremonial magick. They may also turn their talents toward spiritual art or music.

Virgo

Natural healers, Virgos frequently apply their magickal abilities to herbalism and working with the plant kingdom. Let them handle the details of rituals and spellworking. Some are skilled artisans who craft lovely magick tools.

Libra

These sociable people like handling the logistics and atmospheric elements of ritual celebrations and spiritual events, especially the décor. Usually they prefer to work with a magickal partner or coven, rather than solo.

Scorpio

Scorpios are instinctively drawn to occult knowledge and the unseen realms. Many possess keen intuition and divination ability. Their strong wills can help them succeed in all forms of spellworking.

Sagittarius

Spiritual subjects and higher knowledge appeal to Sagittarians, who are often great students of magick as well as teachers. Many enjoy the drama of ritual and make colorful, inspired leaders.

Capricorn

Let the Capricorns in your magickal group handle the money. They also excel at planning, organization, and the practical aspects of the Craft. Prosperity magick, in particular, may appeal to them.

Aquarius

The ideal chaos magicians, Aquarians tend to be unconventional in life and in magick. These innovative people may reject the formality of high magick, preferring to create their own rituals and spells. Many have a natural proclivity for astrology.

Pisces

These sensitive individuals are adept at visualization and usually have highly attuned psychic abilities. Music or art may play a part in their magick work.

Although your sun sign is certainly important, it's only part of your astrological makeup. Other factors in your birth chart will also influence your magickal talents and leanings. Consider the whole chart and all its distinctive features in order to understand the big picture.

Moon Signs and Magick

Witches have always placed great importance on the moon's role in magick, and astrology explains why. Your moon sign, meaning the sign where the moon was positioned at the time of your birth, relates to your emotions and inner self. It also influences your creativity and intuition.

As the moon circles the earth, it travels through all twelve moon signs in approximately twenty-eight days, remaining in one sign for about two and a half days. Each sign favors certain types of magick. To make the most of a spell or ritual, perform it while the moon is in a sign that supports your goals.

- **Aries:** Purification, confronting obstacles and adversaries, courage, starting new ventures, vitality, masculine virility
- **Taurus:** Abundance, fortitude, fertility, plant or earth magick, spells for home or property
- **Gemini:** Communication, learning, mental pursuits, short trips
- **Cancer:** Spells for the home, protection, security, feminine fertility, children, childbirth
- **Leo:** Leadership, career success, courage, recognition, creativity, vitality

- **Virgo:** Health and healing, job-oriented spells, discernment, mental clarity, pets
- **Libra:** Love, legal matters, peace, artistic endeavors, social situations, balance within and without
- **Scorpio:** Power, sexuality, psychic pursuits, overcoming obstacles and fears, banishing, transformation
- **Sagittarius:** Travel, spiritual growth, knowledge, expansion, creating opportunities, good luck
- **Capricorn:** Firm foundations, self-control, financial stability, career success, public image, manifesting goals, binding or banishing
- **Aquarius:** Change, new opportunities, adventure, liberation, friendship, group endeavors
- **Pisces:** Creativity, emotional healing, spiritual pursuits, developing psychic awareness

Let's say, for example, you want to find a better job. Virgo is most closely linked with work and work relationships. But if your main concern is to make more money, do magick while the moon is in Taurus. If financial stability and status are more important, cast your spell while the moon is in Capricorn. If you're seeking fame and glamour, a Leo moon will support your intention. Study the unique properties of each sign to help you choose the right one for your purpose.

Using Moon Phases to Time Magick

The term *moon phase* refers to the part of the moon's face that you see illuminated in the night sky. The relative positions of the sun, moon, and earth shift as the moon orbits the earth, causing the changing phases. In the northern United States, the waxing moon appears as an arc of light on the right side of the moon's face (the left side is dark); as it moves toward its full phase, the arc of light grows. During the waning moon, the light portion is on the left and diminishes as the cycle moves toward new.

For the purposes of magick, witches are mainly interested in four lunar phases: new, waxing, full, and waning. Astronomically these phases are further defined as the new (or dark) moon, waxing crescent, first quarter, waxing gibbous, full moon, waning gibbous, third quarter, and waning crescent.

FACT

The span of time between full moons—called the synodic month—is actually longer than the amount of time it takes the moon to circle the earth. That's because while the moon is orbiting the earth, the earth is also revolving around the sun.

Witches work with lunar energy by doing magick to encourage growth during the moon's waxing phase (the two weeks between the new and full moons). This includes spells to increase prosperity, attract a romantic partner, improve career opportunities, boost vitality, and enhance creativity of all kinds. During the waning moon, they focus on magick for decrease and endings. Spells might be done to end an unwanted relationship, let go of an old habit or behavior, lose weight, or cut costs or responsibilities at work.

To fine-tune your magick, look at both the moon's phase and its zodiac sign. For instance, a new moon in Taurus is a better time to begin a financial venture than when the new moon is in Pisces. If you begin something on the new moon, you'll see development two weeks later when the moon is full. The full moon's bright light also illuminates your path, so you can see what steps to take next on your journey.

Other Celestial Events

Like most people, witches still wish on falling stars and the first star they see in the night sky. In ancient Egypt and Rome, this little bit of "wishcraft" was an active prayer to Ishtar and Venus, respectively.

In times past, the appearance of a meteor or comet was believed to portend some great event (often an unpleasant one). This concept seems to have some support if you look at the history of comet sightings. Comets streaked across the sky about the time Mt. Vesuvius erupted, destroying Pompeii and Herculaneum. A comet in 1665 was blamed for bringing the Black Plague to Europe. Napoleon viewed a comet in 1811 as a sign to attack

Russia. Other comets coincided with the death of Julius Caesar, the fall of Jerusalem, and the Civil War.

Haley's, the most famous comet, showed up before the demise of Herod, coincided with the Turkish invasion of Constantinople, and was said to influence the outcome of the Battle of Hastings. Queen Elizabeth took to her deathbed during one of the comet's returns. Hale-Bopp, a comet discovered in 1997 just outside Jupiter's orbit, was feared by some to herald the end of the world—especially as the millennium was rapidly coming to an end. Should a comet collide with earth, the devastation would be massive. When pieces of the comet Shoemaker-Levy hit Jupiter in 1994, the force was greater than if all the nuclear weapons in arsenals around the world had exploded.

Meteorites are astral debris that reaches earth without being destroyed. When they enter the earth's atmosphere, they burn brightly and produce meteor showers or "shooting stars."

A meteor shower over Czechoslovakia 20 million years ago left behind an unusual translucent green rock, moldavite. This rare stone blends extra-terrestrial and terrestrial properties. Many metaphysicians believe moldavite contains unique magickal properties that can aid human evolution. Moldavite is said to enable its wearers to improve their psychic awareness and release old patterns.

Eclipses frightened early humans, who didn't understand what caused this heavenly occurrence. The darkening of the light held ominous symbolism for our forebears. Sanskrit writings claim that a huge dragon flies between the moon and sun and blocks light. Ancient magi, however, recognized potential in a day that was not a day and in a moon going dark. Modern witches likewise see an eclipse as a perfect in-between time, well suited to magickal gatherings.

To astrologers, lunar eclipses signify periods when solar power—intellect, logic, outer-world activity, and masculine energy—dominates. During solar eclipses, lunar power—intuition, imagination, receptivity, reflection, and feminine energy—dominates. Eclipses can be very important times for spell-casting and rituals that tap these cosmic forces.

By the Numbers

Numerology is a time-honored art with roots in ancient Egypt, Greece, Rome, and Arabia. In folkloric writings, the most common numbers that appear are three, four, seven, and thirteen. Many cultures considered three and seven to be particularly fortunate numbers. Three corresponds to the tri-part nature of divinity, the three phases of human life, and the three dimensions that constitute physical form. Seven relates to the days of the week, the colors in the visible spectrum, the notes on a musical scale, and the body's chakras.

ALERT!

Thirteen is often considered an unlucky number, an idea that stems from the switch to a solar calendar from a lunar one (there are thirteen lunar months in a year). As patriarchal societies replaced matriarchal ones, the number thirteen became vilified. For witches, however, the thirteenth full moon in a year is viewed as a time for miraculous workings.

Early physicians from the time of the Greco-Roman empire into the Middle Ages took numbers into account when timing the course of treatments. To determine whether patients might live or die, healers checked their progress on the fourth, seventh, and ninth days. Arabs applied a different approach, combining the numerical values of the healer's name with that of the messenger sent for assistance. If the sum of the two names was an odd number, the healer would go to the patient because the chances of recovery were strong.

Numerology's Roots

Modern witches look to the Greek mathematician and philosopher, Pythagoras, for insights into numerology. Pythagoras believed in the mystical nature of numbers. He taught that self-divisible numbers and those only divisible by one are the most powerful for magickal purposes. Additionally, each number possesses its own vibration, and each holds clues to the mysteries of the universe.

Pythagoras also devised a system of numerology specifically for telling the future. A prevalent myth credits this divinatory system with Cagliostro's success at predicting Louis XIV's death.

Numbers Within Letters

As mentioned in Chapter 12, the study of number and letter correspondences, known as germatria, is based in esoteric Judaism and the Kabbalah. This practice, which Pythagoras is credited with originating, attaches a number equivalent to each letter in a word; each letter has both a numerical and spiritual value.

1	2	3	4	5	6	7	8	9
A	B	C	D	E	F	G	H	I
J	K	L	M	N	O	P	Q	R
S	T	U	V	W	X	Y	Z	

To kabbalistic witches and magicians, this system, when properly utilized, provides a key to understanding the universe. Many old texts, when the number-letter correlations are analyzed, reveal occult truths that aren't apparent unless you're familiar with this secret code.

Using Numerology to Read the Future

Why are some years filled with activity and adventure, while others seem uneventful or calm? Why do you feel sociable one year and reclusive the next? The answer lies in the predictive side of numerology.

According to this system, each year has its own unique signature. To figure out the numeric value of a year, add the digits together, then consider the sum. The year 2008, for example, when totaled $(2 + 0 + 0 + 8)$ results in 10. When the sum is a double-digit number, add the digits $(1 + 0)$ and reduce it to a single-digit: 1.

The following list describes characteristics and themes associated with the different years:

1	New beginnings, action, independence—This is the time to try something different, assert or challenge yourself, or break away from limitations.
2	Partnerships, balance, developing plans—This year, form mutually beneficial relationships, consolidate financial affairs, and learn the value of cooperation.
3	Expansion, movement, personal growth—This is a good year to travel, undertake studies for personal development, or expand your situation in life.
4	Stability, building, organization—A quiet year after one of activity, this is a good time to consolidate, secure your position or finances, and rest.
5	Communication, change, movement—This year brings changes, surprises, and unique circumstances.
6	Give-and-take, domesticity, comfort, beauty—Now is the time to focus on hearth and home, enjoy the company of loved ones, and pursue creative ventures.
7	Rest, retreat, withdrawal, introspection—Seek peace and quiet this year, focus on healing and tend to inner needs rather than outer-world activities.
8	Responsibility, material success, managing resources—Seek financial growth and abundance this year, focus on career success, or develop your resources and talents in a practical way.
9	Fulfillment, completion, transition—This is a time of closure and finishing up projects, in order to prepare yourself for the next cycle of development.

You can also examine specific months within a year, using the same system. To do so, add the number of the month to the year. For example, to see what the vibration of February 2008 might offer, add 2 + 2 + 0 + 0 + 8 to get 12, then add 1 + 2 = 3. Thus, February would combine the energy of 3 with the qualities of 1—a good time for action and pursuing new opportunities.

To see what each year holds for you, take this concept and apply it to your birth date. Begin by adding the month and day of your birth. If you were born on March 4, for instance, your personal number is 7 (3 + 4). Add this number to any year you want to know more about, then read the description of the sum in the preceding table. In 2009, here's what you'd get: 7 + 2 + 0 + 0 + 9 = 18, reduced to 9 (1 + 8). You now can see that in 2009 you'll be winding up matters in your life and beginning to consider what to undertake next. Using this method, you can look as far into the future as you wish.

CHAPTER 19

Sacred Sites and Magickal Places

Sacred sites celebrate the magick of Mother Earth and allow humans to reconnect with the Divine Feminine on an intimate level. Throughout history, people around the world have journeyed to sacred sites in search of spiritual enlightenment, healing, and other blessings. Springs and lakes, caves and grottos, groves of trees, mountains, canyons, and rock formations all resonate with magickal power and potential. Man-made sites—temples and cathedrals, pyramids, earth mounds, and stone circles—also serve as portals to the world of Spirit.

Sacred Places and Sacred Spaces

Chapter 7 examined the significance and practice of creating sacred space, a temporary gathering of the energies for magickal purposes. The earth, however, is dappled with myriad sites that embody and emit sacred energy all the time. These places of power, whether naturally occurring or man-made, draw people with a sort of mystical magnetic force that may be difficult to explain, but is easy to experience.

The first step to understanding sacred sites is to realize that the earth has an aura, just like human beings. This aura contains hundreds of lines of energy, known as ley lines, that connect to one another along a geometric grid called the *tetragrammaton*. This grid represents the focal point to which sacred geometricians pay attention. These individuals, part scientists and part metaphysicians, believe that if you unravel the intricate pattern of the earth's ley lines, you will find those that have been broken or disrupted by war, pollution, and other sociological causes. Once you identify the wounds, you can learn to heal the earth's aural grid. Doing so will help renew the human relationship with the earth's spirit.

"Each Witch's way of honoring and invoking the Divine will have personal, cultural, and traditional overtones. For instance, in the mornings you might light a candle to welcome Spirit (to say 'good morning,' if you will). It's a small but meaningful touch. As in all magickal things, simplicity isn't the issue—intention is."

—Louise Erdrich

If you map the world's recognized sacred sites, you will notice that many of them lie along specific routes that create a defined pattern. Typically, the patterns are circles, spirals, triangles, octahedrons, and other polygonal forms that keep expanding until they embrace the whole planet. It seems that the ancients were aware of the earth's energy lines, for they built temples and other structures along them to honor and augment that energy. Modern witches can do likewise.

Sacred Sites Around the World

Thousands of sites around the world have been deemed holy and honored for their extraordinary energies. Some of these places, such as the Wailing Wall in Jerusalem, are connected with specific religions or belief systems. Others, especially naturally occurring sites such as Niagara Falls, have no religious connotations and attract visitors of all persuasions.

Some places that are holy to a particular cultural or religious group have specific protocols attached—ways in which visitors must dress, act, and so on. It is important to respect those protocols. The witch's way is one of peaceful coexistence and respect for all spiritual paths. Look beyond the details to the source of energy that inspires such beauty.

Why would places not associated with the Craft be of interest to a witch? Because in the worldview of witches and Wiccans, Spirit is religiously neutral. A witch can visit any sacred place and honor the underlying power there. Here are just a few such sites:

- **Amarnath, Kashmir:** Lord Shiva, the lord of the Dance, is worshiped in a cave here; it was at Amarnath that Shiva imparted the secrets of creation to Parvarti.
- **Angkor Wat, Cambodia:** This archaeological site is covered with temples where pilgrims came from miles around to make offerings and perform rituals. This site is sacred to Vishnu.
- **Bath, England:** The springs here were sacred to the Celtic and Roman goddess Sulis and were reported to have the magickal ability to heal, which is why several of the pools contain hundreds of gold coins as offerings.
- **Blue Grotto, Capri:** This amazing grotto shines with blue light. Locals claim that it was once inhabited by witches.
- **Callanish, Scotland:** At an ancient set of standing stones here, lovers went to declare their vows.

- **Copán, Honduras:** The Mayans used this site for an annual ritual to improve the priest's ability to walk between the worlds and receive guidance from spirits.
- **Denali, Alaska:** In native tradition, this mountain houses a great god who presides over all life.
- **Easter Island:** This island is the home of great stone statues, each of which represents an ancestor or spirit whose power was channeled into the stone during the creation process.
- **Enchanted Rock, Texas:** This region is a fantastic place to witness ghost lights and other natural phenomena (such as the rock itself groaning).
- **Mount Everest, Tibet:** In native tongues, this mountain is called the "mother of the universe."
- **Externstein, Germany:** An ancient site for worship and initiation to followers of the mystery traditions. According to tradition, this region was once the home of the World Tree (the Tree of Life). Sadly, the tree was torn down by Charlemagne. Sacred geometricians believe that many of Germany's ley lines connect here.
- **Giza, Egypt:** Giza is the site of the Great Pyramids, one of the seven wonders of the world, and may have been a site for astronomical and astrological observation.
- **Glastonbury, England:** Legend claims that somewhere on these grounds the ancient Grail found a resting place. Many sacred sites including the Chalice Well and the Tor exist here. There is a strong possibility that the town's abbey was built on an earlier pagan site of worship.
- **Heng Shan, China:** Sacred to Buddhists and Taoists, the mountains around this region contain a powerful spirit that directs positive chi (energy) to this site.
- **Knossos, Crete:** Best known through the legends of the Minotaur, the cliffs of Knossos were also a traditional site where Rhea (an earth goddess) was worshiped.
- **Mammoth Cave, Kentucky:** The calcite crystals in this cave have the amazing capacity to resonate due to the surrounding vaulted ceilings, making a womb of energy.

- **Monte Albán, Mexico:** For ten centuries, this region housed a ceremonial site that included pyramids and an observatory neatly aligned with the Southern Cross.
- **Niagara Falls, New York:** Native Americans called this place "thundering falls." Iroquois warriors worshiped at this site in order to strengthen their courage and vitality.

Obviously, many more places around the world could be listed here, but you get the idea. In some instances, local lore contributed to the manner in which the site was used; in other cases, the natural beauty simply inspired reverence.

"Sacred space offers us a profound vehicle for personal and global healing, and an endless source of spiritual education. It gives us access to the active intelligence of the universe and teaches us how to understand and heal our earth."

—Carolyn E. Cobelo, *The Power of Sacred Space*

At many ancient sacred sites, people left gifts for the spirits of the land. Bread, milk, wine, and other offerings of food were believed to please the spirits. Modern witches still follow this custom, especially when harvesting something from nature.

Tuning in to Earth Energies

Sacred sites (both famous and not) seem to radiate with remarkable energy that all sorts of people—not just witches, shamans, and dowsers—say they can sense. Places such as Lourdes, France, even seem to inspire miraculous healings. Exactly how these locales came by such energy is unknown. Some people think it results from the ley lines that wind around the planet and create an energy grid. Other people believe that an energy vortex or even a localized spirit—an earth god or goddess in residence—may generate a distinct resonance. Still others suggest that the thoughts and feelings of the people who have occupied a space contribute to its energy.

FACT

Ley (pronounced lay) lines are invisible lines of force said to form a network throughout the earth in geometric patterns called the tetragrammation. When two ley lines intersect, a power point is formed. When these lines become disrupted or injured, the associated land may suffer.

Naturally occurring sacred sites are the perfect spots for working magick, if permissible by local law. Not everyone wants wilderness witches tromping across private property to conduct a ritual or enact a spell. You must respect both the land and its owners. Visiting sacred places and sensing the heightened vibrations emanating from these spots will help you understand how to create your own sacred space for worship, rituals, and spellworking.

Indicators of a Vortex, Ley Line, or Power Center

Sacred spots exist in every country and region, perhaps in your own backyard. All you have to do to locate them is attune your awareness to pick up the earth's vibrations. As you seek out places that house special energy, pay attention to these key indicators that tell you you're standing on holy ground:

- Body heat increases (without the sun coming out or other environmental causes).
- Dowsing rods or pendulums react positively, as if finding a hit.
- The place appears repeatedly in your dreams, usually with something magickal or spiritual taking place there.
- An emotional sense of peace and tranquility settles over you like a warm blanket.
- You get a feeling that you're not alone (as if the animals, birds, trees, or other living things are trying to communicate with you through motion, sounds, or symbols).
- Hairs on your arms rise, as if you've been exposed to a current of energy, or you feel a sudden chill.

- There are unusually lush displays of plants uncharacteristic of the region; for example, a streak of bright green grass was once called a faery trail, and these usually follow ley lines.
- Your totems and power animals appear there regularly.
- You experience a sense of timelessness, as if there is only now.

You can also dowse an area to assess its energy. A pendulum will pick up speed and spin enthusiastically in the presence of a ley line or power center. Dowsing rods tip down toward the ground when they connect with this vibrant earth energy. As mentioned in Chapter 17, you can even dowse a map to find a sacred site near your home.

Liminal Zones

Liminal zones are in-between spaces, where two distinctly different types of terrain or elemental forces meet. The edge of a forest, the entrance to a cave, and the mouth of a volcano are examples of liminal zones. Places where natural changes occur continually, so that the energy there is always ebbing and flowing, might also be considered liminal zones. At the ocean, the area between the low tide and high tide marks constitutes a powerful liminal zone.

The shadowy periods at dawn and dusk are liminal zones, too. Although many witches prefer to do magick at night, the moments between light and darkness afford opportunities for unifying the masculine energies of daytime with the feminine powers of the night.

Witches and shamans move between the temporal and spirit worlds when they do magick. Earthly spots where topography defines the border between different "realms" in the physical world can serve as portals or facilitate different states of awareness. If you know of such a place, consider it sacred and work magick there.

Sacred Architecture

Structures can also house sacred energy, as shrines, temples, and cathedrals clearly demonstrate. The ancient Europeans erected stone circles as places for worship and ritual, just as people today erect churches. Stonehenge, on the Salisbury Plain in England, is probably the best-known stone circle, although its true origins and purposes remain a mystery. Human beings placed those stones with great care and intent, remaining sensitive to the energies of the locale.

During the Medieval and Renaissance periods, a select guild of craftsmen known as the Freemasons built the great cathedrals in Europe and Britain. These men worked in the service of a higher power whom they referred to as The Great Architect of the Universe. Their knowledge of occult truths can be seen in the symbols woven into the architecture of these holy buildings.

"The architecture I consider sacred is that which has a common root in the life of the soul and spiritual vision, rather than merely in forms which qualify as being religious."

—A. T. Mann, *Sacred Architecture*

Buildings, whether ancient or modern, that exhibit a sense of sacredness may have been created by someone who was sensitive to mystical energy. Perhaps the building site lies on a natural vortex, ley line, or power center. Buildings retain the vibrations of the people who inhabit them for a very long time; the emotions and thoughts generated in a space continue to reverberate long after the people who expressed them have gone. A sanctuary where prayers and sacred chants have been uttered is likely to feel peaceful and comforting.

Creating Your Own Sacred Site

Visiting famous sacred sites can be a profound and illuminating experience. Not everyone can travel the world to experience such magickal energy, however. Moreover, it is important for the witch or Wiccan to be able to find sacred sites near where she lives, where she can commune with nature and the Divine on a regular basis. By paying close attention to the world around you and developing a rapport with the earth, you contribute to the overall healing of the planet.

Sacred places are perfect locations for meditation. Being present at a sacred site is much like plugging into an electrical outlet that goes directly to Spirit. When you hook yourself up to that circuit, it's much easier to move into altered states of awareness.

Finding sacred sites is not as difficult as you might think. Look back on your childhood, for example. Where did you go when you needed private time or when you were upset? Perhaps a creek, a tree, a cave, or a nearby park? That's a great place to start looking, if you still live in the area. Or seek out spots that remind you of those youthful sanctuaries.

Here are ten steps to follow to improve your connection with sacred space.

1. Relax, sit quietly, and take a few deep breaths to quiet your mind.
2. Release any expectations.
3. Remain alert in body, mind, and spirit.
4. Try to look beyond fears or barriers, if they appear.
5. Tune in; wake up to the potential around you.
6. Align yourself with that energy and experience it as fully as you can.
7. Meditate on what you experience, and what rises into consciousness.
8. Internalize and integrate the experience.
9. Make notes in a spiritual journal.
10. Visit this sacred spot regularly.

Although a witch's journey to a sacred space is a physical one, the intention behind it affects the whole of being—body, mind, and spirit. This is as much an inward quest as one that's upward and outward. The sacred site is a catalyst for that quest.

Empowering and Honoring Sacred Sites

Many witches like to decorate their living spaces in a manner that reflects their faith and practices. These "decorations" may appeal to a witch's personal sense of aesthetics as well as offering a magickal function; for example, a pretty piece of rose quartz that sits on a bookshelf might also function as a component in love magick. Sensitively applying your own decorative touches to a sacred site can actually augment its powers.

FACT

In Sanskrit, the word for "mindful" also means "remember." Being mindful means remembering your connection to the Mother, to Spirit, to your inner world, and to magick.

To honor and empower a sacred site, look to your ancestors for inspiration and ideas. In times past, people used standing stones and stone altars to mark sacred sites. Spirals, circles, and labyrinths made of stones not only defined the boundary between sacred and secular space, but the patterns themselves actually focused and augmented the natural energies present. Often stone configurations aligned with astrological patterns; Stonehenge is a good example of this. Some traced ley lines. As the builders positioned the stones, they created a web of power aimed at protecting and energizing that space.

If you live in an area that's large enough (and private enough), you might want to build your own outdoor labyrinth or circle of standing stones. If that's not an option, you could ring a room (or section within a room) with crystals or pillar candles and set up an altar inside the circle. Some witches draw a spiral or labyrinth on a large piece of paper or cloth, so it can be laid down for rituals and spellworking, then folded up and stored when not in use. Again, the most important part of honoring and empowering sacred space is your intention. Any place can become sacred if you fill it with your magickal energy and thoughts.

Gardening in Your Sacred Site

In many cultures, the garden is a symbol of sanctuary, a place of peace, abundance, and beauty. Gardens play a central role in spiritual art and literature—the biblical story of creation presents Paradise as a garden. The word *paradise* even comes from the Old Persian word for a walled garden. Today, gardens provide respite from the stress of modern life. Whether in the middle of Manhattan or your own backyard, a garden is a haven where you can reconnect with nature and your inner self.

When you cultivate a garden you become a co-creator working in harmony with the devic forces, participating in the magick of fostering life. Planting a garden also offers a lesson in karma, where you can clearly see that you reap what you've sown.

If you are fortunate enough to have a spot where you can create a garden of your own, consider combining components to represent the four elements—earth, air, fire, and water—in order to establish balance and wholeness in your sacred space. Here are some suggestions:

- **Earth:** Soil, plants, and rocks depict the earth element. Ceramic planters and stone statuary add aesthetic touches.
- **Air:** Accentuate the air element with wind chimes, mobiles, flags, bells, and other features that the wind can activate.
- **Fire:** Hang faceted crystals to reflect sunlight, or include lanterns, electric lights, or votive candles to represent the element of fire.
- **Water:** A stream, pond, or fountain is an obvious water feature, but a birdbath or even a bowl of water will work.

For centuries, witches have planted their gardens with herbs and flowers for healing purposes as well as magickal ones. In your sacred space, choose plants that correspond to your own intentions: basil for protection, mint for prosperity, roses for love, lavender for insight, and so on. (Refer to

Chapter 9 for more information.) To further enhance the beauty, tranquility, and magickal properties of your garden, consider the following tips:

- Use only native plants so as to not upset the ecosystem.
- Plant medicinal herbs at water-oriented sites (to support healthful energies).
- Plant culinary items in an earth-oriented site (honoring earth's providence).
- Sow flowers in colors that relate to the four directions: yellow in the east, red in the south, blue in the west, green in the north.
- Plant trees or bushes that correspond to the energies of the four directions—for example, azalea in the east, holly in the south, willow in the west, and birch in the north.
- Over vortexes, plant or arrange flowers in a spiral pattern.
- Design a small mandala or labyrinth near the center of the site.

In a sense, all gardens might be considered sacred sites. Maintaining a garden is an ongoing process—your garden will evolve and reflect your own personal growth over time. As you cultivate your garden and your relationship with the nature spirits who reside there, you'll come to see your garden as a metaphor for life.

Elemental Energies in Your Site

At each sacred site, one element predominates. If you feel drawn to a particular site, it may be because the dominant element there influences your birth chart in a positive way. If you wish to strengthen or balance certain energies in your life, you could choose to spend time in a place that resonates with an element that's weak in your birth chart. The following list shows the main elements present in various locales.

- **Earth:** Caves, pastures, forests, grasslands, valleys
- **Air:** Cliffs, crags, hills, mountains, peaks, windy shores
- **Fire:** Deserts, hot springs, the tropics, volcanoes
- **Water:** The ocean, geysers, lakes, rainforests, streams and rivers, waterfalls

Of course, most places blend more than one element. The ones that incorporate all four are often the most powerful and appealing, which is why people flock to the seashore. As you venture out into the natural world, pay attention to your feelings and impressions in different places—your sensations will help you discern which elemental energies reside there.

Earth

Any region that makes you feel centered and grounded is a predominantly earthy site. You might experience a sense of security, protection, or stability. If you extend your psychic senses into such a region, you may notice that it throbs like a drumbeat. Caves, in particular, can demonstrate this magickal response.

Each locale affords opportunities for certain types of magickal work. Predominantly earth sites are good places to do spells for prosperity, growth, steady progress, career advancement, fertility, stability, and protection.

Air

The air element is a little elusive, but any region that inspires a playful, creative, liberated feeling within you is likely dominated by the air element. Windy spots and high peaks where you feel you can touch the sky are airy sites. If you extend your psychic ears, here you might hear what sounds like bells or chimes. Notice the music of the winds; each wind has a unique voice and emotion.

Magickally, you can tap the energy in an area where air energy is strong to increase your mental and communicative abilities. These are good places to do spells for friendship and social situations, creativity, motivation, happiness, intellectual pursuits, legal matters, and inventiveness.

Water

The water element has a gentle, soothing quality. At a water site, you might feel peaceful, nurtured, clean, renewed, or refreshed. In the vicinity of water, you could hear waves breaking or the rippling of a brook, but even if no physical water is present you may notice astral sounds that are similar to those you hear when you put a seashell to your ear.

At a water locale, your psychic abilities tend to improve; these are good places to connect with nonphysical entities or to do divination. Spells for healing, love and relationships, creativity, fertility, emotional balance, spiritual connection, purification, and peace are supported by the water element.

Fire

Fire is dynamic and, according to shamans, the hardest element to master. It purifies, energizes, activates, destroys, and creates. In a place that's dominated by the fire element, you may feel hot (physically or internally), inspired, invigorated, restless, clear, stimulated, or expansive. Typically, fire sites have a distinctive "crackle" about them, like static or the sparking of a flame.

Such regions offer lots of power that can be tapped magickally, but it must be carefully controlled. Fire sites support magick for vitality, courage, strength, success, fame, clarity, overcoming obstacles, and inspiration.

Spirit

A fifth element—spirit—serves as the connection between all the other elements. It is the source of magick. Places where spirit abides feel timeless. When you're there, you sense a oneness with all things, karmic awareness, and an awareness of your divine nature. Listen for "deafening silence." Spirit only speaks when you quiet your heart and mind, and truly listen.

A locale where spirit is strong will enhance all forms of magick, particularly when you need to reconnect with your soul-self and manifest a miracle. In these places, you can work the highest forms of white magick—that is, align yourself with Divine Will and gain spiritual wisdom for the good of all.

CHAPTER 20

Where to Go from Here

Some witches choose to work alone, pursuing their spiritual path and vision in a solitary way. Nonetheless, human beings are social creatures who enjoy companionship, especially with like-minded people. The ever-expanding circle of Wiccans and witches worldwide provides opportunities to express your beliefs in a supportive community and to align your abilities with others to bring about a better world for everyone. This chapter will help you decide whether to seek a group to interact with, and if so, how to find the right group.

Covens

The word *coven* originated from the Latin term *coventus*, meaning "assembly" or "agreement." (Covenant comes from the same root.) The term first appeared in Scotland around the 1500s to denote a witch's meeting or a local group of practicing witches. However, the word was rarely used until the modern witchcraft movement became more public and popularized.

In her book *The Spiral Dance*, Starhawk describes a coven as "a Witch's support group, consciousness-raising group, psychic study center, clergy-training program, College of Mysteries, surrogate clan, and religious congregation all rolled into one." That about sums it up. In short, a coven is a spiritual family in which each member is committed to the principles of the Craft and to one another.

The traditional coven has thirteen members, although some groups may choose to include more or fewer. Keeping the group small enables intimacy to grow among members and reduces the likelihood of developing into a pack of disciples led by a guru.

Traditional covens have thirteen members. Why? A year contains thirteen lunar months. Wicca and witchcraft are closely aligned with the moon and its feminine energy; thus, the number thirteen represents the lunar calendar and signifies wholeness.

Wicca and witchcraft tend to appeal to people who dislike hierarchy and rigid dogma. Many modern witches were raised in patriarchal religions that didn't encourage free thinking; they have chosen Wicca (or another pagan path) because it allows them to follow their own truth.

Covens offer a lot to practitioners of Wicca and witchcraft. It's nice to have "kinfolk" with whom to share information about magick and spirituality. Covens provide an opportunity for learning on all levels. It's also fun to celebrate meaningful holidays and events with people who feel as you do. In a world that still doesn't completely accept witches and magick, a coven brings individuals into a community where they can feel safe, accepted, and valued. Furthermore, the power a group can raise when they work together for the good of all far exceeds what one witch could muster alone.

ALERT!

The challenge, which faces groups of all kinds, is to get past egos, unrealistic expectations, and self-esteem issues, and just allow the group connectedness to happen. Dedication, commitment, and work on the part of each individual in the coven are necessary to bring about strength and harmony.

As you can well imagine, thirteen independent-minded witches are likely to have lots of differing opinions, ideas, and objectives. At times things can get pretty dicey. Some covens split up over trivial matters, while others work through problems and find solutions. If you decide to become part of a coven, you'll want to ask yourself if you are willing to devote the effort necessary to make the coven work. Being part of something greater than yourself requires cooperation, respect, and tolerance.

Benefits of Working with a Coven

You can learn a lot—about magick and life—through working with a coven, especially when it comes to foundational information that a well-established coven can provide. In particular, you will have the opportunity to:

- Learn what modern magick is in practice versus popular ideas and misrepresentations.
- Discover the history of a specific magickal tradition.
- Receive instruction on how to meditate and focus effectively (in a group setting).
- Learn how to raise and direct energy through group spells and rituals.
- Explore divine images and their meanings to a specific group.
- Acquire the tools of witchcraft and use them in a coven setting.

Unless the group is eclectic, these points will be conveyed according to the coven's particular traditions, but that doesn't reduce the value of learning at the feet of good teachers. Everything you glean can (and will) be applied to other magickal methods and situations, either as a solitary witch or within a group.

Coven Culture

The best covens are made up of individuals who take their responsibility to the group seriously. You want a group whose practices honor both the person and the Circle.

Consider the coven's tradition and the constructs that different traditions provide. Some covens follow specific "lineages" and ideologies, such as Celtic or Egyptian, Dianic or Alexandrian. If a coven holds to a particular tradition that doesn't interest you or with which you feel uncomfortable, you're in the wrong place.

As you decide whether a coven is right for you, ask yourself the following questions:

- What kind of attendance and study requirements are expected of you?
- Do these mesh with your mundane schedules and responsibilities?
- Does the group you're considering have a specific initiation ritual? What is it like? Is there anything in that ritual that doesn't fit your vision?
- Does the group require secrecy? If so, what's the reason behind it and how hush-hush is everything?

Ask the coven leader for permission to attend an open Circle or other function before you consider pursuing membership. This will allow you to observe how the coven operates and how the people involved interact. Keep your senses open, allowing yourself to imagine what it would be like to work within that structure.

"In a strong coven, the bond is, by tradition, 'closer than family'; a sharing of spirits, emotions, imaginations. 'Perfect love and perfect trust' are the goal."

—Starhawk, *The Spiral Dance*

Only you can determine whether joining a coven is right for you, and if it is, which coven best suits your objectives. Take your time and don't rush. Bear in mind that every group you review will have its strengths, weaknesses, and idiosyncrasies—that is part of being human. Find a group with whom you feel a common bond and focus on the big picture; the nitpicky stuff you can work on over time.

Finding a Coven That's Right for You

If a witch carefully considers the pros and cons of joining a coven, and decides to move forward, how would she go about finding a coven to join? It's not as if covens are listed in the Yellow Pages!

Modern witches—and witches-to-be—have a tremendous advantage over seekers twenty years ago. Today you'll discover a wealth of resources and information online. The first place to look is *www.witchvox.com*. Witchvox .com is the largest repository of information about the Craft, including listings of groups around the world.

You may find a coven or several in your own hometown, or at least in your state. Get in touch with a group's contact person—he should be able to give you more information about any nearby covens, study groups, and gatherings. If no group exists in your area, you could connect with one of the many online covens and pagan groups on the Web.

Also check bulletin boards at bookstores, health food cooperatives, yoga centers, and New Age shops. A nearby Unity or Unitarian Universalist

Church could steer you in the right direction—it might even provide space for Circles and other spiritual events.

Leadership and Members

If you're lucky, you'll find several groups to choose from. Pay particular attention to two key points: the aptitude of the leaders and the cohesiveness of the membership. These two factors can make or break a coven.

The best leaders don't seem to need titles. They are great facilitators, communicators, and honorable diplomats. They remain sensitive to the individuals and to the greater whole. They work hard to teach, inspire, and motivate the coven. When deciding between covens, ask yourself whether any of the leaders stand out as having these qualities and whether they have earned the respect of the coven for their wisdom, responsibility, openness, and consistency.

The best members are those who work together for the greater good, placing their individual preferences and desires second to the group's. They are dedicated to the group's goals and the magickal tradition to which they belong. They support and encourage one another, and refrain from gossiping, criticizing, or bickering among themselves. They welcome you into the collective and respect you, without judging or trying to control you. They willingly share information with you and seek your input.

Cautions and Caveats

There are several "ten-foot-pole rules" you'll want to keep in mind when reviewing a coven's leadership and members. In other words, if you see any of these warning signs, don't get near 'em with a ten-foot pole!

1. Any group that says you *must* do something in a particular way, even if it goes against your personal taboos or moral guidelines, is not an ethical group.
2. Seeing members grovel before the coven's leader should raise a warning flag. A leader needs help and assistance, but should not order coven members around like servants.
3. Be wary of any coven that charges dues for membership, unless there is a valid reason for such fees (and proper accounting is in place). Most

witches believe that learning should be free. It's okay to ask for help with the gas, or munchies for a meeting, but there's a huge difference between this and making a fast buck off someone's spiritual thirst.

4. A group whose members brag about their numbers, claim they are all-powerful, or purport a 100 percent success rate in their magick isn't worth your time. There is no such thing as fundamental Wicca and no "right" way to pursue spiritual growth.

Many spiritual groups have been guilty of these problems—not just Wiccans and magickal societies, but organized religions as well. Spiritual hubris is one of the most seductive and destructive forms of arrogance. Of course, witches aren't ego-free, nor are they enlightened beings. They are humans, trying their best to become better people every day in every way.

Joining a Coven

If you have found your ideal coven and would like to join, the next step is to have an old-fashioned chat with the group's leader. Tell him or her of your interest (specifically, what attracted you to this particular coven). Ask if the coven is open to new members and how to go about getting more involved. Find out when they hold initiations. The initiation process will vary from group to group, but in any case you'll probably have some studying ahead of you and some things to learn before an actual initiation occurs.

There's nothing to prevent you from leaving a coven if you find you've made the wrong choice. Although covens would like people to stay for a while for the sake of continuity, witches recognize that each individual's path changes every day. Try to part on good terms. As the witches say: "Merry meet, merry part, and merry meet again!"

Start thinking ahead. What role do you see for yourself in this group? Do you seek a specific function that utilizes your skills and talents? If, for example, you're a musician you might enjoy playing at rituals. Or if you're a good writer, perhaps you could craft some specialized spells, incantations, or rituals for the group.

This attitude will show the prospective coven your sincerity—and that you're thinking in terms of the group and not just about yourself. Also, it will help you define your place in the coven if and when you choose to take the next step (initiation).

Initiation into a Coven

The initiation is a very important moment of bonding. At this stage, coven members extend their Circle, in all its quirky intimacy, to another person. Every person in the group should be present for this activity.

Each coven will enact its own, unique initiation ritual, even though there may be similarities from group to group. The ritual reflects the philosophy, traditions, objectives, and orientation of the group.

One nice welcoming ritual involves braiding or knotting yarn to symbolize that the new member's path is tied in with the rest of the coven. The initiate brings a length of yarn, which is tied into the bundle created by the current members. In some cases, the coven's priest or priestess will keep the bundle or wear it as a belt as a sign of office.

At the time of initiation, new members can choose the magickal names they wish to use in sacred space. They then go to each person present, introduce themselves by that name, and greet them as a brother or sister in the Craft (perhaps with a kiss on the cheek or a hug).

"Some traditions have degrees of initiation," explains Debbie Michaud in her book *The Healing Traditions & Spiritual Practices of Wicca*. "At each degree, more 'mysteries' are revealed to the initiates. Structured rituals are performed using images, forms, and languages in a religious, magickal, and mystery context."

Forming Your Own Coven

Sometimes you can't find an existing coven that meets your needs. Or you may have belonged to a coven, but over time things have changed and it's time to try something else. If you don't wish to be solitary, you might consider forming your own coven.

Organizing a coven is kind of like baking. You need the right ingredients and timing to make everything turn out well. This isn't a social club, it's a spiritually mindful group and establishing it should be done with sincerity. Sometimes people form covens for the wrong reasons (for instance, to show off to friends or weird out the parental units). Do some preliminary soul-searching—you really need to know yourself and be honest about your intentions.

Getting Down to Details

If you determined this is the right move for you, decide how many people you want to be involved. Thirteen is the traditional number of witches in a coven, but you don't have to follow that custom. Set a reasonable limit on membership. Quantity is less important than quality—in fact, a large quantity may diminish quality.

Next, ask yourself what kind of coven you want. Do you intend to focus on a specific magickal tradition? Do you want your group to be religious or secular? Do you want a rotating leadership or one defined leader? How will you choose the leader(s)? In other words, consider all the factors that will define and flesh out your group. These parameters will make it easier for others to decide whether your coven is right for them.

Here are some other issues to consider:

- What will the correct line of authority be?
- Will your coven work with magick for magick's sake, or will you be integrating religious aspects into your Craft?
- Where will your coven meet?
- Will you have requirements about how many meetings a year a person must attend to remain a member?
- Will you have study requirements?

- Will your members participate in activities together outside the coven setting?
- Do you plan to keep a Book of Shadows for your group (and if so, how and where will it be maintained)?
- Will you need to have specific tools or regalia for your coven meetings?
- What seasonal festivals will you observe?
- What other types of gatherings do you want to make available to your members (for instance, to respond to a member's personal needs)?
- What types of members' personal problems should the coven avoid getting involved in?
- How will someone attain the role of priest or priestess in your group?
- Who will make the decisions? Will you run your coven democratically, or will the leader's word be the final authority in every matter?

After these details have been ironed out, politely approach those individuals you think would be interested. Talk over the type of coven you envision and listen carefully to the way each person responds. It's okay for them to ask questions. If they don't, you should be worried. Nonetheless, somewhere at the bottom line, their vision of the group has to mesh with yours, or there are going to be problems.

Moving Forward

Once you've found a core group, the next stage is the "shake 'n' bake" period. Consider instituting a time period (for example, a year and a day) before anyone is considered a full, formal member of the coven (and before they are initiated into that group). This trial period gives everyone a chance to see if the relationship between the members is going to work. It also allows time to learn the skills necessary for working magick together. Rome wasn't built in a day, and neither is a good coven!

During this growing stage, try out a variety of rituals, spells, and meditations together, taking notes about each event. Find out what sensual cues work best for everyone. Note what goes really wrong, and what goes really right. By reviewing these notes regularly, you will begin to see the spiritual pattern you effectively use to build energy as a cohesive group.

At the end of the trial period, everyone should sit down and powwow. Discuss your accomplishments. Talk about what has and has not worked. Ask each person if he or she would like to continue in a more formalized manner. If the answer is yes, great! If not, separate as friends and spiritual helpmates. Just because you're not working magick together doesn't mean your other interactions will end.

Those who decide to move forward now have an even greater task ahead, that of keeping things going. Establish a line of authority and really start organizing. And, of course, it's time to start formally meeting as a coven.

Solitary Practice

Some witches practice alone—in solitary—rather than with a group. Perhaps no coven is available, or a witch may prefer to follow solitary practice because it suits her particular purposes, temperament, or lifestyle. Some people may work alone for a period, then join a coven for a period. Witches who don't belong to a coven may still gather with "kindred spirits" to celebrate the sabbats or other events, in a sort of extended Circle.

For seasoned witches, a solitary path may be simply a choice. For the beginner, however, working alone can be lonely. It can also be more difficult than being guided by other, more experienced colleagues. On the other hand, a solitary pursuit enables you to develop your own style of magickal expression, rather than taking on the ideology or outward form of an established group. Fortunately, today many books—including this one—exist to teach a novice the basics of Wicca and witchcraft.

As a solitary witch—especially if you're just starting out—some guidelines can help you proceed safely and successfully:

- Read lots of books by different authors, to gain a variety of insights and perspectives.
- Meditate regularly to improve your mental focus and your connection with your higher self.

- Set a schedule for yourself that makes magickal study and work part of your everyday life.
- Apply what you learn—study alone won't make you a witch.
- Start with simple rituals and spells, then work up to more complicated ones.
- Don't get discouraged if something doesn't work out the way you'd planned; try to determine what went wrong and why, and learn from your mistakes.
- Practice, practice, practice—magick is like every other skill: the more you do it, the better you get.
- Keep a journal (grimoire) of your experiences.

After you've spent time studying and practicing on your own, you'll have a better idea of what type of magick appeals to you and which path you want to follow. At some point, you may decide to find a teacher or a group of like-minded individuals to work with. Working with a teacher can help you advance more quickly and may steer you away from some pitfalls along the way. Good teachers tend to be selective about the students they take on. If you can show that you've done your homework through solitary study, you'll have a better chance of convincing a teacher to help you reach the next level. Remember the old saying, "When the student is ready, the teacher will appear."

Living a Magickal Life

The witch's world is rich and rewarding. Now that witchcraft has "come out of the broom closet" and people around the world are sharing their knowledge openly, the field is growing ever richer. Everyone's experiences contribute to the development of the whole. Wicca and witchcraft are not static ideologies; they are constantly evolving, just like the women and men who are part of these wisdom traditions.

Once you put on the witch's mantle, your entire perspective will change. You'll never again see the world as you did before. You realize that nothing happens in a vacuum and nothing happens accidentally. You become aware of your connection with all life on earth and with the universe, the physical and the nonphysical. You know that your thoughts create your reality, and everything you think, feel, and do affects the whole.

As Donald Michael Kraig writes in his book *Modern Magick*, "Magick is not something you do, magick is something you are." For a witch, magick is a way of life, a way of thinking, feeling, and interacting in the visible world as well as the unseen one.

Being a witch means living consciously, in harmony with the rest of existence to the best of your ability. It also involves using your will responsibly to produce the results you desire for yourself and others. According to Aleister Crowley, "Every intentional act is a magical act." As you move through the world as a witch, you'll notice that everyone you meet is your teacher, and you in turn teach something to everyone you meet.

Magick transforms you. Magick exists everywhere, all the time. You are part of the magick.

Glossary of Magickal Terminology

adept
Someone considered accomplished in at least one magickal art and able to teach it to others effectively.

affirmation
A statement of intent, written or spoken in a positive way and always in the present tense.

All Hallows' Eve
An alternative name for Halloween; witches and Wiccans call this holiday Samhain.

altar
A surface on which the witch's tools and other sacred items are placed; it is also an area around which many rituals and spells take place.

amulet
An item worn or carried for protection or to deter negative influences.

animism
The belief that natural phenomena or items have an indwelling spirit that can be appeased or called upon for aid.

Asatru tradition
A Northern European tradition of magick that also honors the old gods as described in the *Edda*, the ancient compendium of Icelandic lore, and legally recognized in Iceland in 1972.

asperge
To sprinkle water in a ritual to clear a space of negativity and provide purification.

astral travel
The ability for the spirit to leave the body and visit other places and times.

athame
The ritual knife of Wiccans, usually with two edges to represent the two-edged nature of magick (boon and bane).

augury
The art, ability, or practice of divination by signs and omens.

aura
A term that means "invisible breath." Witches see an aura as a kind of energy atmosphere that surrounds each living thing. Some psychics can see auras. The patterns and colors within the aura are indicators of a person's physical, mental, and spiritual state.

balefire
An outdoor fire Wiccans gather around for dancing and working magick.

banishing
Turning away negative energy or spirits.

bard
A formally trained storyteller often entrusted with the oral history of a group.

blessing way
The ritualistic dedication of young children (similar to a baptism).

Book of Shadows
Also called a grimoire, this is a witch's or group's collection of practical magick. A Book of Shadows may contain recipes, spells, charms, invocations, and rituals.

Book of the Dead
An Egyptian treatise on the afterlife that includes hundreds of magickal instructions for everything from invocations to charms.

Burning Times
A time in history, from the late fourteenth to the eighteenth centuries, when many thousands of people were punished and killed for purported acts of witchcraft, which at that time was considered heresy.

cauldron
Any three-legged pot, which many witches and Wiccans use to represent the threefold Goddess.

chakra
A Sanskrit word that literally means "wheel," "disk," or "vortex." It usually refers to one of the body's seven major energy centers that align from the base of the spine to the crown of the head.

chalice
One of the four principal tools used by witches and other magicians, often for sharing potions or other magickal libations.

chant
A series of meaningful words that a witch repeats to focus his will and raise energy toward a specific goal. A chant specifically designed for personal improvement is called an affirmation.

charm
A magick spell, often spoken, or a simple token, a charm is frequently one you create for yourself.

chi
In Eastern philosophy, chi (pronounced kee) is the enlivening force in the universe that animates all life (also spelled qi).

cingulam
A knotted cord worn with ritual robes; it often denotes connection to a coven or degreed status (also see *measure*).

conjuration
A means of invoking a helpful spirit for a specific task.

coven
A group of witches who practice together. A coven can be of any number but traditionally comprises thirteen members (one for each full moon of the year).

Crone
The third, and eldest, aspect of the Goddess. The masculine version would be the Grandfather.

crystallomancy
Divination using crystals.

cunning folk
An old name for people who practiced folk magick because they lived by their cunning, insightful abilities.

curse
An appeal to supernatural powers for injury or harm to another person.

degrees
Some witches have specific levels of skill within their Craft. Degrees designate progressive levels of skill and knowledge in witchcraft acquired by witches.

deosil
Moving clockwise (this generates positive energy).

devas
A natural order of spirits with elemental essence (akin to nature faeries).

Dianic Wicca
A sect of witchcraft named for the goddess Diana and strongly tied into the feminist movement.

divination
The art of predicting the future, often through a specific medium such as crystal-gazing or tarot

cards. It literally means to let the divine realm manifest.

dowsing
Searching for water or precious items (or anything desired) using a pendulum, Y-shaped branch, or other types of rods whose movements indicate a "hit." German miners brought this art to Europe in the fifteenth century.

druid
Priest or priestess of Celtic Europe who performed many social and religious functions; usually druids were knowledgeable in astrology, divination, and healing, as well as other magickal arts.

earth magick
A form of witchcraft that focuses on natural symbols and components and attempts to remain aware of our stewardship of the earth.

elementals
Nonphysical beings said to live within the energy force of a specific element. For example, sylphs are air elementals.

elixir
A kind of potion used to energize and restore overall health to the person drinking it.

equinox
A word meaning "equal night." Twice a year, the duration of daylight and night are equal. This is a traditional time for many Wiccan celebrations, marking two of the four major points on the Wheel of the Year (the other two being the solstices).

Esbats
Wiccan full-moon celebrations.

ESP
An acronym for extrasensory perception; an ability to perceive facts outside the range of the usual five senses and independently of any reasoning process.

faery tradition
A sect of witchcraft started in the United States predominantly by Victor Anderson and Gwydion Penderwen that focused on the lore and magick of the fey.

familiar
An animal that acts in the capacity of a magickal partner, guide, and teacher to a witch.

father
The second, more mature aspect of the God, similar to the Christian idea of God the Father.

fetch
An old name for the ghostly image of a living person that appears outside the body just prior to death (it acts as an omen of death).

fetish
Any object believed to have a specific magickal power for which that object is then carried, buried, burned, or otherwise utilized magickally.

folk magick
The practice of using natural symbols and the superstitions of common people combined with personal will to manifest change. Akin to a hedge witch in many ways.

Gaia
A name for the earth's spirit; also a Greek goddess who presided over the earth.

germatria
A practice that attaches a number equivalent to each letter in a word. Germatria was initially connected with the Hebrew language; however, its tenets can be applied to any language.

glamoury
The art of creating a sphere of energy within one's aura, akin to putting on an ambiance or atmosphere that presents a specific image to the outside world. Faeries are said to be highly adept in this art.

gnomes
Earth elementals.

Grandfather
The third, and eldest, aspect of the God.

Great Rite
A celebration of the God and Goddess in literal or figurative terms, which often includes sexual intercourse, so the two forces can be united to create balance and increased power for magick.

Green Man
An image of the God aspect of Divinity that is strongly connected with nature. Many witches believe that the Green Man (who is often horned like a stag) is the image from which Christianity drew the portrait of Satan to try to frighten superstitious people.

grimoire
A witch's secret journal of magick spells and rituals, also known as a Book of Shadows.

grounding
Shutting down psychic or magickal energy to return to an ordinary level of awareness and mundane thinking.

guardian
Member of the spiritual "security staff" at magickal rituals and festivals.

handfasting
A Neo-Pagan version of a wedding that does not necessarily correspond to a legal marriage. Many handfastings act as an agreement between the couple to be together for a year and a day (or other contract).

hedge witch
A hedge witch, traditionally, is a solitary practitioner who depends on self-study, insight, creativity, and intuition as guideposts. Such a witch may be self-dedicated, but is rarely publicly initiated, with practices similar to those of the village shamans and cunning folk who provided spells and potions for daily needs.

hermetic texts
A collection of books dated to about 3 C.E., which contains information about astrology, rituals, education, and much more. These books treat magick as a science of the mind, an outlook that continues to influence modern practices.

higher self
A spiritual part of humankind that has access to the universal mind and all the knowledge and wisdom of our past lives.

high magick
The more elaborate and symbolic form of magick that deals with issues of the mind and spirit, as opposed to the more practical "low magick." Also called ceremonial or ritual magick.

imitative magick
Used a lot by ancient hunters and farmers, imitative magick involved enacting the desired outcome of the spell or ritual as a reality, such as drawing the image of a captured animal on a stone just before the hunt begins.

incantation
A rhymed affirmation.

incubation
The practice of going to a sacred space alone for a time to receive divine inspiration.

initiation
A formal welcoming of a new witch into a group (or a public dedication for a solitary witch).

intention
A consciously designed wish or objective.

Kabbalah
The occult theosophy with rabbinical origins. It is an esoteric interpretation of Hebrew scriptures with strong ritualistic overtones. Pronounced ka-BAH-lah, it is also spelled Cabala, Qabalah, and with other variations.

karma
A concept borrowed from Eastern traditions, karma is quite simply the law of cause and effect. All acts in our lives are said to balance out; all ills visit back on us, as do all good things, in this life or the next.

left-hand path
Black magick, which is used to manipulate free will or cause harm.

ley lines
Invisible lines of force said to network throughout the earth in geometric patterns. When these lines are disrupted or injured, the associated land may suffer.

magi
Plural of *magus.*

magick
The unique spelling of this word came about to set this practice apart from stage illusion and magic tricks.

magick circle
The space within which many witches and covens work their magick. This is a sacred space, erected temporarily by words and actions (along with a variety of symbolic objects).

magus
A sorcerer or magician. Also called a mage. Plural is *magi.*

Maiden
The youngest aspect of the Goddess, characterized as energetic and beautiful.

measure
A practice that still takes place in some covens, it entails measuring various parts of a person's body with thread. This thread (or cord) is then kept by the group's leader in trust for the duration of a person's involvement, implying that person's promise to keep the secrets of that order.

medium
A person with the ability to become a middle ground between our world and the world of the dead, thus allowing the dead to speak through her.

Mother
The second, more mature aspect of the Goddess who is fertile and nurturing.

occult
Something hidden, especially secret mystical knowledge.

offering
Giving a small token to a deity by way of thanks, or as a means of invoking assistance. This token should be meaningful and valuable to the person who gives it. Typical offerings include grains, wine, coins, handmade goods.

Ogham
The ancient Celtic tree alphabet consisting of twenty letters, each of which corresponds to a tree. Ogham (pronounced oh-am) letters also serve as mystical and magickal symbols.

oracle
A direct link—either a human being or a tool such as tarot cards or runes—between your conscious self, your subconscious, and Divine Wisdom.

pendulum
An item suspended by string or thread that, when in motion, indicates the answer to specific questions. Romans used pendulums to try to determine the outcome of forthcoming battles. Witches use them for divination and dowsing.

pentagram
A five-pointed star with a circle around it. An important symbol of protection, it's often used in magick ceremonies or worn as an amulet. The five points symbolize the five "points" of the human body (arms, legs, and head).

poppet
A figurine made to resemble a person or animal to which specific magick is being directed.

potion
A liquid contrived with magickal components and through magickal processes to produce a specific result. Although most potions are meant to be consumed, some might be asperged, poured out to the earth, or tossed on a fire, depending on their intended function.

rituals
Specific movements, words, and actions designed to produce specific results. Witches and Wiccans hold seasonal rituals, personal rituals, rituals for times of need in the community, and so on; a ritual may be compared to a church service.

runes
Letters derived from an ancient, usually old Teutonic, alphabet. Each rune is both a letter and a mystical glyph used to convey complex meanings, especially in divination.

sabbats
The eight main festivals of Wiccans, which take place throughout the year (also see *Wheel of the Year*). Sabbats are based on the sun's position relative to the earth and are celebrated approximately six weeks apart, on the solstices, the equinoxes, and the halfway points between these dates.

sacred space
Witches often create a sacred space in which to work their magick. This entails putting up a protective sphere of energy (sometimes called a magick circle) that holds energy in place and keeps negative influences outside. At the end of the working, the sacred space is dismissed.

salamanders
Fire elementals.

scrying
A form of divination that involves gazing into a reflective surface, such as a crystal ball, to see the future.

shaman
Someone who understands both the spirit world and the natural world, and journeys between them to obtain knowledge that can provide healing, guidance, and protection to his people.

sigil
A uniquely personal symbol you create in order to produce a specific result. Although there are various techniques for designing sigils, the easiest one involves fashioning an image from letters in a word of power or affirmation.

skyclad
A term used by Neo-Pagans to describe ritualistic worship without clothing (in other words, clothed in nothing more than the sky).

solitary
A witch who chooses to practice alone, outside a coven.

solstice
The two times of the year when the sun is at either its farthest northern or farthest southern point of the celestial equator. Wiccans often celebrate the Summer Solstice as a fire festival to honor the sun, the Winter Solstice as a time of rebirth and renewal.

Son
The youngest aspect of the God, characterized as energetic and handsome.

Summerland
The place between lives where a witch's soul goes after death to await reincarnation.

sylphs
Air elementals.

sympathetic magick

This kind of magick relies heavily on the power of symbolism to create a specific magickal result. For example, a person who is ill might wash in a well known for its pure water to wash away her sickness. Here the healthy/clean "sympathy" of the water empowers the spell.

talisman

A charm designed to attract something its owner desires. Gemstones and jewelry have long been favored as talismans.

tarot

Pronounced TARE-oh, this illustrated deck of cards (usually seventy-eight) dates back to medieval times or earlier. It can be used as a form of divination or as a guide to spiritual/personal growth.

undines

Water elementals.

wand

A magician's tool made of metal or wood, used to direct, draw, or cast energy.

waning moon

The period following the full moon, when the lunar sphere gradually shrinks or wanes.

wards

Mystical energy patterns designed to safeguard an area (or person) from negative influences. Wards, such as pentagrams, are often drawn in the air at the four quarters of a sacred space to enforce the protective energy.

Watchtowers

A name for the elemental guardians of the four quarters of a sacred space (earth/north, air/east, fire/south, and water/west). These powers "watch" over the sacred space when invoked and honored.

waxing moon

The period following a new moon, when a small crescent appears and grows larger until it becomes a full moon.

Wheel of the Year

The annual circle of eight major observances that are important to Wiccans, and that many witches and Neo-Pagans also observe.

widdershins

Moving counterclockwise, widdershins is used in magick for banishing or decreasing.

Resources and Further Reading

Abadie, M. J. *The Everything® Candlemaking Book*. Avon, Mass.: Adams Media Corporation, 2002.

Adler, Margot. *Drawing Down the Moon*. New York: Viking Penguin, 1997.

Alexander, Skye. *The Everything® Spells & Charms Book*. Avon, Mass.: Adams Media/F + W Publications, Inc., 2007.

Alexander, Skye. *The Only Tarot Book You'll Ever Need*. Avon, Mass.: Adams Media/F + W Publications, Inc., 2008.

Alexander, Skye. *The Everything® Tarot Book*. Avon, Mass.: Adams Media/F + W Publications, Inc., 2006.

_____. *Naughty Spells/Nice Spells*. Avon, Mass.: Adams Media/F + W Publications, Inc., 2006.

_____. *10-Minute Magic Spells*. Gloucester, Mass.: Fair Winds Press/Rockport Publishers, 2002.

_____. *10-Minute Tarot*. Gloucester, Mass.: Fair Winds Press/Rockport Publishers, 2003.

_____. *10-Minute Crystal Ball*. Gloucester, Mass.: Fair Winds Press/Rockport Publishers, 2002.

_____. *Magickal Astrology*. Franklin Lakes, N.J.: New Page Books/The Career Press, 2000.

_____. *Planets in Signs*. West Chester, Pa.: Whitford Press/Schiffer Publishing, 1988.

Andrews, Ted. *Animal-Speak*. St. Paul, Minn.: Llewellyn Publications, 1993.

Anthony, Carol K. *A Guide to the I Ching*. Stow, Mass.: Anthony Publishing, 1982.

Astrolabe, Inc. *The Astrolabe World Ephemeris 2001-2050*. West Chester, Pa.: Whitford Press/Schiffer Publishing, 1998.

Ash, Steven. *Sacred Drumming*. New York: Sterling Publishing, 2001.

Beyerl, Paul. *The Master Book of Herbalism*. Custer, Wash.: Phoenix Publishing Co., 1984.

_____. *A Compendium of Herbal Magick*. Custer, Wash.: Phoenix Publishing Co., 1998.

Bonewits, Isaac, and Philip Emmons Bonewits. *Real Magic*. York Beach, Maine: Red Wheel/Weiser, 1991.

Budapest, Zsuzsanna. *Grandmother of Time*. Harper San Francisco, 1989.

Budge, E.A. Wallis. *Amulets and Superstitions*. New York: Dover Publications, 1978.

Campanelli, Pauline, and Dan Campanelli. *Ancient Ways: Reclaiming Pagan Traditions*. St. Paul, Minn.: Llewellyn Publications, 1991.

Cavendish, Richard. *A History of Magick*. New York: Penguin USA, 1991.

Cobelo, Carolyn E. *The Power of Sacred Space*. Santa Fe, N.M.: Akasha Productions, 2000.

Cooper, J. C. *Symbolic and Mythological Animals*. New York: Harper Collins, 1992.

Cunningham, Scott. *Cunningham's Encyclopedia of Crystal, Gem and Metal Magic*. St. Paul, Minn.: Llewellyn Publications, 1988.

_____. *The Magic of Food: Legends, Lore, and Spellwork*. St. Paul, Minn.: Llewellyn Publications, 1996.

Currot, Phyllis. *Book of Shadows*. New York: Broadway Books, 1998.

Drew, A. J. *Wicca for Men*. Secaucus, N.J.: Carol Publishing Group, 1998.

Dyer, Dr. Wayne W. *The Power of Intention*. Carlsbad, Calif.: Hay House, Inc., 2004.

Frost, Gavin, and Yvonne Frost. *Good Witch's Bible*. New Bern, N.C.: Godolphin House, 1999.

Gordon, Lesley. *Green Magic: Flowers, Plants, and Herbs in Lore and Legend*. New York: Viking Press, 1977.

Graves, Robert. *The White Goddess*. San Francisco: The Noonday Press, 1997.

Green, Marian. *Natural Witchcraft: The Timeless Arts and Crafts of the Country Witch*. London: Thorsons, 2002.

Hall, Manly Palmer. *Secret Teachings of All Ages*. San Francisco: Philosophical Research Society, 1994.

Hutton, Ronald. *The Triumph of the Moon*. San Francisco: Oxford University Press, 2001.

Kaser, R. T. *I Ching in Ten Minutes*. New York: Avon Books, 1994.

Knight, Sirona. *Dream Magic*. San Francisco: Harper San Francisco, 2000.

_____. *A Witch Like Me*. Franklin Lakes, N.J.: New Page Books, 2001.

Kraig, Donald Michael. *Modern Magick*, 2d Ed. St. Paul, Minn.: Llewellyn Publications, 2002.

Kunz, George Frederick. *The Curious Lore of Precious Stones*. New York: Dover Publications, 1971.

Lawless, Julia. *The Encyclopaedia of Essential Oils*. Shafesbury, Dorset, England: Element Books, 1992.

Leach, Maria, and Jerome Fried, eds. *Funk and Wagnall's Standard Dictionary of Folklore, Mythology, and Legend*. Harper San Francisco, 1984.

McArthur, Margie. *Wisdom of the Elements*. Freedom, Calif.: The Crossing Press, Inc., 1998.

Mann, A. T. *Sacred Architecture*. Shafesbury, Dorset, England: Element Books, 1993.

Matthews, John. *The World Atlas of Divination*. Boston: Bulfinch Press, 1992.

Mella, Dorothee L. *Stone Power*. New York: Warner Books, 1986.

Michaud, Debbie. *The Healing Traditions & Spiritual Practices of Wicca*. Los Angeles: Keats Publishing, 2000.

Roche, Lorin. *Meditation Made Easy*. San Francisco: Harper San Francisco, 1998.

Simms, Maria Kay. *A Time for Magick*. St. Paul, Minn.: Llewellyn Publications, 2001.

Starhawk. *The Spiral Dance*: A Rebirth of the Ancient Religion of the Great Goddess, 20th Anniversary Edition. New York: HarperCollins Publishers, 1999.

Sutton, Maya Magee, Ph.D., and Nicholas R. Mann, *Druid Magic*. St. Paul, Minn.: Llewellyn Worldwide, 2000.

Telesco, Patricia. *Dancing with Devas*. Freedom, Calif.: Crossing Press, 1996.

_____. *Exploring Candle Magick: Candle Spells, Charms, Rituals, and Divination*. Franklin Lakes, N.J.: New Page Books, 2001.

_____. *The Healer's Handbook*. York Beach, Maine: Samuel Weiser, Inc., 1997.

_____. *A Kitchen Witch's Cookbook*. St. Paul, Minn.: Llewellyn Publications, 1994.

_____. *The Language of Dreams*. Freedom, CA: Crossing Press. 1997.

Wasserman, James. *Art and Symbols of the Occult*. Rochester, Vt.: Destiny Books, 1993.

Walker, Barbara G. *The I Ching of the Goddess*. San Francisco: Harper San Francisco, 1986.

Watson, Nancy B. *Practical Solitary Magic*. York Beach, Maine: Samuel Weiser, Inc., 1996.

Whitcomb, Bill. *The Magician's Companion*. St. Paul, Minn.: Llewellyn Publications, 1998.

Wilhelm, Richard, and Cary F. Baynes, *The I Ching or Book of Changes*. Princeton, N. J.: Princeton University Press, 1950.

Williamson, Marianne. *A Return to Love*. New York: HarperCollins, 1992.

Wilson, Colin. *The Atlas of Holy Places and Sacred Sites*. New York: DK Publishing, 1996.

Index